CLAUDE S. GEORGE, JR.
University of North Carolina

THE

HISTORY

OF

MANAGEMENT

THOUGHT

PRENTICE-HALL, INC., Englewood Cliffs, New Jersey

for Ella

ISBN: P 13-390187-4
       C 13-390295-5

Library of Congress Catalog Card No. 70-38415

10 9 8 7 6 5 4 3 2

PRENTICE-HALL INTERNATIONAL, INC., *London*
PRENTICE-HALL OF AUSTRALIA, PTY. LTD., *Sydney*
PRENTICE-HALL OF CANADA, LTD., *Toronto*
PRENTICE-HALL OF INDIA PRIVATE LIMITED, *New Delhi*
PRENTICE-HALL OF JAPAN, INC., *Tokyo*

CONTENTS

THE MANAGERIAL CONTINUUM

PREFACE

1   MANAGEMENT IN ANCIENT CIVILIZATIONS   1
Prehistoric Era
Ancient Civilizations
Summary

2   MANAGEMENT DURING THE MEDIEVAL PERIOD   29

Feudal Organization
Early Writings
The Merchants of Venice
The Arsenal of Venice
Sixteenth Century Writers
Summary

3   A MANAGERIAL AWAKENING   49

Organizing for Production
Early Managerial Practices and Concepts
Sir James Steuart
Adam Smith
Richard Arkwright
A Transition Phase
Early Scientific Management. The Renaissance of Application
Summary

4   EARLY MANAGEMENT WRITERS   67

The Classical Economists
Other Writers
Summary

5   A PRELUDE TO SCIENTIFIC MANAGEMENT   81

Henry Poor
Daniel C. McCallum
The Scientific Management Movement
Henry R. Towne
Henry Metcalfe
Frederick Halsey
Summary

6   SCIENTIFIC MANAGEMENT   89

Frederick W. Taylor
Awakening Interest in Scientific Management
Impact of Scientific Management
Aims of Scientific Management
New Views Generated by Scientific Management
Frank B. and Lillian M. Gilbreth

7   EARLY TWENTIETH CENTURY CONCEPTS   103

Henry L. Gantt
Hugo Munsterberg
Walter Dill Scott
Harrington Emerson
Harlow Stafford Person
Henry Fayol
Summary

8   MINOR WRITERS AND CRITICS   117

Alexander H. Church
Hugo Diemer
John C. Duncan
Louis D. Brandeis
James Hartness
Meyer Bloomfield
Robert F. Hoxie
Horace B. Drury
Morris L. Cooke
Carl C. Parsons
William H. Leffingwell
Herford, Hildage, and Jenkins
Summary

9   THE MANAGERIAL PHILOSOPHERS   131

Oliver Sheldon
Elton Mayo
James D. Mooney
Mary Parker Follett
Chester I. Barnard
James Burnham
Lyndall Urwick
Summary

10   EMERGING SCHOOLS OF MANAGEMENT THOUGHT   145

Background for an Emerging Management
Traditional School: Scientific Management
Behavioral School
Management Process School
Quantitative School
Summary

11   THE QUANTITATIVE SCHOOL   157

Development of Quantitative School
World War II Applications
Postwar Uses
Business Applications
Associations
Quantitative Techniques

12   A GENERAL THEORY OF MANAGEMENT   169

Maslow and Management Theory
Management and Managers
A General Theory of Management
The Managerial Composite

13   HISTORY AND CONTEMPORARY MANAGEMENT   181

Personnel-Human Relations
New Managerial Approaches
Efficiency
Employee Welfare
Wages
Decision Making
Social Responsibility
The Contemporary Manager

SELECTED BIBLIOGRAPHY OF MANAGEMENT
LITERATURE   189

INDEX   217

THE MANAGERIAL CONTINUUM

Approximate Year	Individual or Ethnic Group	Major Managerial Contributions
5000 B.C.	Sumerians	Script; record keeping.
4000	Egyptians	Recognized need for planning, organizing, and controlling.
2700	Egyptians	Recognized need for honesty or fair play in management. Therapy interview—"get it off your chest."
2600	Egyptains	Decentralization in organization.
2000	Egyptians	Recognized need for written word in requests. Use of staff advice.
1800	Hammurabi	Use of witnesses and writing for control; establishment of minimum wage; recognition that responsibility cannot be shifted.
1600	Egyptians	Centralization in organization.
1491	Hebrews	Concepts of organization, scalar principle, exception principle.

Approximate Year	Individual or Ethnic Group	Major Managerial Contributions
1100	Chinese	Recognized need for organization, planning, directing, and controlling.
600	Nebuchadnezzar	Production control and wage incentives.
500	Mencius	Recognized need for systems and standards.
	Chinese	Principle of specialization recognized.
	Sun Tzu	Recognized need for planning, directing, and organizing.
400	Socrates	Enunciation of universality of management.
400 B.C.	Xenophon	Recognized management as a separate art.
	Cyrus	Recognized need for human relations. Use of motion study, layout, and materials handling.
350	Greeks	Scientific method applied. Use of work methods and tempo.
	Plato	Principle of specialization enunciated.
325	Alexander the Great	Use of staff.
321	Kautilya (India)	Science and art of statecraft.
175	Cato	Use of job descriptions.
50	Varro	Use of job specifications.
20 A.D.	Jesus Christ	Unity of command. Golden rule. Human relations.
284	Diocletian	Delegation of authority.
900	Alfarabi	Listed traits of a leader.
1100	Ghazali	Listed traits of a manager.
1340	L. Pacioli (Genoa)	Double-entry bookkeeping.
1395	Francisco Di Marco	Cost accounting practiced.
1410	Soranzo Brothers	Use of journal entries and ledger.

Approximate Year	Individual or Ethnic Group	Major Managerial Contributions
1418	Barbarigo	Forms of business organization; work in process accounts used.
1436	Arsenal of Venice Venetians	Cost accounting; checks and balances for control; numbering of inventoried parts; interchangeability of parts; use of assembly line technique; use of personnel management; standardization of parts; inventory control; cost control.
1500	Sir Thomas More	Called for specialization; decried sins of poor management and leadership.
1525	Niccolo Machiavelli	Reliance on mass consent principle; recognized need for cohesiveness in organization; enunciated leadership qualities.
1767	Sir James Steuart	Source of authority theory; impact of automation.
1776	Adam Smith	Application of principle of specialization to manufacturing workers; control concepts; payback computations.
1785	Thomas Jefferson	Called attention to concept of interchangeable parts.
1799	Eli Whitney	Scientific method; use of cost accounting and quality control; applied interchangeable parts concept; recognized span of management.
1800	James Watt Matthew Boulton Soho, England	Standard operating procedures; specifications; work methods; planning; incentive wages; standard times; standard data; employee Christmas parties; bonuses announced at Christmas; mutual employee insurance society; use of audits.
1810	Robert Owen New Lanark, Scotland	Need for personnel practices recognized and applied; assumed responsibility for training workers; built clean row homes for workers.
1820	James Mill	Analyzing and synthesizing human motions.

Approximate Year	Individual or Ethnic Group	Major Managerial Contributions
1832	Charles Babbage	Scientific approach emphasized; specialization emphasized; division of labor; motion and time study; cost accounting; effect of various colors on employee efficiency.
1835	Marshall, Laughlin, et al.	Recognition and discussion of the relative importance of the functions of management.
1850	Mill, et al.	Span of control; unity of command; control of labor and materials; specialization—division of labor; wage incentives.
1855	Henry Poor	Principles of organization, communication, and information applied to railways.
1856	Daniel C. McCallum	Use of organization chart to show management structure. Application of systematic management to railways.
1871	William S. Jevons	Made motion study of spade use; studied effect of different tools on worker; fatigue study.
1881	Joseph Wharton	Established college course in business management.
1886	Henry Metcalfe	Art of management; science of administration.
	Henry R. Towne	Science of management.
1891	Frederick Halsey	Premium plan of wage payment.
1900	Frederick W. Taylor	Scientific management; systems applications; personnel management; need for cooperation between labor and management; high wages; equal division between labor and management; functional organization; the exception principle applied to the shop; cost system; methods study; time study; definition of scientific management; emphasis on management's job; emphasis on research, standards, planning, control, and cooperation.

Approximate Year	Individual or Ethnic Group	Major Managerial Contributions
	Frank B. Gilbreth	Science of motion study; therbligs.
1901	Henry L. Gantt	Task and bonus system; humanistic approach to labor; Gantt charts; management's responsibility for training workers.
1910	Hugo Munsterberg	Application of psychology to management and workers.
	Walter Dill Scott	Application of psychology to advertising and personnel.
	Harrington Emerson	Efficiency engineering; principles of efficiency.
	Hugo Diemer	Pioneering text in factory administration.
1911	Harlow S. Person	Initiated first scientific management conference in United States; gave academic recognition to scientific management.
	John C. Duncan	Comprehensive college text in management.
1915	Horace B. Drury	Criticism of scientific management—reaffirmed initial ideas.
	Robert F. Hoxie	Criticism of scientific management—reaffirmed initial ideas.
	F. W. Harris	Economic lot size model.
	Thomas A. Edison	Devised war game to evade and destroy submarines.
1916	Henri Fayol	First complete theory of management; functions of management; rpinciples of management; recognized need for management to be taught in schools.
	Alexander H. Church	Functional concept of management; first American to explain the totality of managerial concepts and relate each component to the whole.
	A. K. Erlang	Anticipated waiting-line theory.

Approximate Year	Individual or Ethnic Group	Major Managerial Contributions
1917	William H. Leffingwell	Applied scientific management to office.
	Meyer Bloomfield	Founder of personnel management movement.
1918	Carl C. Parsons	Recognized need for applying scientific management to offices.
	Ordway Tead	Application of psychology to industry.
1919	Morris L. Cooke	Diverse applications of scientific management.
1923	Oliver Sheldon	Developed a philosophy of management; principles of management.
1924	H. F. Dodge H. G. Romig W. A. Shewhart	Use of statistical inference and probability theory in sampling inspection and in quality control by statistical means.
1925	Ronald A. Fisher	Various modern statistical methods including chi-square test, Bayesian statistics, sampling theory, and design of experiments.
1927	Elton Mayo	Sociological concept of group endeavor.
1928	T. C. Fry	Statistical foundations of queuing theory.
1930	Mary P. Follett	Managerial philosophy based on individual motivation. Group process approach to solving managerial problems.
1931	James D. Mooney	Principles of organization recognized as universal.
1938	Chester I. Barnard	Theory of organization; sociological aspects of management; need for communication.
	P. M. S. Blackett, et al.	Operations research.
1943	Lyndall Urwick	Collection, consolidation, and correlation of principles of management.

Approximate Year	Individual or Ethnic Group	Major Managerial Contributions
1947	Max Weber Rensis Likert Chris Argyris	Placed emphasis on psychology, social psychology, and research in human relations in organization theory; incorporation of an open-system theory of organization.
1949	Norbert Wiener Claude Shannon	Emphasized systems analysis and information theory in management.
1951	Frank Abrams Benjamin M. Selekman	Reintroduced managerial statesmanship in managerial thinking.
1955	Herbert Simon Harold J. Leavitt Robert Schlaifer	Placed emphasis on human behavior in decision making, viewed as an identifiable, observable, and measurable process; increased attention given to managerial psychology.

PREFACE

The first edition of this book saw an increased interest in the study of management history, as well as the instigation of many new courses in the history of management thought. These events, together with publications by prominent educators, have moved us still further along the continuum of managerial acumen. But even with all this awakening interest, we find ourselves far short of a comprehensive understanding of the whole of management. Despite this condition, however, many scholars see management's future as one emerging along a professional vein—one that will eventually help us find solutions to many of the problems that plague our contemporary society.

Ferreting out managerial thought today is no easy task because men, though managers, did not write about or recognize management as such until fairly recent times. The management historian must therefore interpret man's actions in a managerial light. And this selective and interpretative process makes the whole what it is. This history of management thought, therefore, is influenced by what is left out as well as by what is included. This is the writer's prerogative, but it vitally affects the finished product.

While I recognize that many facets that were omitted might have been included in this volume, to do so would have made it unnecessarily long. A true and comprehensive history of management, of course, would be a history of man. Inasmuch as it is not possible to be all-inclusive in a single volume, I have tried, instead, to select and bring together the most pertinent examples of managerial thought and unite them into a logical whole that would provide an outline of management thought and afford a framework for subsequent endeavors.

This book is not in any sense intended to be a substitute for reading from the primary sources listed in the Bibliography. Rather, it is meant to provide a framework for understanding the development of management thought and unify the broad field of management for scholars and practitioners alike.

I am indebted to scores of persons for help, encouragement, research aid, and criticism. I am, however, especially indebted to Maurice W. Lee, Dean of the Graduate School of Business Administration, University of North Carolina at Chapel Hill, for his encouragement and my release from administrative duties, and to the Business Foundation of North Carolina for its financial aid in providing research assistants. Many of my former students have made contributions through their individual research efforts and interests, but I am especially indebted to Professor Robert H. Trent for virtually all the research and composition in Chapter 11. In addition, I am appreciative of the scholarly interest and meticulous research of Professors Geoffrey H. Churchill, Robert B. Conrad, Rudolph P. Lamone, and Robert E. Schellenberger. To all of these and to the publishers who so generously gave me permission to quote, I should like to express my sincere appreciation.

Finally, I am indebted to Professor Emeritus Gustave T. Schwenning of the School of Business Administration, University of North Carolina at Chapel Hill, who first opened the doors of management history to me.

Claude S. George, Jr.

1

MANAGEMENT

IN ANCIENT CIVILIZATIONS

Despite its importance to every man, management is one of the most nebulous and at the same time most ubiquitous functions in all societies, being found in the homes, churches, governments, and economic undertakings of all peoples. It is and always has been the strong right hand of all leaders. In fact, all the truly great leaders of history were managers—managing countries, managing explorations, managing wars, managing other men's efforts.

From an almost unrecognized position in 1900, management has risen today to be the central activity of our age and economy—a powerful and innovative force on which our society depends for material support and national well-being. Management is at one and the same time the determiner of our economic progress, the employer of our educated, the amasser of our resources, the guide for our effective government, the strength of our national defense, and the molder of our society. It is the central core of our national as well as personal activities, and the way we manage ourselves and our institutions reflects with alarming clarity what we and our society will become.

Although we may recognize the importance of management to our well-being and development, its history is difficult to reconstruct. Man's records, if any, of his early undertakings are vague and often remote: a broken piece of clay with inscriptions, a picture on the wall of a cave, or a partially destroyed skin. Interpreting these findings is frequently as troublesome as discovering them in the first place. In addition, early civilizations did not recognize the practice of

1

management as a function of consequence, and as a result, their references to it are few.

When to these difficulties we add the sense of secrecy that competition forced every good manager to surround himself with, we can easily understand the paucity of any clearly recorded thoughts that early man might have had about the practice of management. To examine the records of history and from them reconstruct the development of management thought is almost overpowering in its magnitude. Ours, therefore, is a difficult task. The path is far from distinct and clear, but if we are diligent in our search, we shall find enough evidences of previous wayfarers to point a way.

PREHISTORIC ERA

The first milestone, which is the starting point of this search, comes shortly after the retreat of the glaciers northward—the last great glacial age being dated about 10,000 to 9000 B.C.[1] The retreating glaciers brought about a gradual disappearance of the large herds of herbivorous animals which were replaced by more scattered and more agile animals. The adaptations to these conditions produced cultures known as the Mesolithic. Men were food-gatherers, making their living by hunting, fishing, and collecting berries and nuts.

It was at this time that family groups at first, and then later entire tribes, moved in companies for mutual assistance on the hunt and mutual protection from enemies. Little is known, however, about these very primitive men—just a few scattered bones, remains of campfires, simple tools, and a few drawings on the walls of caves are all that is left. There is, as a consequence, a fair amount of conjecture about the way in which mankind learned and developed. These Mesolithic cultures were, of course, eventually replaced in most regions by cultures using elementary agriculture and domesticated animals to give the major contributions of good production and conservation.

In our atomic age of moon trips and satellites, we frequently assume that primitive man and his society of ten thousand years ago possessed little in the way of law, government, education, and management. In many ways, however, primitive society was probably as complex as our own. It had its codes for the conduct of business, rules regarding the roles of parents, punishment for wrongdoing, rites for the worship of gods, manners prescribing proper ways to eat, and the like. But even more important was the understanding of the need for authority and the necessity for a system of management. Young men of the tribe surely grew up with a veneration and a fear of the "old man," or leader—and with just cause: he was *alive* and *old* because of his cunning and

[1] James Mellaart, *Earliest Civilizations of the Near East* (London: Thames and Hudson, 1965), p. 11.

wisdom. Perhaps they, too, could learn from him; hence their veneration for him and his source of authority.

With the advent of practiced agriculture, man ceased roaming the countryside to hunt and collect, and with this cessation came a settled existence and the genesis of small villages. With these aggregations of people in communities the need arose for some crude method to manage the common affairs of the group. And, as one would expect, this bit of management devolved to the cunning, the alert, the wise, and the shrewd. As these small villages grew and civilization evolved, the managers, too, grew and evolved. They became the priests, the kings, and the appointed ministers holding power and wealth in their societies even before highly organized social, political, and military structures had been devised. Taxation, effective utilization of resources, division of labor, and trade arrangement and agreements, and the making of war and peace, were surely typical problems to these managers of the first full-scale primitive civilization.

ANCIENT CIVILIZATIONS

The origins of a number of so-called modern concepts and practices of management are easily traceable to the ancients. Solomon, the famed biblical ruler, directed the establishment of elaborate trade agreements, managed construction projects, and molded peace agreements in the tenth century B.C.

Prior to the existence of such rulers as Solomon, however, there arose the need for some way, some system, to govern and manage the people. Many ancient rulers used their trusted servants to carry out their wishes, giving such servants the necessary authority to act for the ruler. These servants collectively then became the council or advisory board for the chiefs. As their power and reputation grew, many of these chiefs assumed theocratic positions in their tribes. They were both earthly and spiritual leaders of the people. To manage, they developed rules and taboos of conduct. Through their spiritual position they used fear of the supernatural as well as fear of earthly ridicule to insure adherence to their rules. It is in this light that we first view the ancient civilizations.

Sumer

Some of the earliest written documents in the world, found in the Sumerian civilization of five thousand years ago, are evidences of managerial control practices.[2] The Sumerian temple priests through their vast tax system

[2]V. G. Childe, *Man Makes Himself* (New York: The New American Library, 1951), p. 143.

collected and managed tremendous amounts of worldly goods, including flocks, herds, revenues, and estates. Being mortal, these priests were required to give an account of their stewardship to the chief priest—a managerial control practice. Because of the magnitude and variety of wealth amassed, however, the priests encountered a job with problems unprecedented in human history. For this account of their stewardship, memory could not be trusted about dues paid, transactions consummated, and the like. Nor could they rely on crude devices such as a notch in a stick, commonly used by private individuals to indicate that their dues had been paid.

The Sumerian priests thus found themselves managing the wealth and operations of a religious organization or business that was immortal but using the ways of mortal man. This mortal facet of man added to the confusion because when a priest died some system of managerial control had to be established to assure, for example, that a loan would be repaid and that the repayment would be exacted by the controlling priest's successor. To do this, the Sumerian priests developed a system of writing or recording data to account for all the transactions entered into by the many priests in the vast holdings of the religious "corporation." Because these Sumerian people recognized this need for managerial control, it is no wonder that virtually the earliest written documents in the world are the five-thousand-year-old accounts of their inventories. It is highly probable that the managerial needs of this early civilization prompted the invention of the Sumerian script.[3] The impetus, of course, was economic; and although developed by the priests, the script's first use was for managerial control purposes and not for liturgical ends.

Hard on the heels of the Sumerian development came the rise of Egypt, with its architectural structures, its government, and its writings to give further evidences of managerial development.

Egypt

Structures. The building of the pyramids with a technology that would be considered primitive by modern standards affords us mute testimony of the managerial and organizational abilities of ancient Egypt from 5000 to 525 B.C. The great pyramid of Cheops, for example, covers thirteen acres and contains 2,300,000 stone blocks each weighing an average of two and one-half tons.

Construction is estimated to have taken the labor of over one hundred thousand men for twenty years. In today's terms, this would mean managing and directing the efforts of a city of one hundred thousand over a twenty-year period—truly a managerial task of massive proportions! When we consider the planning, organizing, and control that had to be exercised in this undertaking, it is clear that the managerial concepts and techniques that we know were not born

[3]*Ibid.,* p. 145.

of the twentieth century. The incidental problems of feeding, transporting, and housing such a multitude stagger the imagination.

The managerial planning of where the stones were to be quarried, when, what size, and how they were to be transported required the practice of what today might well be called long-range planning. The quarrying, for example, took place during the winter and the spring with each stone marked when it was ready for removal to the site of the royal tomb, and the top side of the stone clearly marked. Transportation took place during the annual flood season to minimize land transport. And finally, all blocks were cut to shape and numbered on the site before being put into position. This mining of quarries and the movement of blocks for such tombs afford us an excellent illustration of the Egyptian system of organization.

Quarries were usually chosen for their proximity to the Nile because it furnished convenient transportation. Nevertheless, Hammamat, one of the most-used quarries, lay two to three day's journey from the Nile, and mining expeditions there required hundreds of men and animals to accomplish the work and transport provisions for the workers.[4]

During the New Empire under the reign of Ramses IV, one expedition to quarry stone at Hammamat was carried out in quite a regal style. The expedition was under the titular leadership of the high priest of Amon (because the monuments were for a god) and other attendants of the king, none of whom made any consequential contribution. The men who, in effect, were in charge were military officers inasmuch as work of this nature usually fell on the army. On this expedition 110 officers of each rank, 50 civil officials and ecclesiastics, 130 stone masons, 2 painters, and 4 engravers furnished the leadership. The work of transport was done by 5,000 common soldiers, 200 members of the king's court, 800 barbarians, and 2,000 bondservants of the temple. Altogether, the expedition consisted of 8,368 men.[5]

By using masses of organized labor the Egyptians were able to accomplish tasks that astonish us. While their system of organization may appear unwieldly, cumbersome, and even wasteful, they actually had no reason to economize on labor, since more peasants, mercenaries, and slaves were always available simply for the asking. That they were able to do the job with the available resources is to their credit, and their remaining edifices clearly indicate their managerial effectiveness and sophistication.

Writings. In addition to their architecture, many instances are found in Egyptian literature of management thought, frequently posed as advice from a father to his son. The book of instruction of Ptah-hotep is supposed to have been composed by a vizier of King Issi about 2700 B.C., but the validity of this

---

[4]Adolf Erman, *Life in Ancient Egypt,* trans. from the German by Helen M. Tirard (London: Macmillan & Co., Ltd., 1894), p. 472.

[5]*Ibid.,* p. 475.

claim is doubtful. It is, however, a very ancient work and had already been reedited in 2000 B.C., and as late as 1500 B.C. it was used in schools.[6] As an example of what the book contains, the instruction of Ptah-hotep to his son reads:

> If thou art a leader commanding the affairs of the multitude, seek out for thyself every beneficial deed, until the business be free from wrong. Maat [translated as order or truth] is great, and its effectiveness is lasting. . . . Wrongdoing has never brought its undertaking to port.
>
> If thou art one to whom petition is made, be calm as thou listenest to what the petitioner has to say. Do not rebuff him before he has swept out his body or before he has said that for which he came. . . . It is not [necessary] that everything about which he has petitioned should come to pass, [but] a good hearing is soothing to the heart.[7]

Compare this ancient advice with that found in a contemporary personnel book:

> Listening can be valuable to both parties. Whatever other benefit a disturbed worker derives from the interview, he cannot fail to experience a therapeutic value if he is allowed to get the problem "off his chest" to a sympathetic and intelligent listener.[8]

The Egyptian managers, too, recognized the value of planning and the use of staff advice, as indicated by the following from a manuscript entitled *aboyet* ("instruction") from a father to his son:

> Proclaim thy business without concealment. . . . One ought to say plainly what one knoweth and what one knoweth not. *[A call for honesty in managerial dealings.]*
>
> The leader ought to have in mind the days that are yet to come. *[The need for planning.]*
>
> Great is a great one whose counselors are great. *[The value of staff advice to a manager.]*
>
> Write with thine hand, read with thy mouth, and ask counsel of them that have more knowledge than thou. . . . Persevere in asking counsel, neglect it not. . . . *[The use of staff by managers.]*[9]

We find also that the Egyptians were aware of sound managerial practices

---

[6]Adolf Erman, *The Literature of the Ancient Egyptians,* trans. Aylward M. Blackman (New York: E. P. Dutton & Co., Inc., 1927), pp. 55-60.

[7]John A. Wilson, *The Culture of Ancient Egypt* (Chicago: University of Chicago Press, 1951), p. 84.

[8]Paul Pigors and Charles A. Myers, *Personnel Administration* (New York: McGraw-Hill Book Company, 1956), p. 84.

[9]Adapted from Erman, *The Literature of the Ancient Egyptians,* pp. 59, 76, 195, and 242. (Italics are mine.)

and principles. They understood and appreciated, for example, managerial authority and responsibility, and they recognized the value of spelling out job descriptions in detail. These are illustrated, for example, by the following instructions which were delivered at the appointment of every vizier or manager:

> It is an abomination of the god to show partiality. This is the teaching: thou shalt do the like, shalt regard him who is known to thee like him who is unknown to thee, and him who is near like him who is far . . . an official who does like this, then, shall flourish greatly in the place.
>
> Be not enraged toward a man unjustly, but be thou enraged concerning that about which one should be enraged.
>
> The going out of all that goes out of the king's house shall be reported to him; and the coming in of all that comes into the king's house shall be reported to him.
>
> The overseers of hundreds and the overseers of (word not translated) shall report to him their affairs.
>
> Furthermore, he shall go in to take counsel on the affairs of the kind, and there shall be reported to him the affairs of the two lands in his house every day.
>
> It is he who brings in the officials of the district; it is he who sends them out; they report (to) him the affairs of their district.
>
> One shall put every petition in writing, not permitting that he petition orally. Every petitioner to the king shall be reported to him, after he puts (it) in writing.
>
> They shall report to him all that happens among them on the first day of every four month season; they shall bring him the writing thereof, in their hands together with their local council.
>
> Let every office, from the first to the last, proceed to the hall of the vizier to take counsel with him.
>
> Inspection of every craft (untranslated word), in order to cause every man to know his duty according to the stipulation of every affair.[10]

These are operative, managerial rules or principles used by the Egyptians in their early civilization. Advisory in nature, these principles could easily be applied to many governmental uses today.

Government. The study of the Egyptian government through the periods of the Old Kingdom, the Middle Kingdom, and the New Empire provides us with illustrations of their recognition of the principle of control of an extended operation through a centralized organization.

They first established in their empire a loosely decentralized form of government. From 2160 to 1788 B.C. the government was so highly decentralized that the tax commission was the only real tie between the central

---

[10]J. H. Breasted, *Ancient Records of Egypt* (Chicago: University of Chicago Press, 1906), pp. 269, 274, 277-78, and 291.

government and the sub-states. The head of each of these states, of course, owed his loyalty to the Pharaoh. However, control was so remote that these states could easily be compared to the feudal estates of middle European history.[11]

Recognizing that this loose control resulted in a loss in revenue and loyalty, the rulers of the New Empire period, beginning around 1600 B.C., began recentralizing by means of a military take-over.[12] Since it was a military take-over, the officers of the army stepped into administrative positions and reorganized the central government. This centralization placed all the land into the hands of the royal officials with the Pharaoh at the head. Authority was centralized in the Pharaoh who delegated local authority to the territories through governors or mayors appointed by the central government. The new governors did not operate independently, as did the governors of the Old Kingdom, but merely carried out the directives of the Pharaoh. The army was maintained by the central government and taxes were collected by it. To aid him, the Pharaoh had a prime minister who actually took part in administering the state, making frequent inspections of the territories.[13] Thus the Egyptians apparently recognized (after nearly a thousand years!) that dispersed holdings requiring a decentralized government was an effective form of managerial organization only if effective central controls were established.

Later during the New Empire (1530-1050 B.C.) the provincial governments of the Old Empire completely disappeared, and the royal power became real as well as titular. The centralization of the government was accomplished during the rule of the Hyksos, who drove out the foreign invaders in the provinces and assumed complete control.[14] The king thereby came to own all the property in Egypt and to exact an annual rental payment from the country, usually 20 per cent, and in the form of grain.

If control via records and paper work is the hallmark of an advanced civilization, the Egyptians of the New Empire would have to be considered civilized indeed. Their scribes were kept busy maintaining detailed records. In their business and governmental affairs, they kept documents to show exactly how much was received, from whom, and when, with the details of how it was used. Nothing in the government was done without supporting documents. The following excerpt from a business letter suggests the ancient Egyptian's penchant for this documentation:

> I write this to you, that it may serve as a witness between us, and you must keep this letter, that in the future it may serve as a witness.[15]

[11]*Ibid.*, p. 157,
[12]*Ibid.*, p. 233.
[13]*Ibid.*, pp. 231-45.
[14]Erman, *Life in Ancient Egypt*, p. 102.
[15]*Ibid.*, pp. 112-13.

The Egyptians also recognized the importance of specialization in total organization, as is indicated by their passing laws stating that no tradesman could pursue any trade save that handed down by his parents. Each trade was thus continually competing to perfect its own type. Tradesmen were also barred from participating in political affairs inasmuch as this might tend to distract them, proving detrimental to their primary endeavors.[16]

The Nile region, however, was not alone in its development of high levels of civilization during this period. The Babylonian empire developing along the Tigris and Euphrates also affords us many examples of early managerial practices.

Babylonia

Under Hammurabi, king of Babylonia, the cities along the valley were forced to unite to keep peace, with laws being developed to cover personal property, real estate, trade and business, the family, and labor. Virtually all the laws coming to us from the Babylonian civilization are of a business nature dealing with such items as sales, loans, contracts, partnerships, agreements, and promissory notes.

As one would expect from such an advanced civilization, Babylonian business transactions were highly documented on tablets as a means of control. Fortunately, these tablets also provide us with one of the first recognitions of the principle that responsibility cannot be delegated. This is illustrated in a letter from the king ordering ten men to work at constructing a canal. In the letter it was noted that if the work were not accomplished properly, it was the supervisor of the men, and not the men, who would be punished.[17] The Akkadian Code of Eshnunna, with its price controls and criminal penalties, is the oldest known code to have been used in Babylonia and is thought to predate the Code of Hammurabi by over 150 years.

Hammurabi. Probably the most significant contribution of the Babylonians to management thought, however, was the Code of Hammurabi, ruler for some period between 2000 and 1700 B.C. This Code, like the Akkadian Code, is one of the oldest known codes of law in the world and affords us real insight into their thinking on management. The following excerpts are illustrative.

On minimum wages: If a man hire a field laborer, he shall pay him 8 gus of grain per year.[18]

[16]Sir Gardner Wilkinson, *Manners and Customs of Ancient Egyptians,* 2nd ed. (London: John Murray [Publishers] Ltd., 1842), p. 8.

[17]Georges Contenau, *Everyday Life in Babylon and Assyria* (London: Edward Arnold [Publishers] Ltd., 1954), p. 86.

[18]Robert F. Harper, *The Code of Hammurabi, King of Babylon* (Chicago: University of Chicago Press, 1904), p. 157.

On control: If a man give to another silver, gold, or anything on deposit, whatever he gives he shall show to a witness and he shall arrange the contracts and then he shall make the deposit.[19]

If a merchant give to an agent grain, wool, oil, or goods of any kind which to trade, the agent shall write down the value and return the money to the merchant. The agent shall take a sealed receipt for the money which he gives to the merchant. If the agent be careless and do not take a receipt for the money which he has given to the merchant, the money not receipted for shall not be placed in his account.[20]

On responsibility: The mason who builds a house which falls down and kills the inmate shall be put to death.[21]

If a wine merchant allows riotous men to assemble in his house and does not expel them, he shall be killed.[22]

If a man's child has died under the care of the nurse, and the nurse has substituted another (nurse) without consent of his father and the mother, the breasts of that nurse shall be cut off.[23]

If a doctor operates on a wound with a copper lancet, and the patient dies, or on the eye of a gentleman who loses his eye in consequence, his hands shall be cut off.[24]

Nebuchadnezzar. After over one thousand years of decline following the reign of Hammurabi, Nebuchadnezzar became king in 604 B.C. and raised Babylonia to another epoch of brilliance. From the textile mills of this period we find examples of production control and incentive wage payment. Color, for example, was used as a control means for yarn entering the mill each week. Thus, the yarn for this week might be color tagged with a red tag, next week with a blue tag, and so on, thereby affording management a clear control device to determine how long the raw material for a particular lot had been in the mill. The same type of system was used in Nebuchadnezzar's granaries. When the grain was harvested, it was stored in large earthenware jars and a colored reed was placed in the seal of each jar. Each year has its own color, so that it was immediately evident how long the grain in a particular jar had been in the storehouse. And, finally, wages were paid the women engaged in spinning and weaving operations in the form of food, the amount depending on the individual production of each worker.[25] Truly a basic and highly motivating incentive.

[19]*Ibid.,* p. 122.

[20]*Ibid.,* pp. 104-5.

[21]E. A. Wallis Budge, *Babylonian Life and History,* 2nd ed. (London: Religious Tract Society, 1925), p. 130.

[22]*Ibid.,* p. 126.

[23]*Ibid.,* p. 128.

[24]*Ibid.,* p. 218.

[25]L. P. Alford, *Laws of Management* (New York: The Ronald Press Company, 1928), p. 37.

Hebrews

It has been said of the Hebrews that no other people in history so few in number and so weak politically, with the possible exception of the Greeks, have so greatly influenced civilization.

One of the great Hebrews was Moses, a leader and manager whose ability in government, law making, and human relations makes him worthy of some note. His preparation, organization and execution of the exodus of the Hebrews from the bondage of the Egyptians was a tremendous managerial undertaking, and following the advice of his father-in-law, Moses did a magnificent job of personnel selection, training, and organization. The entire account is found in chapter 18 of Exodus and clearly illustrates the principle of delegation as well as the exception principle: "Every small matter they shall judge, but every great matter they shall bring to thee."

This scriptural account affords us one of the earliest and most commonly available records of a philosophy and plan for organization. The advice of Jethro, Moses' father-in-law, indicates a recognition of the need for delegation of authority based on the job assignment, as well as the effectiveness of the exception principle. Here for all to study is a simple record of a fundamental managerial concept.

China

The Chinese have long been known for their wisdom, but little if any real research has been undertaken to understand their feelings toward management. The ancient records of Mencius and Chow (1100 to about 500 B.C.) do, however, indicate that the Chinese were aware of certain principles bearing on organizing, planning, directing, and controlling.

Chow. The constitution of Chow, probably written about 1100 B.C., is a directory of all civil servants to the emperor, from the prime minister down to the household servants, with their jobs and duties carefully listed. In speaking of the powers of the prime minister, for example, it records the following:

> Eight things he holds to help the king handle his numerous officers: The first is rank that controls their distinction. The second is emolument that controls their wealth. The third is favor that controls their fortune. The fourth is appointment that controls their conduct. The fifth is attention that controls their blessing. The sixth is confiscation that controls their poverty. The seventh is removal that controls their failings. The eighth is death that controls their excessiveness.

> Eight regulations he holds to govern the different departments of government. The first pertains to their organization so that the government of the state may be established. The second pertains to their functions so that the government of the state may be clarified. The third

pertains to their relationships so that the government of the state may be cooperative. The fourth pertains to their procedure so that the government of the state may be efficient. The fifth pertains to their formalities so that the government of the state may appear permanent. The sixth pertains to their control so that the government of the state may be complete. The seventh pertains to their punishments so that the government of the state may be corrected. The eighth pertains to their reckoning so that the government of the state may be audited.

Eight methods he holds to govern the country. The first is ritual and worship, so as to control its spirit. The second is statutes and regulations, so as to control its great officers. The third is removal and appointment, so as to control its petty officers. The fourth is emolument and rank, so as to control its scholars. The fifth is taxes and tributes, so as to control its resources. The sixth is ceremonies and customs, so as to control its people. The seventh is punishment and reward, so as to control its strength. The eighth is farming and other employments, so as to control its multitude.[26]

Thus over three thousand years ago we find in China concepts that have a contemporary managerial ring: organization, functions, cooperation, procedures to bring efficiency, and various control techniques.

Use of Staff. Emperor Yao, who according to legend is said to have reigned from about 2350 to 2256 B.C., made constant use of his advisory staff by consulting them about every major decision.[27] Shun, too, employed the staff principle, meeting with his top cabinet officers throughout his kingdom, seeking their advice on how to open all doors of communication between the court and the empire so that he could see with the eyes and hear with the ears of all his subjects.

Later (1766-1754 B.C.) T'ang, founder of the Shang dynasty, followed the staff principle by letting his able ministers have a free hand in running the government in order to make full use of their wisdom and talents.[28]

Because of the success and power of these and other early monarchs, the use of the staff principle became a traditional part of China's government. This tradition was so strong that when the young Emperor T'ai Chai (1753-1721 B.C.) of the Shang dynasty repeatedly ignored the counsel of his advisers, his prime minister who had served for many years under the Shang dynasty caused the young emperor to be deposed for a period of three years, reinstating him only after he had repented and had agreed to respect the future counsel of his staff.

With the passage of time, the staff principle began to be used by rulers of lower rank. King Wu (1122-1116 B.C.), founder of the Chow dynasty, promoted

[26]Kuo-Cheng Wu, *Ancient Chinese Political Theories* (Shanghai: The Commercial Press, Ltd., 1928), pp. 40-41.

[27]James Legge, trans., *The Chinese Classics* (Hong Kong: Hong Kong University Press, 1960), p. 26.

[28]*Ibid.,* pp. 180-81.

the use of an advisory staff among his vassal kings and even specified in his appointment of Prince Ching that he hold councils for advice before making any major decision.[29]

Mencius. Turning now to the writings of Mencius, we find that he believed that laws alone were insufficient for business—that every going concern should adhere to a standard of operation which was ordained by the law of God, and used as a model for government.

Writing about 500 B.C., Mencius clearly indicated the need for system, methodology, and models in effective management when he said:

> Whoever pursues a business in this world must have a system. A business which has attained success without a system does not exist. From ministers and generals down to the hundreds of craftsmen, everyone of them has a system. The craftsmen employ the ruler to make a square and the compass to make a circle. All of them, both skilled and unskilled, use this system. The skilled may at times accomplish a circle and a square by their own dexterity. But with a system, even the unskilled may achieve the same result, though dexterity they have none. Hence, every craftsman possesses a system as a model. Now, if we govern the empire, or a large state, without a system as a model, are we not even less intelligent than a common craftsman?[30]

Specialization was also emphasized by the ancient Chinese in that each of the crafts was hereditary and an artisan was committed to his industry for a lifetime. The artisans lived together in special districts, separate from the remainder of the citizens such that they could easily learn their trade in the absence of distraction.[31] Mencius also addressed himself to this topic when he asked:

> But why does not Hsü himself act as potter and blacksmith, supplying his needs with articles made on his own premises? Why this multifarious dealing with all sorts of craftsmen?

Mencius answered:

> ...men of high and low station alike have their own proper business and any one man has to be supplied with the products of other men's industry. If he had to manufacture them all for his own use, everybody in the empire would be turned out upon the roads.[32]

---

[29]*Ibid.,* p. 57.

[30]*Ibid.,* p. 226.

[31]Chen Huan-Chang, *The Economic Principles of Confucius and His School* (New York: Columbia University Press, 1911), I and II, 408-9.

[32]*Ibid.,* p. 59.

Sun Tzu. Written about 500 B.C., *The Art of War* by Sun Tzu is the oldest military treatise in the world. And today, even though the chariot is gone and the weapons have changed, this ancient master holds his own because he dealt with fundamentals. To those military leaders and modern managers who would care to study his treatise it is still a valuable guide, as indicated by the following excerpts.

> *On planning:* Now the general who wins a battle makes many calculations in his temple ere the battle is fought. The general who loses a battle makes few calculations before hand. It is by attention to this point that I can see who is likely to win or lose.[33]
>
> *On directing:* If the words of command are not clear and distinct, if orders are not thoroughly understood, the general is to blame. But if his orders are clear, and the soldiers nevertheless disobey, then it is the fault of their officers.[34]

Finally, over two thousand years ago when speaking on *organization,* Sun Tzu warned: "When the general is weak and without authority; when his orders are not clear and distinct; where there are not fixed duties assigned to officers and men; the result is utter disorganization."[35]

The scientific selection of workmen by means of examinations was started by the Chinese government about 120 B.C. Because the clerks and the officers were unable to read the edicts and laws of the government, Prime Minister Kung-Sun Hung established a system of examinations and those who scored highest were given the government positions. In 219 A.D. this system was further expanded by classifying men into nine different grades, dependent upon a man's ability, knowledge, experience, and character. The classification was undertaken by an impartial judge. However, the judge was not quite so impartial and the system was replaced in 606 A.D. (after trying it for four hundred years!) by a governmental examination.[36]

Greece

The Greeks, Phoenicians, and Minoans, rising to power somewhat later than the Chinese, Babylonians, and Egyptians, exhibited a real skill and capacity for management in the operation of trading companies. Greece developed a democratic government with all the necessary managerial complications that

---

[33]Thomas P. Phillips, *Roots of Strategy* (Harrisburg: Military Service Publishing Co., 1955), p. 23.

[34]*Ibid.,* p. 75.

[35]*Ibid.,* p. 73.

[36]Hu Shish, "Historical Foundations for a Democratic China," *Edmund J. James Lectures on Government,* 2nd Series (Urbana: University of Illinois Press, 1941), as quoted by Albert Lepawsky, *Administration* (New York: Alfred A. Knopf, Inc., 1949), p. 428.

such a government entails, and in the Grecian civilization we find the origin of the scientific method. *History* became the Greek word meaning search for true knowledge. By questioning all kinds of knowledge and ideas, the Greeks discovered the research point of view and introduced scholarship and science in many spheres. The influence of the scientific method on management is obvious. This objective type of inquiry was later to become the ultimate goal of such men as Frederick W. Taylor, Henri Fayol, Frank B. Gilbreth, and a host of other leaders in the management field.

The Greeks developed a new type of city government, the *polis,* which encouraged a free exchange of ideas. The polis provided practice and experience in open discussion, and through it the Greeks furnished positive examples and ample evidence of the values of that process which in management we refer to as *consultation* or *consultative supervision.*[37]

Principles of Management. The Greeks early recognized the principle that maximum output is achieved through the use of uniform methods at stipulated tempos. This was especially true for hard, monotonous, repetitive work where time was set by music. The flute and the pipe governed the motions, with songs for each task and for each operation in it.[38] Thus they introduced rhythm, standard motions, and work tempos by working in harmony with music. When to these advantages we add the positive psychological effect of music, we can understand why the result was an increase in output and a decrease in wasted effort and fatigue.

As in other civilizations, trades were hereditary in Greece and specialization was the order of the day. Specialization was carried so far that stonemasons did not sharpen their own tools, and Plato even stated in his laws that no man should work in both wood and iron at the same time because of his inability to excel.[39]

Indeed, in his *Republic* Plato gave to the economic sciences their first theory of specialization or the division of labor when he stated:

> Which would be better—that each should ply several trades, or that he should confine himself to his own? He should confine himself to his own. More is done, and done better and more easily when one man does one thing according to his capacity and at the right moment. We must not be surprised to find that articles are made better in big cities than in small. In small cities the same workman makes a bed, a door, a plough, a table, and often he builds a house too. . . . Now it is impossible that a workman who does so many things should be equally successful in all. In the big

[37]Curtis H. Gager, "Management throughout History," *Top Management Handbook,* ed. H. B. Maynard (New York: McGraw-Hill Book Company, 1960), p. 58.

[38]Gustave Glotz, *Ancient Greece at Work* (New York: Alfred A. Knopf, Inc., 1926), pp. 272-75.

[39]Jules Toutain, *The Economic Life of the Ancient World* (New York: Alfred A. Knopf, Inc., 1930), pp. 133-34.

cities, on the other hand . . . a man can live by one single trade. Sometimes he practices only a special branch of a trade. One makes men's shoes, another women's, one lives entirely by the stitching of the shoe, another by cutting the leather. . . . A man whose work is confined to such a limited task must necessarily excel at it.[40]

One of the first accounts of the principle of the universality of management is found in a Socratic discourse as recorded (or imagined) by Xenophon, one of Socrates' disciples. It clearly indicates that even in the fifth century B.C. men were aware or beginning to be aware that a good manager for a soap company would work equally well as head of an automobile concern or as secretary of defense. Xenophon records the discourse as follows:

Seeing Nicomachides, one day, coming from the assembly for the election of magistrates, Socrates asked him, "Who have been chosen generals, Nicomachides?"

"Are not the Athenians the same as ever, Socrates?" he replied; "for they have not chosen me, who am worn out with serving from the time I was first elected, both as captain and centurion, and with having received so many wounds from the enemy (he then drew aside his robe and showed the scars of the wounds), but have elected Antisthenes, who has never served in the heavy-armed infantry, nor done anything remarkable in the cavalry, and who indeed knows nothing, but how to get money."

"Is it not good, however, to know this," said Socrates, "since he will then be able to get necessaries for the troops?"

"But merchants," replied Nicomachides, "are able to collect money; and yet would not, on that account be capable of leading an army."

"Antisthenes, however," continued Socrates, "is given to emulation, a quality necessary in a general. Do you not know that whenever he has been chorus manager he has gained the superiority in all his choruses?"

"But, by Jupiter," rejoined Nicomachides, "there is nothing similar in managing a chorus and an army."

"Yet Antisthenes," said Socrates, "though neither skilled in music nor in teaching a chorus, was able to find out the best masters in these departments."

"In the Army, accordingly," exclaimed Nicomachides, "he will find others to range his troops for him, and others to fight for him!"

"Well, then," rejoined Socrates, "if he find out and select the best men in military affairs, as he has done in the conduct of his choruses, he will probably attain superiority in this respect also."

"Do you say, then, Socrates," he said, "that it is in the power of the same man to manage a chorus well, and to manage an army well?"

"I say," said Socrates, "that over whatever a man may preside, he will if he knows what he needs, and is able to provide it, be a good

[40]Francis Cornford, *The Republic of Plato* (New York: Oxford University Press, 1959), pp. 165-67.

president, whether he have the direction of a chorus, a family, a city, or an army."

"By Jupiter, Socrates," cried Nicomachides, "I should never have expected to hear from you that good managers of a family would also be good generals."

"Come, then," proceeded Socrates, "let us consider what are the duties of each of them, that we may understand whether they are the same, or are in any respect different."

"By all means," he said.

"Is it not, then, the duty of both," asked Socrates, "to render those under their command obedient and submissive to them?"

"Unquestionably."

"Is it not also the duty of both to appoint fitting persons to fulfill the various duties?"

"That is also unquestionable."

"To punish the bad, and to honour the good, too, belongs, I think to each of them."

"Undoubtedly."

"And is it not honourable in both to render those under them well-disposed towards them?"

"That also is certain."

"And do you think it for the interest of both to gain for themselves allies and auxiliaries or not?"

"Certainly; but what, I ask, will skill managing a household avail, if it be necessary to fight?"

"It will doubtless, in that case, be of the greatest avail," said Socrates; "for a good manager of a house, knowing that nothing is so advantageous or profitable and prejudicial as to get the better of your enemies when you contend with them, nothing so unprofitable and prejudicial as to be defeated, will zealously seek and provide everything that may conduce to victory, will carefully watch and guard against whatever tends to defeat, will vigorously engage if he sees that his force is likely to conquer, and, what is not the least important point, will cautiously avoid engaging if he finds himself insufficiently prepared."

"Do not, therefore, Nicomachides," he added, "despise men skillful in managing a household; for the conduct of private affairs differs from that of public concerns only in magnitude; in other respects they are similar; but what is most to be observed, is, that neither of them are managed without men; and that private matters are not managed by one species of men, and public matters by another; for those who conduct public business make use of men not at all differing in nature from those whom the managers of private affairs employ; and those who know how to employ them, conduct either private or public affairs judiciously, while those who do not know, will err in the management of both."[41]

---

[41]Xenophon, *Memorabilia and Oeconomicus,* trans. E. C. Marchant, The Loeb Classical Library ed. (Cambridge: Harvard University Press, n.d.), pp. 186-87.

And thus Socrates reviews the duties of a good businessman and a good general to show that they are, in fact, the same. It is the duty of both to make their subordinates willing and obedient, and to put the right man in the right place. Moreover, both should punish the bad and reward the good. Both will do well to win the goodwill of those under them. It is to the interest of both to attract allies and helpers. Both should be able to keep what they have. In their own work both should be strenuous and industrious.

Nicomachides agrees that these duties are common to both, but fighting is not. And Socrates points out that certainly both are bound to find enemies and that it is important for both to get the better of them. Since victory results in profits, and defeat results in loss, the good businessman will be eager to seek and furnish all aids to victory and will be careful to consider and avoid what leads to defeat. And, finally, Socrates enjoins Nicomachides not to look down on businessmen; that managing private concerns and public concerns employ the same principles and men; and that the successful manager is the one who understands these principles and employs them in whatever area the undertaking might be—and fails if he does not understand this universality of application.

Art of Management. Xenophon also clearly indicated that he recognized and believed management to be a separate and distinct art when he wrote:

> Is domestic management the name of an art, as that of healing, or of the working in brass, or of building? "It appears to me," said Critobulus, "He who is skilled in building can do for another equally well what he can do for himself; and surely he who is skilled in domestic management can act similarly . . . but as to that which is common to all pursuits, whether agricultural, or political, or domestic, or military, namely that he who would excel in them must be capable of directing others. . . ."[42]

India—Kautilya's *Arthasastra*

Although many individuals today know of Machiavelli, few have heard of Kautilya, his counterpart, who predated him by two thousand years. Brahman Kautilya, also named Vishnugupta, was a great scholar who played a dominant part in the establishment, growth, and preservation of the Indian Empire during the fourth century B.C.

Kautilya's principal work is *Arthasastra,* the science of polity, written about 321 B.C. His major theme is the political, social, and economic management of the state. Dealing with a large variety of subjects, he covers almost every aspect of the theory of government. He discourses on the duties of the king, his ministers, and his councillors, and on council meetings, departments

---

[42]J. S. Watson, *Xenophon's Minor Works* (London: G. Bell & Sons, Ltd., 1898), pp. 73, 74, and 145.

of government, diplomats, war, and peace. In addition, he covers the organization and management of trade and commerce, law and law courts, municipal government, social customs, marriage and divorce, rights of women, taxation and revenue, agriculture, mines and factories, markets, corporations, census operations, slaughterhouses, and on and on. Because of the objectivity and disregard for morality and human compassion in his writings, in India Kautilya's name has become synonymous with sinister and unscrupulous management. His main purpose, however, was no different from that of Machiavelli (whom we will discuss later), that being simply to analyze the practices that had brought political success in the past and to deduce from them what principles ought to be followed for political success in the future. His *Arthasastra*, therefore, was an honest attempt at scientific inquiry—not moral oughtness. He showed what men are wont to do—not what they ought to do. Not an advocate of the wicked and immoral, he simply ignored all concepts of morality and stated that if political success was what one wanted, then to achieve it one must do thus and so.

In his discussion of the administration of an empire, he covers defense of the state, finance of the state, personnel, public works, urban affairs, and law and order—and much more. His job specification for a state officer, in fact, covers many of today's demands:

> Native born of high family, influential, well trained in arts, possessed of foresight, wise, of strong memory, bold, eloquent, skilful, intelligent, possessed of enthusiasm, dignity, and endurance, pure in character, affable, firm in loyal devotion, endowed with excellent conduct, strength, health and bravery, free from procrastination and ficklemindedness, affectionate, and free from such qualities as excite hatred and enmity— these are the qualifications of a ministerial officer.[43]

An excerpt from his job description for superintendent of commerce also strikes a familiar note:

> The superintendent of commerce shall ascertain demand or absence of demand for, and rise or fall in the price of various kinds of merchandise which may be the products either of land or of water, and which may have been brought in either by land or by water path. He shall also ascertain the time suitable for their distribution, centralisation, purchase, and sale.[44]

And thus the highly innovative work proceeds. To Kautilya, the state was an institutional necessity for human advancement. Believing this, he outlined almost everything that the state should do and described how it should be managed for the improvement of the individual. Probably one of the earliest and

[43]R. Shamasastry, trans., *Kautilya's Arthasastra* (Mysore: Sri Raghuveer Printing Press, 1956), p. 14.
[44]*Ibid.*, p. 104.

most comprehensive works on the organization and management of human affairs of state, Kautilya's *Arthasastra* deserves a wider audience.

Early Military Contributions

Cyrus. From the military come many examples of early management thought. The life of Cyrus both as a military leader and as a ruler affords us several illustrations of the advanced state of thinking about management at that time. His father, for example, advised Cyrus "not to adopt such plans only as you have been taught, but to be yourself a contriver of stratagems. . . ."[45] Likewise on planning, we might well remember his "Consider at night what your men shall do when it is day; and consider in the day how matters may be best settled for the night."[46]

Cyrus was aware of the need for specificity in work assignment as well as clarity of instructions. In addition, he recognized the value in good personnel or human relations. These points are illustrated by the following discourse:

> They [the commanders] went off to their tents, and, on their way, observed among themselves how retentive a memory Cyrus had, and how, as he gave his orders to those to whom he assigned their places, he addressed each of them by name. This Cyrus was enabled to do by giving his attention to it; for he thought it very strange, if, while artificers know the names of their tools, each in his own art, and a physician knows the names of all the instruments and medicines that he uses, a general should be so foolish and not to know the names of the commanders under him, whom he must necessarily use as his instruments whenever he wishes to seize on any post, to keep on guard, to encourage his men, or to strike terror into the enemy; and when he desired to do honour to any one, he thought it became him to address him by name. He was of opinion, too, that those who thought themselves known to their commander, would thus be more eager to be seen performing some honourable action, and more anxious to abstain from doing anything that was disgraceful. He thought it very foolish also, when a person wished anything to be done, for him to give orders as some masters give theirs. . . . "let somebody go for water, let somebody cleave the wood"; for when orders were given in such a manner, all the servants seemed to him to look one at another, and no one to execute what was ordered; and while all appeared to be in fault, yet no one was ashamed or afraid on account of his culpability, because he shared the blame equally with several others. For these reasons, he named every one when he gave his orders.[47]

[45]J. S. Watson and Henry Dale, trans., *Xenophon's Cyropaedia and the Hellenics* (London: G. Bell & Sons, Ltd., 1898), p. 41.

[46]*Ibid.*, p. 42.

[47]*Ibid.*, p. 153.

In addition to the foregoing, Cyrus recognized the need for order, placement, and uniformity of actions. He was one of the first practitioners on record of motion study, layout, and materials handling, as illustrated by the following:

> . . . he paid the utmost attention to propriety of arrangement. . . . The other parts of the army were so disposed, that each knew its own ground both as to dimension and position. When they are to prepare for marching, each man packs up such baggage as *he is appointed to use,* while others *place it upon the beasts of burden;* so that all the baggage carriers come up, *at the same time,* to the baggage appointed to them to carry, and all, *at the same time,* place it, severally, upon their beasts. *So that the same time suffices for one and for all the tents to remove.* . . . The case is the same with regard to the pitching of the tents. In order, too, that everything necessary may be done at its proper time, it is appointed to each man, *in like manner,* what he is to do; and, by this means, *the same time* suffices for doing things in one part and in all . . . [Italics are mine.] [48]

He was also cognizant of the principles of division of work, unity of direction or command, and order (a place for everything and everything in its place); and he recognized the need for teamwork, coordination, and unity of purpose in his organizations. In fact, he placed greatest emphasis upon this principle.

When war was over, Cyrus turned his attention to the management of his empire. And here, too, by recognizing that managing an army and managing an empire are in most respects the same, he illustrated the principle of universality of management.

Uniform Methods. Another illustration of the prevalence of motion study is found in an anonymous treatise on the art of war as recounted in Spaulding's *Pen and Sword in Greece and Rome.* Written in the sixth century, this treatise shows that the writer recognized the advantages to be gained by using uniform methods of performing tasks, indicating in detail how squads are assigned to tents, and *exactly* and *precisely* how the men should arrange all the articles of their equipment and clothing at night so that in case of alarm they may dress and arm themselves in the least amount of time and without confusion. Rations and mess equipment are placed in the middle of the tent; pikes upright in the ground, with shields leaning against them, concave side toward the men; clothing and equipment at each man's left in a prearranged order as he sleeps. The men are trained, in dressing and arming, to begin at the feet and work up ". . . so that no piece of equipment, already put on, shall interfere with the adjustment of a later piece."[49]

[48]*Ibid.,* p. 267.
[49]O. Spaulding, *Pen and Sword in Greece and Rome* (Princeton, N.J.: Princeton University Press, 1937), pp. 102-3.

The special interest of military history to the student of management, of course, does not lie in the character of its objectives, which have no parallel in other fields, but rather in the efficiencies that have grown out of the nature of these objectives. Many of the efficiencies have direct management applications. Of particular interest is the development of the staff system of organization.

Staff Principle. The staff principle in military organization is as old as war itself. Great individual commanders attained outstanding victories, but their success was largely dependent upon the thinking done by them before battle-staff planning. Where major forces were involved, not even martial geniuses were endowed with sufficient physical and mental capability to attend to all the details incident to the organization, administration, maintenance, and field operations of an army. Instead, the commander's staff helped in formulating plans, putting them in writing, and coordinating the subordinates in their activities.

The first significant indication of the use of the staff system occurred during the reign of Alexander the Great (336-323 B.C.). Alexander commanded one of the greatest military machines in all history through thirteen years of continuous campaigns that extended over all the world then known in the West. Genius that he was, not even Alexander would contend that his pageant of conquest was a one-man show. Although his command was a highly personalized one, the basis of his organization was a group of officers who were under his personal direction. Today we would call them chiefs of staff, adjutants, and aides-de-camp. Although we have no clear-cut description of their duties, evidence clearly indicates that each was entrusted with a specific function. Hephaestion, for example, was often charged with the matters of supply; Diades was the engineer; and Laomedon served as provost marshal. As Tarn puts it, ". . . Alexander had about him a body of men of high position . . . ., these men acted as an informal council."[50]

Alexander's military methods and his organization and management of his men influenced the ideas of Hannibal, Caesar, Frederick, and Napoleon. By the time of Caesar the military mind was able to differentiate between intelligence and operational functions, a significant development in the evolution of the concept of staff in organizing military forces. During the early seventeenth century Gustavus Adolphus took these contributions and added some touches of his own, with the result that many historians date modern warfare from this period.[51]

If we compare the management of industrial organizations with that of war machines, we shall find the conditions vital to managerial success markedly similar. There is the same man with his needs, motivations, and feelings; the same protection is required against carelessness, laziness, jealousy, fear, and

[50]W. W. Tarn, *Alexander the Great* (Boston: Beacon Press, 1957), p. 12.
[51]J. D. Hittle, *The Military Staff* (Harrisburg: Military Service Co., 1949), p. 36.

selfishness; and the same reliance is placed upon intelligence, initiative, energy, and loyalty. For success in management a plan is essential, and the preparation of a completely coordinated plan requires collective and coordinated staff effort. Discipline, delegation of authority, and recognition of line and staff distinctions—all important in management—have been borrowed in many instances from the military. In fact, the military's contribution to the science of organization is its greatest single legacy to management.

Estate Management

Leaving military history, we continue to see evidences of managerial thought and practice. In Xenophon's writings on estate management, for example, the estate, according to him, should consist of two major divisions: indoor and outdoor. The tasks of the outdoor division (ploughing, sowing, grazing, etc.) supply the product which must be stored and kept under cover by the indoor division. Specifically, the indoor manager was instructed to remain indoors and send out those servants whose work was outside, and to superintend those who were to work indoors. He was to receive the "incoming" of the estate and distribute so much of it as must be spent, but taking care that the sum laid by for a year not to be spent in a month—a clear indication of his understanding of planning and budgeting. The practice of inventory control is substantiated by the story of the servant who knew each particular section so exactly that he could tell even when away where everything was kept and *how much* there was of it, with things consumed month by month separated from the supplies *calculated* to last for a year!

On incentives, Xenophon states that workers should be trained to be eager for the improvement of the estate ". . . by allowing them to share in our success."[52] An ancient touch of the modern Scanlon!

Rome

With single-minded determination and superior managerial talents, the Romans gained control over an estimated fifty million people, extending from Great Britain in the west to Syria in the east, and including Europe and all the north of Africa. Mismanagement, however, caused the downfall of Rome, but the very fact that the Romans were able to build a governmental and military structure of such giant proportions and operate it so successfully for so many years is a tribute to their superior and advanced managerial capacities and abilities.

Empire Organization. Forced by the conquest of new territories and new

[52]Xenophon, *Memorabilia and Oeconomicus,* pp. 421-69.

peoples, the Romans early turned their thoughts to the most effective way to organize and control their empire. Management has learned much from Rome's successes as well as from her mistakes in the area of organization—actually the world's first experiment in organizing a truly far-flung empire. The problem, of course, was how to maintain control, loyalty, and taxes in a geographically dispersed empire. Too much delegation on a local level tempted the military and others to divide or sever their loyalty to Rome. And because of the distance involved and the need for local "autonomy" to meet local peculiarities, a highly centralized form of organization did not prove workable.

In the year 284 A.D. Diocletian became emperor and instigated a new system of organization which emphasized the successive delegation of authority. Realizing he could not control the far-flung reaches of the empire without delegating more of his authority, he divided the empire into 101 provinces. These, in turn, were grouped to form thirteen dioceses, with the latter grouped to form four major geographical divisions. He appointed three assistants (one with the title of "Augustus" and the other two with the titles of "Caesar") to rule three of the divisions, keeping one for himself. He appointed "vicarii" to rule the dioceses and "governors" to rule the provinces. To each he delegated only the authority related to civil government, permitting them no control of the military stationed within their provinces and removing them two levels from the emperor.

Diocletian's aim was to strengthen and solidify the imperial authority, and by thus extending the scalar principle, the old provincial governors, directly responsible to the emperor, disappeared, leaving successive gradations of delegated authority. The net effect was to solidify the organization—by reducing the importance of the province as a unit of government.

Some writers refer to the Roman organization as one of decentralization. This appears, however, to have been true only during the Roman Republic and perhaps an earlier period of the empire when the government was plagued with internal problems as a result of the tremendous power held by the provincial rulers. Under Diocletian's system of centralization, however, it became incomparably more difficult for provincial and other rulers to defy or overthrow the central power. Today managers are applying these same Diocletian principles of organization when they employ a graduated system of central control in an effort to stabilize centralized authority.

Farm Management. The study of the treatises of Cato and of Varro on Roman farm management would be profitable to today's farmer regardless of how practical or scientific he might be. As we shall see, two thousand years ago Romans were studying the same problems that exist today and were solving them by intelligent reasoning and good management.

Cato, for example, indicates that when the owner inspects his fields he should observe how the work has progressed, what has been done, and what remains to be done. He should then summon his overseer and call for a report of what has been done and ask why it has not been possible to complete the rest. According to Cato, the overseer of antiquity will have a very modern reply: "Some of the workers have been sick, others absent; the weather has been bad. . . ." After listening to these and other excuses, Cato indicates that the overseer's attention should be called to the program of work laid out for him on the previous visit and he should compare it with the results obtained. If bad weather prevented certain work from being accomplished, then Cato advises that the owner rehearse with the overseer what work could have been done despite rain, such as cleaning out the barns, sorting the grain, cleaning seed, and mending gear. Finally, the owner should give orders for the completion of the work that has been neglected, orders that should be clear and thoroughly understood by the overseer.

Cato states that the accounts of money, supplies, and provisions should then be considered to find out what wine and oil has been sold, what price obtained, what is on hand, and what remains to be sold. Finally, Cato indicates that the owner should give the overseer *in writing* a work plan for the year![53]

Turning to the overseer, Cato lists among his duties the following.[54]

> He should maintain discipline.
>
> He should respect the rights of others and steadfastly uphold his own.
>
> He should settle all quarrels among the hands; if any one is at fault he should administer the punishment.
>
> He should show appreciation of courtesy, to encourage others to practice it.
>
> He should keep the hands busy.
>
> He should give heed to those whom the master has recommended to him and should maintain relations with two or three other farms so that he can exchange things needed in an emergency.
>
> He should go over his accounts with his master frequently. Soothsayers, fortune tellers, necromancers, and astrologers should not be consulted!
>
> He should pay the highest compliments to the team masters who keep their cattle in the best condition.
>
> Finally, he should plan all the work in ample time, for if one thing is done late everything will be late, and even though work stops, expenses still go on!

And the duties of today's foremen? Getting out production, maintaining plant and equipment, maintaining communications, maintaining discipline,

---

[53]Adapted from Cato, *De re rustica,* trans. by a Virginia farmer, *Roman Farm Management* (New York: The Macmillan Company, 1913), pp. 51-290.

[54]*Ibid.,* p. 33.

managing human relations, planning ahead, participating—all of which were either stated or implied by Cato who lived between 234 and 149 B.C.

During the past fifty years a good deal of attention and emphasis has been placed on personnel selection and placement, but Varro living between 116 and 28 B.C. had this to say on the selection of farm hands:

> Select for farm hands those who are fitted for heavy labor and have some aptitude for agriculture, which can be ascertained by trying them on several tasks and by inquiring as to what they did for their former master. The foreman should have some education, a good disposition and economical habits, and it is better that he should be older than the hands, for they will be listened to with more respect than if they were boys. The foreman should be very experienced in agricultural work so that workers may appreciate that it is greater knowledge and skill which entitles the foreman to command. The foreman should never be authorized to enforce his discipline with the whips if he can accomplish his result with words. It is wise to choose a foreman who is married because marriage will make him more steady and attach him to the place. The foreman will work more cheerfully if rewards are offered him . . .[55]

SUMMARY

It is highly probable that the management process first began in the family organization, later expanded to the tribe, and finally pervaded the formalized political units such as those found in early Babylonia. In these organizations, a type of financial control and record keeping was invented which usually took the form of clay tablets with inscriptions. The recognition of the concept of managerial responsibility was clearly evidenced through the Code of Hammurabi. Later the Egyptians provided us with one of the first examples of a dispersed, decentralized organization with little or no control, with its consequent poor end results. This system of organization is the first recorded instance of the utilization of a decentralized form of organization to manage an empire, and it illustrates the inherent weaknesses of this system which eventually led to its demise. The Egyptian skill in planning and organizing the construction of public edifices, however, is evident in their pyramids and buildings. The Hebrews, too, made their contribution to organization theory and first illustrated the use of the exception principle.

The ancient Chinese philosophers were the first to recognize the need for methodological means of employee selection and staffing, which they supplied through their civil service system. Throughout these early civilizations we see evidences time and again of the early recognition of the use of staff as well as the

---

[55]Varro, *Rerum rusticam libritres,* trans. by a Virginia farmer, *Roman Farm Management* (New York: The Macmillan Company, 1913), p. 277.

principle of specialization, noting, especially in the writing of Mencius, its application in such areas as divisions of a trade, and hereditary trades. The science of *polity,* the management of cities and states, first appeared in India in the writings of Kautilya.

Perhaps the Greeks more than any other people provide us with the most extensive documentation of management principles in Xenophon's writing about the universality of management, specialization, management as an art, employee selection, delegation of authority, and motion study. These and other instances from early history point clearly to the "originality" of our "modern" managerial practices!

The Romans, as we have seen, made the same mistake that the Egyptians made in the organization of their empire on a decentralized basis with little or no control. But civilizations never seem to learn from others' mistakes, and during the Middle Ages the principle of decentralization was again violated in the feudal system of management, with the same ultimate demise.

Looking at the entire continuum of management thought during this early period of history, we can conclude that management was strictly on a trial-and-error basis, with little or no theory and virtually no exchange of ideas and practices. Perhaps inadequate records, poor communication, and failure to analyze the reasons for nonsuccess lay behind this lack of profiting from the earlier experiences of others. Evidences of managerial practices clearly indicate, however, that some principles of management were recognized in these early times and communicated at least locally on a how-to-do-it basis.

In general, it appears that the managerial principles employed were born out of the necessity of having to accomplish goals, and these principles were "discovered" over and over again by numerous individuals in history as they went about attempting to reach needed objectives.

Thus, in these early times, management thought existed, but only in a somewhat nebulous and unsophisticated state. Management as a separate process was not verbalized until Plato and Socrates. Even then, however, the principles were not united in a scheme of management thought, nor is there evidence of any chronological building of various managerial techniques upon previously conceived ones.

2

MANAGEMENT DURING THE MEDIEVAL PERIOD

With the fall of the Roman Empire, the peoples of Western Europe were reduced to filling the basic need of self-preservation. The prime necessity facing an individual was protection against murder, robbery, and violence. To secure this protection, the individual frequently sought the protection of a person more powerful than himself; and, in return for the protection he paid the price of subservience, including the loss of individual freedom and the rise of a feudal relationship.

Given these economic and environmental conditions the growth of the institutions of feudalism was both natural and inevitable. The feudal system itself, of course, was actually nothing more than an extension of practices that appeared in the final days of the Roman Empire. The wealthy Roman landowner, for instance, was granted many civil powers by the crown. And following this came the growing practice of poor and small landowners giving up ownership of their lands in exchange for protection. Thus, some conditions of feudalism already existed in Roman times.

FEUDAL ORGANIZATION

Perhaps a brief description of the main features of the feudal organization that existed between the fall of the Roman Empire and the early conceptualized forms of management would help to give us a better idea of the system of state organization that dominated Europe during these four centuries known as the Dark Ages.

The organization of feudalism was basically a scalar one, with descending grades of delegated authority. At the top of the great feudal pyramid stood the emperor or the king, and all the land in his dominions belonged to him. He kept large areas for his personal use and invested the highest nobles with the remainder. The great vassals of the crown held these fiefs on condition of rendering certain specified services, mainly military and financial. In like manner, these vassals in turn exacted services similar in kind from their sub-vassals. This system of subinfeudation resulted in successive graduations down to the smallest feudal unit, the knight's fee, which in turn had its dependent tenantry, classified as freeholders down to serfs.

The process of decentralization represented by this pyramid was further emphasized by the growth of the institution of immunity. Under this system the vassal won the right to govern his own territory as he wished. The feudal unit, the manor, became in some respects a governmental unit with its one-man court. Feudalism, therefore, represented another large-scale venture in decentralization and involved the same conditions and problems as those faced by contemporary governmental and business organizations.

As one might expect, however, the primary problem then as now was to determine how to preserve the proper balance between centralized authority and local autonomy. Decentralized *operation* was necessary to provide the immediate attention and flexibility needed to adjust policies to local conditions. Centralized *authority,* on the other hand, was equally important to insure that all the advantages arising out of the total interaction of all the parts on the whole, or the whole on all parts, would be realized. According to Mooney and Reiley, this balance is not merely a question of management; it also involves the form of organization through which management can best operate and become effective.[1] On this point the lessons of feudalism taught managers a great deal. It taught them that strength of organization was gained through scalar control. Additionally, it showed that with a common interest this type of organization would work, *but, they found, the common interest concept must exist.* The one major defect of feudalism was the inaccurate assumption that this common interest did exist. The same assumption was also made by the organizers of the Roman, Egyptian, and Greek empires.

Finally, feudalistic organization taught management that delegation of authority is not an abdication—that the delegatee always has the authority to take back what he delegated and that the delegation was a *con*ferring and not a *trans*ferring of authority. The inappropriate delegation of authority by *transfer* showed clearly that if a manager wished to organize a function on a

---

[1] James D. Mooney and Alan C. Reiley, *Onward Industry!* (New York: Harper & Bros., 1931), p. 149.

decentralized basis, the organization must be accomplished on a base of *conferred* authority, otherwise the sought-after decentralization would turn into disintegration.

EARLY WRITINGS

During the Dark Ages, virtually no books were written concerning the concepts of management. This is not surprising when we stop to consider the environment, the authors, and their readers.

People lived under hostile conditions: Self-preservation was a prime concern; and little or no attention was given to concepts as opposed to physical things. Those who wrote were either scribes, members of religious orders, or well-educated leaders of the court. Books were written laboriously by hand, and only the most important concepts were worth recording under these tedious and trying circumstances. The typical subjects included religion, governing a kingdom, waging war, and the laws of the land. Those who "knew their letters" and could read these books were the priests and scribes, the rulers and nobles, and the landed gentry. The art of management, though important to each of these groups, was not given a high priority. Managing or running a manor, for example, was often turned over to one of the underlings while the learned lord concerned himself with the more "important" matters of the day, such as hunting, riding, and gaming. Under these circumstances, it is not surprising that little or no writing on management was done during the medieval period; however, we do find some evidence of managerial acumen and know-how. About the year 900, for example, Alfarabi, in writing about managing a kingdom or state, noted that:[2]

> In the model state there must be a hierarchy of rulers coming under the control of a supreme head or prince. This prince, head of the model state or of the whole earth, must possess certain traits: great intelligence, excellent memory, eloquence, firmness without weakness, firmness in the achievement of good, love for justice, love for study, love for truth, aversion to falsehood, temperance in food, drink and enjoyments, and contempt for wealth.
>
> All these traits must be found in one man alone placed in charge of directing the complicated machinery of the state. In case all these traits cannot be found in one man alone, then inquiry should be made to determine whether there are two or more who possess the required traits jointly. If there are two, they should both rule the model state. If there are three, then these three should rule. If more are needed, more should rule.

What a model list of traits this is for contemporary managers! In addition,

---

[2]Robert Hammond, *The Philosophy of Alfarabi* (New York: The Hobson Book Press, 1947), p. 51.

it points up the wisdom of dual managership or control by a complementary group.

Two hundred years later, in 1100, Ghazali stated in his book of counsel for kings:

> Oh King of the World, four things must you always keep with you: (i) justice; (ii) intelligence; (iii) patience; and (iv) modesty. Four things must you never have with you: (i) envy; (ii) arrogance; (iii) narrow-mindedness; and (iv) malice. . . . The [kings] who preceded you have all passed away, and the coming of others is arranged. Until they come, try hard to make all the kings and subjects feel that they would miss you.[3]

Again, sage managerial advice.

Beginning with the fourteenth century, however, we can more easily reconstruct managerial thinking from the somewhat more plentiful writing—though it was still meager by modern standards. The populace did, however, keep records of actions and transactions, and from these historians have been able to reconstruct many managerial practices.

In 1494, for example, Luca Pacioli published a treatise describing the double-entry bookkeeping system. Pacioli did not invent the double-entry system; he indicated that the system employed in Venice should be adopted and he recommended it over all others.[4] To management scholars, Pacioli's work is of significance for several reasons. Technically, the accounting methodology suggested in his treatise is applicable to a great deal of our modern accounting practice. Many excerpts from Pacioli's writing could be inserted into our current accounting textbooks with virtually no changes in wording. In addition, Pacioli pointed to the need for a concern with internal managerial controls. Along this line he recommended that the memorandum, journal, and ledger be numbered and dated, that documents for all transactions be complete in detail and permanently filed, and that periodic audits be made for internal checks.[5] When we consider that Pacioli was not a businessman, but a scholar and teacher in such diverse fields as mathematics, theology, architecture, and military tactics, his attention to and writing about these managerial needs suggest that the study of business management was gaining some respectability as a subject worthy of academic effort.

One modern historian, Frederic C. Lane, has written two unusual books which give us insight into some of the early managerial practices. The first, *Venetian Ships and Shipbuilders of the Renaissance,* is an economic history of the Venetian shipbuilding industry; the second, *Andrea Barbarigo: Merchant of*

---

[3]F. R. C. Bagley, trans., *Ghazali's Book of Counsel for Kings (Nasihat al-Muluk)* (London: Oxford University Press, 1964), p. 83.

[4]R. E. Brown and K. S. Johnston, *Pacioli on Accounting* (New York: McGraw-Hill Book Company, 1963), p. 26.

[5]*Ibid.,* pp. 99-102.

Venice (1418-1449), is a biography of an early "businessman." These books provide detailed accounts of the advanced state of commerce and industry in Italy in the fourteenth, fifteenth, and sixteenth centuries and are a valuable addition to the field, since little has been written about the period prior to the fifteenth century.

THE MERCHANTS OF VENICE

Andrea Barbarigo: Merchant of Venice (1418-1449) pictures the flourishing trade of Venice in the fifteenth century. Lane chose Barbarigo as the subject for a biography because the records of Barbarigo's business transactions were available and because he was a typical Venetian merchant. The two main areas of interest to the modern student of management are the types of business organization employed and the Venetian use of accounting as a managerial device.

The partnership and the joint venture were the two chief types of business organization in Renaissance Italy. The partnership was designed for and used mainly by business firms, while the joint venture was usually employed in one-time deals, explorations, or ventures.[6]

Many of the large firms, Cosimo de' Medici of Florence, for example, were tightly organized partnerships in which one man, owner of a large amount of capital, would bring in with him partners of lesser power and wealth. The contracts of partnerships used by the Medici specified how long a partnership would last, usually three to five years. Normally these were renewed.[7]

The Medici partnership, although a family organization, was tightly centralized. However, in the typical family partnership, the organization was loose and rather decentralized. Frequently these family partnerships were actually household partnerships in which brothers pooled their inheritance.[8]

Sometimes the Venetian family partnerships became a combination investment trust and holding company in which the holdings were spread among real estate, government bonds, merchandise, and commercial accounts payable. The family firms with their enormous prestige and wealth were often able to exert powerful economic and political pressures.[9]

In international commerce, Andrea Barbarigo and other merchants made wide use of two legal relationships: joint ownership and agency. Joint ownership was usually a joint venture in which the owners had limited liability. The combinations which were formed to charter merchant galleys from the state split

[6]Frederic C. Lane, *Andrea Barbarigo: Merchant of Venice (1418-1449)* (Baltimore: Johns Hopkins Press, 1944), p. 91.
[7]*Ibid.,* p. 86.
[8]*Ibid.,* p. 87.
[9]*Ibid.,* p. 89.

the ownership into shares, and shareholders shared proportionately in the expenses and profits of the venture.[10] Comparable to the absentee corporation shareholders of the twentieth century were depositors with no direct interest in the ventures who could nevertheless invest their capital for a profit.[11]

Venetian joint ventures commonly used commission agents, and Andrea Barbarigo usually did business abroad by assigning merchandise to such agents. The early Italian practice of paying agents a share of the profits gave way to the custom of paying a fixed percentage of the transaction. Barbarigo often consigned goods to agents who might in turn convey the goods to other agents unknown to Barbarigo.[12] He was adept in persuading the commission agents to supply him with information of the commercial centers abroad, thus establishing an international news service of his own.[13]

This loose form of Venetian business organization, often dropped once the venture was consummated, made it possible for merchants to shift from venture to venture, from one type of merchandise to another, and from agent to agent. The trader who specialized in one type of goods was at a distinct disadvantage in competing against the trader who was not afraid to shift from one line to another. The big profits went to the trader who could recognize changing conditions in supply and demand and was resourceful enough to shift his emphasis to the more profitable enterprise. Then as now it was the entrepreneur of vision and initiative who succeeded.

The involved commercial and financial deals of the Venetian merchants perforce entailed a system of documentation and record keeping. During the time of Andrea Barbarigo (early fifteenth century), Venice was beginning to use double-entry bookkeeping, but the use of bookkeeping elsewhere in Italy preceded the Venetians. The essentials of double-entry bookkeeping were in use in ledgers of Genoese bankers as early as 1340, and the books of Florentine merchant-bankers of that generation contained some but not all of the elements.[14]

The books of the Soranzo Brothers of Venice (1410-16) show that the important function of the journal was to serve as the basis for the ledger. The Soranzos recorded all transactions in the *memoriale* and then in the journal before posting to the ledger so that ". . .if by any chance you should lose this ledger through robbery, fire, or shipwreck . . . you can by means of this book always make up the ledger with the same entries, day by day."[15]

Andrea Barbarigo employed other bookkeeping features which correspond to modern practices. When he sent cloth out to be dyed, he had an account for

[10]*Ibid.,* pp. 91-92.
[11]*Ibid.,* p. 93.
[12]*Ibid.,* pp. 93-96.
[13]*Ibid.,* pp. 120-21.
[14]*Ibid.,* p. 153.
[15]*Ibid.,* p. 158.

"wool given to be worked on," which corresponds to goods in process. Before he drew up his trial balance, Barbarigo made some important consolidations of accounts in order to simplify the statement of his net worth. A profit and loss account was also used by Barbarigo.[16]

Though not as detailed and sophisticated as those of Barbarigo, records relating to cost accounting have been found in the account books of Francisco Di Marco, a merchant of Florence (1358-1412). Wages of spinners, weavers, and dyers were detailed, with one page giving details for each spinner: weight and price of wool given him, weight and yardage of wool returned, and wages. In fact, one 1395 book details the costs of producing two bolts of woolen cloth.[17]

THE ARSENAL OF VENICE

As Venice's maritime power grew, her citizens saw the need for an armed fleet to protect her trade, which was crucial to her livelihood. For a while the city depended on private shipyards to build the military fleet, and in times of crisis she could draw ships from the commercial fleet. As her trade and influence and the concomitant need for protection grew, the city had in operation in 1436 its own government shipyard, the Arsenal. In this Venetian shipyard bookkeeping was just as important as it was in business, but employed somewhat differently. The supervisors were directed personally to handle and record the use of appropriations, but by the middle of the fifteenth century bookkeepers and pages were hired for the purpose. In an attempt at efficiency, the shipyard kept a strict accounting of moneys, materials, and men. An early form of cost accounting was also used. All accounts were consolidated into two journals and one ledger, with one of the journals kept by the lords of the shipyard for comparison with the ledger. Three types of expense accounts were recognized: fixed, variable, and extraordinary. A meticulous record was kept of everything that entered and left the shipyard as well.[18]

In the sixteenth century when the Venetian state and navy were at their zenith of power, methods of large-scale production were needed to build the war fleet and maintain its reserve.[19] The Arsenal of Venice, as a consequence, became what was perhaps the largest industrial plant of the world. It covered sixty acres of ground and water and employed from one to two thousand workers. Many of the problems created by size (accounting, arrangement of material,

---

[16]*Ibid.,* pp. 170-75.

[17]A. C. Littleton, *Essays on Accountancy* (Urbana: University of Illinois Press, 1961), pp. 22-23.

[18]Frederic C. Lane, *Venetian Ships and Shipbuilders of the Renaissance* (Baltimore: Johns Hopkins Press, 1934), p. 4.

[19]*Ibid.,* p. 127.

and discipline of workers, for example) were solved with an efficiency that modern industry might well emulate.[20]

Arsenal management was noted for its checks and balances. Although three lords of the Arsenal were officially in charge, the commissioners, who were the connecting link between the Venetian senate and the Arsenal, also had influence. The senate itself often managed or interfered with the management of the Arsenal. The commissioners and the lords were so closely involved in the financial management, purchasing, and similar functions that they were unable to direct the actual shipbuilding. Foremen and technical advisers headed the large operating divisions of the shipyards. So vital was the work of the Arsenal to the life of Venice that no one man or group was alone trusted to manage it.[21]

The Arsenal did more than build ships. It had a threefold task: (1) the *manufacture* of galleys, arms, and equipment; (2) the *storage* of the equipment until needed; and (3) the *assembly* and *refitting* of the ships on reserve.[22]

The lords of the Arsenal were required to keep on reserve ships which could be outfitted and sent to sea on short notice. In the fourteenth century a modest reserve of six ships was required.[23] But with the growth of Venice's maritime power, the reserve fleet was increased to fifty and later to one hundred ships in the sixteenth century.[24] The reserve requirements were not idle precautions, for the entire fleet could be wiped out in one or more battles.

The galleys built by the Venetians were small by present standards. This light ship (perhaps "boat" would be more nearly correct), which was the mainstay of the sixteenth century Venetian navy, was approximately 106 feet long and had one deck with a beam of 15 to 22 feet. The deck was divided into three parts: a fighting platform in the bow, a larger and higher stern castle, and in between, running almost the whole length, the rowing space divided down the middle by a gangway. The oars were 29 to 32 feet long and weighed 120 pounds.[25]

Several areas of management practiced in the Arsenal are worthy of our attention: (1) numbering and warehousing of finished parts; (2) assembly line outfitting of the galleys; (3) personnel practices; (4) standardization of parts; (5) control by accounting; (6) inventory control; and (7) cost control.

Warehousing

To be prepared to outfit the reserve fleet on a moment's notice, the Arsenal needed not only the ships but also the necessary gear and rigging. At any

---

[20]*Ibid.*, p. 146.
[21]*Ibid.*, pp. 148-52.
[22]*Ibid.*, p. 164.
[23]*Ibid.*, p. 133.
[24]*Ibid.*, p. 142.
[25]*Ibid.*, pp. 9-10.

moment, therefore, the warehouses might have had the following equipment on hand for emergency issue: five thousand benches, one hundred rudders, one hundred masts, two hundred spars, five thousand footbraces, five thousand to fifteen thousand oars, plus cordage arms, pitch, and ironwork.[26]

The task of outfitting the galleys was facilitated by the warehousing of the equipment. All of it was numbered and stocked in a designated space. Systematic arrangement of material saved time and labor, and the assignment of definite warehouses to various products helped to implement the assembly line procedure as well as the accuracy of the inventories.[27]

Although the finished products were neatly numbered and stocked, the Arsenal was slow to adopt a system for orderly storage of unprocessed wood. When a worker needed a piece of wood, he had to search through a huge stack until he found a suitable piece. As we shall see later, all the wood was eventually kept in one place, assorted by type, to avoid having it cost three times as much to find a log as the log was worth.[28]

Assembly Line

When the time came to outfit the ships on reserve, the Arsenal employed a system similar to our modern assembly lines. The warehouses were arranged along a canal so that the galleys could be brought to the equipment rather than the equipment to the galleys.[29]

As the galley was towed along the canal past the warehouses, the arms and equipment were passed through the windows of the warehouses. The location of the warehouses was such that the parts were placed on the galleys in the proper sequence of outfitting.[30]

For the emergency outfittings, the officers of the Arsenal were assigned specific departments by types of equipment. One foreman was responsible for carpentry, a second for masts, a third for the caulking, a fourth for oars, and so on.[31]

The Arsenal dazzled distinguished visitors with its dispatch in the final assembly and outfitting of a galley. One Spanish traveler, Pero Tafur, wrote in 1436:

> And as one enters the gate there is a great street on either hand with the sea in the middle, and on one side are windows opening out of the houses of the Arsenal, and the same on the other side, and out came the galley towed by a boat, and from the windows they handed out to them

[26]*Ibid.,* p. 159.
[27]*Ibid.,* p. 160.
[28]*Ibid.,* p. 158.
[29]*Ibid.,* p. 172.
[30]*Ibid.*
[31]*Ibid.,* p. 160.

from one the cordage, from another the bread, from another the arms, and from another the balistas and mortars, and so from all sides everything which was required, and when the galley had reached the end of the street, all the men required were on board, together with the complement of oars, and she was equipped from end to end. In this manner there came out ten galleys, fully armed, between the hours of three and nine.[32]

When Henry III of France visited Venice in 1574, a galley was assembled, launched, and completely armed within one hour. The galleys on reserve were, of course, ready for launching except for caulking and other minor finishing.[33]

When the need arose, the Arsenal could accomplish astonishing feats. On January 28, 1570, for example, when the Turkish plan to attack Cyprus became known, the senate ordered that a total of one hundred ships be put in order by the middle of March. The Arsenal did not fall behind expectations, completing the order by the beginning of April.[34]

Personnel

No industrial organization as big as the Arsenal could long function without rather close supervision of the rank and file workers. And supervise them the Arsenal did. Working hours—starting time and quitting time—were strictly enforced. Entrance into the shipyard was closely guarded to prevent thievery.[35]

Depending on the job, both piecework and day wages were paid. Piecework was the rule in the making of oars; the foremen closely scrutinized the work and gave credit only for satisfactory work.[36] Day wages were paid for menial labor as well as for painstaking jobs such as fastening exposed timbers and planks.[37]

Artisans who made the equipment worked in separate craft shops under those foremen skilled in the craft, who gave out the material, accepted only well-made products, and kept an account of the output. The foremen were able to concentrate on their duties as technical directors by assigning other responsibilities to subordinates: paymasters checked hours, gang bosses handled discipline, and so forth.[38]

The Arsenal exercised control over the admission of apprentices to mastership, although in the sixteenth century the main distinction between apprentice and master was the wage differential. However in some shipyard

[32]*Ibid.*, p. 172.
[33]*Ibid.*, p. 14.
[34]*Ibid.*, p. 144.
[35]*Ibid.*, p. 193.
[36]*Ibid.*, p. 166.
[37]*Ibid.*, p. 204.
[38]*Ibid.*, p. 164.

crafts, carpentry in particular, prospective workers were required to pass examinations prior to employment.[39]

Today personnel managers stress the importance of a systematic employee rating plan as an aid to supervisors in evaluating the performance of their subordinates and in making personnel decisions. During the sixteenth century the Arsenal also used a merit-rating plan administered by a committee that met in March and in September to review the merits of each master employee and to raise his pay if he deserved advancement.

An interesting personnel sidelight is the Arsenal's policy on the "wine break," analogous to our modern coffee break. Considered a regular part of their pay, wine was supplied to the masters five or six times a day while they worked. From this practice arose the need for a wine steward who would be as sparing as possible in distributing the wine and who would buy only good wine so that, as sometimes happened, it would not spoil and incapacitate the masters.

Standardization

That the advantages of standardization were recognized is evident in the policy drawn up by the Arsenal's planning committee. This policy stated that (1) all bows were to be made so that arrows would fit any of them, (2) all sternposts were to be built of the same design so that each rudder would not have to be especially fitted to its sternpost, and (3) all rigging and deck furnishings were to be uniform. One general manager disapproved of giving each master builder the opportunity to make a galley of his own design because this policy would result in wasteful building and imperfect galleys. Thus, over five centuries ago the Venetians recognized the advantages of standardization in both the assembly and the handling of their ships. In assembly standardization would speed production and reduce costs; in utilization it would make the ships handle the same way, with the same speed and maneuverability, thereby permitting them to operate as a fleet and not as a series of individual ships.

Control by Accounting

Of the various business problems resulting from the growth of the Arsenal, accounting was the first to be recognized and accepted as a technique of control in the management of the Arsenal. Insofar as the Arsenal performed the functions of a supply detachment, strict ordering of accounting was the obvious first consideration in the minds of those regulating its management. Complete and accurate accounts appeared the chief requirement, whether the Arsenal bought in the open market or contracted for products with craftsmen whom it supplied with the materials and paid by the piece. There was also required a

[39]*Ibid.*, p. 182.

strict accounting of money, of materials, and finally of men and the use of their time.

By regulations established by the Arsenal about 1370, all accounts were consolidated in two journals and one ledger. One journal was kept by the lord of the Arsenal who tended the cash box. The chief accountant entered the items in the ledger from a second journal which was kept by the second accountant. Every few months two lords of the Arsenal working together checked their journal with the ledger to see that there had been no mistake. Each September the ledger was balanced, each account separately, the balance was carried over to a new ledger, and the old books were sent to the treasurer's office to be audited.

In 1564 an attempt was made to divide all the expenses of the Arsenal into three accounts. The first covered fixed expenses; the second, necessary but unlimited expenses; and the third provided for extraordinary expenses. This division of the income of the Arsenal into separate funds for different purposes led to such a multiplication of the number of books kept that in 1555 it was again necessary to stipulate that, while funds were to be separately accounted for, the one ledger and the two journals should receive all transactions. The point here is that the Arsenal wanted and succeeded in getting a method for keeping track of all expenditures as well as a means for evaluating the expenditures made.

Although the Arsenal employed books of entry and ledgers, as we have shown, the origin of modern bookkeeping can be traced back to 1494, the year in which Luca Pacioli, a Franciscan friar, published a work on double-entry bookkeeping. Fifty years later the book was translated into English. By the end of the seventeenth century, the principles and practices of double-entry bookkeeping, in virtually their modern form, were widely known among the industrial and commercial centers. In fact, Thomas Watts referred to this method of keeping accounts as his "darling science," and he had only contempt for those who kept single-entry books. The systematic modern accounting that originated at this time represents one of the first general methodologies of management. It is significant as a quantitative method, and underlying the problems of accounting were problems of observation and measurement, systems analysis, model construction, and decision theory—all necessitated by the early manager's quest for accurate records to be used in decision making.

Inventory Control

For inventory control, we find that a detailed record was kept by the arms steward of what munitions were sent out and where they were sent, regardless of who issued the orders for shipment.

The actual physical oversight of all that passed out of the Arsenal was left to the doorkeepers. They were to stop anything from leaving without the signed permits of the lords of the Arsenal.

The arms steward also kept records of goods received, but special officials were used to keep track of certain goods bought by the Arsenal. These inspectors, or "appraisers" as they were called then, were responsible for inspecting timbers offered, seeing that good wood was delivered, and reporting its value to the lords who formally contracted for it. They were also responsible for inspecting finished products.

Cost Control

Although adequate provision was made for recording goods received, no regular system was devised before 1564 for the orderly arrangement after delivery of the goods. When a worker wanted a piece of wood—the chief raw material—he would search around through the piles of lumber until he found one to suit his need. This casual handling of the lumber stocks contrasted sharply with the orderly disposal of the finished products as previously discussed. Lane's study, however, indicated that this inefficiency attracted the attention of officials only after being expressed in terms of money lost. Thus, in 1564 an accountant testified that five hundred ducats a year were spent in finding wood and moving it around the Arsenal. Furthermore, whenever a ship was launched, it was necessary to clear the lumber out of the way. This activity required an expenditure of twelve hundred ducats each year. An accountant found that it cost three times as much to find a log as the log was worth. Here, then, is an example of the early use of a quantitative method as an aid in decision making. As a result of these cost studies a separate place was established for a lumberyard in which all timber was arranged in an orderly manner, with a full appreciation of the savings in time and labor as well as the value of an accurate inventory.

In addition to these business operations, further insights into managerial concepts of the period have been furnished by sixteenth century writers such as Sir Thomas More and Machiavelli. Both these writers present interesting evidences of managerial thinking.

SIXTEENTH CENTURY WRITERS

Sir Thomas Moore

Utopia, like many other books on the subject, is Sir Thomas More's literary attempt to create the ideal state. Trained in the law but perhaps even more famous as a churchman and a scholar, More conceived his state as, above all, a good state.

It was inevitable that More's ideal society would be a good society. He was, in fact, a truly noble man who ultimately went to his death simply because he could not reconcile his principles with his king's desires.

Born in London in 1478, for a time More considered entering the Catholic priesthood but chose the law instead and rose to become sheriff of London and lord chancellor of England. He first incurred the royal wrath of King Henry VII by opposing the latter's request for an extravagant subsidy. Later when King Henry VIII insisted on divorcing Catherine of Aragon to marry Anne Boleyn, More resigned as lord chancellor. He was willing to accept the Act of Succession which made Anne Boleyn's children heirs to the throne, but he would not take an oath to impugn the pope's authority over the church of England. For defying the king, More was tried as a traitor, condemned, and beheaded in 1535.

The intended readers of More's *Utopia* were his contemporaries rather than posterity. His ideal state would correct the managerial injustices and abuses as he saw them in England and Europe of his day. Book I of *Utopia* outlines the shortcomings of his society; Book II describes the ideal state.

More blamed the economic ills of England on mismanagement by the ruling class of noblemen. As he viewed them, the noblemen were unproductive parasites who lived on the labors of their farm tenants. Surrounding the noblemen was another unproductive group, their entourages, men who had neither learned a trade nor earned a livelihood.[40] To compound the troubles of the tenants, many noblemen had turned their acreage into pastures for sheep and had driven the farmers off the land and into unemployment. These erstwhile farmers were often thrown into prison as vagrants, although they would gladly have offered their services for hire if employment had been available.[41]

As a moralistic economist, More viewed the pleasures and diversions of both rich and poor as a further source of their economic troubles. He was contemptuous of the conspicuous consumption of the rich, their ostentatious dress, and their excessive indulgence in eating. Meanwhile, the poor brought on their own economic ruin by squandering their meager earnings in dives, brothels, wine shops, games of chance, and quoits.[42] In his ideal state More proposed through better management to eliminate the wasteful consumption of the rich and the diversions of the poor and channel the funds into more useful purposes.

In *Utopia* the crafts are characterized by the principles of specialization of labor and maximum utilization of manpower. Aside from a few chosen individuals who would devote their lives to scholarship (and that would have to be of the useful variety!), all persons, of both sexes, would at an early age be forced to learn a craft that would occupy them for the remainder of their productive years. Most individuals would normally learn the craft of their parents, but they would be permitted to choose another craft if it better suited their abilities and inclinations. The useful crafts, according to More, would include linen-making, wool-making, masonry, metalworking, and carpentry.[43]

---

[40]Sir Thomas More, *Utopia*, ed. Edward Surtz (New Haven: Yale University Press, 1964), pp. 21-22.
[41]*Ibid.*, p. 25.
[42]*Ibid.*, p. 27.
[43]*Ibid.*, p. 69.

Although More was not addressing himself to the subject of organization and management in *Utopia*, he nevertheless contributed a few noteworthy points. His communal dining halls highlight the economies of mass production. He also stressed the advantages of specialization of labor in discussing the crafts in his ideal state. In a rather cursory section on the government of Utopia, he outlined a system of government by elective officials—a new type of kingdom management that was anathema to the king of England.

More's Italian contemporary, Niccolo Machiavelli, would never have accepted the humanistic doctrine presented in *Utopiaa*. In fact, had he read *Utopia* he would have scoffed at many of More's managerial reforms, as well as at the war strategy of the pietistic Utopians who, because they disapproved of war, would hire their neighbors to do their fighting for them![44]

Aside from its religious and social issues, however, *Utopia* is a caustic attack on the management practices of the ruling nobles of England, and More's managerially organized life of *Utopia* probably represents considerable improvement over the miserable existence of the peasants at the time. More's book is important to us because it reflects the recognition and importance given to management between 1480 and 1550 by one of England's great sons, although Sir Thomas More, of course, would not have recognized his book as a managerial work. Nevertheless, More's comments on management may well have served to open the eyes of some English leaders and to provide a framework for future changes toward better management of men and other resources.

Niccolo Machiavelli

Although Thomas More was canonized, posterity has paid Niccolo Machiavelli the greater tribute of emulation. These two Renaissance contemporaries are an interesting study in contrast. More, the pious preacher, was a leading figure among the humanists; Machiavelli, the shrewd philosopher and observer of the affairs of state, eyed the world with practical realism. Statesmen and world leaders have for centuries been guided by the sagacious counsel of Machiavelli; no less have they admired Sir Thomas More for his espousal of virtue. A man searching for a true philosophy of life might well attempt a synthesis of the ideas of these two Renaissance intellectuals.

It is unfortunate that over the years Machiavelli has acquired such an unsavory reputation. Shakespeare and other playwrights have used him as a model for greedy, designing, unscrupulous characters. His name, to most persons, connotes evil shrewdness.

Born in 1469 to a family of impoverished gentry in Florence, he secured a position at the age of twenty-nine in the employ of the city-state. Skilled in the use of words and in the writing of documents, he quickly distinguished himself

[44]*Ibid.*, p. 122.

as the Renaissance counterpart of the twentieth-century bureaucrat and brain truster. Recognized as a perspicacious student of government and men, he was sent on assignments as unofficial emissary to every important city-state in Italy and several outside countries. As a diplomat he had the opportunity to observe men and governments in action. The reports that he sent back to Florence were sharp and discerning. In a brilliant letter to Raffaello Girolami, who had been appointed as an ambassador, Machiavelli told the young man what to look for and how to cultivate friendships at court for the purpose of securing intelligence. The letter is undoubtedly autobiographical.[45]

Were it not for a period of enforced idleness, Machiavelli might never have written *The Prince* or *The Discourses,* the two works for which he is best known. In 1512 he lost his position in the Florentine government when the Medici family was restored to power, and for the rest of his life he pleaded in vain to be reinstated to a position in government. Thus he devoted his declining years to writing.[46]

And write he did—literally volumes. His works include poetry, letters, plays, history—every literary form. *The Discourses,* which have no central theme, are a commentary on the first ten books of Livy's *History of Rome. The Prince,* which was distilled from *The Discourses,* is a comprehensive treatise dedicated to one of the young Medici princes in a futile bid to regain favor. According to Max Lerner, *The Prince* is anything but original. A traditional literature on this subject stretched all the way back to the Middle Ages. However, it was Machiavelli's approach that alarmed his peers. Discarding the theology, metaphysics, and sanctimonious quality of the traditional treatises on rulers, he dared to reveal the inner machinations of power behind the city-state. Everyone knew about these realities, but no one talked or dared to write about them.[47]

The principles of leadership and power that occupied Machiavelli are applicable to almost every endeavor that is organized and purposeful. Were he writing today he would probably be analyzing the power structures of our large corporations in order to advise young executives how to reach the top of the corporate hierarchy. Or in these days of mushrooming conglomerate take-overs, he might advise us to put small management teams of our own into one or two key factories, otherwise we would have to use up half of our staff in giving orders, issuing requests, and checking to see whether they had been properly executed. He might add that a management team would not cost much and that the only people who would be upset would be the displaced managers whose jobs had been taken over—and since they were no longer in the firm they could cause little trouble. Meanwhile, the rest of the staff would not protest as long as

---

[45] Niccolo Machiavelli, *Machiavelli: The Chief Works and Others,* trans. Allan Gilbert (Durham, N.C.: Duke University Press, 1965), I, 116.

[46] Niccolo Machiavelli, *The Prince* and *The Discourses* (New York: Random House, Inc., 1950), p. xxvii.

[47] *Ibid.,* p. xxvi.

they maintained their old jobs, and particularly so if they remembered the example of the fired managers. Machiavelli's guiding principle here is that senior men in taken-over firms should be either warmly welcomed and encouraged—or fired. His reasons: If they are fired they are powerless; if they are simply downgraded, however, they will remain united and resentful and determined to get their old glory back.[48]

Pertinent to management in the twentieth century are several broad principles which recur throughout *The Prince* and *The Discourses:*

1. Reliance on Mass Consent. Machiavelli often reiterated the theme that the continued existence of all governments, whether monarchical, aristocratic, or democratic, depends on the support of the masses. Princes may usurp power or they may inherit it, but to win firm control of the state they must somehow win the approval of the people. This states clearly Machiavelli's understanding of the acceptance theory of authority—that authority flows from the bottom up and not from the top down—a concept regarded by many scholars as originating in the twentieth century.

Continuing along this line, Machiavelli indicates that if a prince can choose between gaining power through the nobility or through the people, he should definitely choose the latter.[49]

2. Cohesiveness. Like the other principles of Machiavelli, the principle of cohesiveness in organization is intended to insure the continued viability of the state. In this principle he indicates that the most effective way in which a prince can maintain organic unity is by retaining a firm hold on his friends. He should watch them carefully and placate them in order to use them to advantage. On handling foreign dominions, he advises the prince to live in the conquered territory, where he can exercise vigorous control.

The crucial element of organizational cohesiveness was insuring that the people know that they can expect of their prince and in return what is expected of them—the principle of clear-cut responsibility. A prince who has no laws but vacillates from one policy to another can quickly demoralize the entire state.[50] The people should know exactly what penalties are meted out for crimes and should not be able to avoid punishment by performing other meritorious acts. A man who has committed a crime should be chastized without regard to his previous merits.[51]

3. Leadership. Machiavelli wrote of two kinds of leaders (or managers): the natural or innate type and the type whose techniques are acquired. The sole object of *The Prince,* of course, was to assist a young prince in acquiring the

[48]Antony Jay, *Management and Machiavelli* (New York: Holt, Rinehart & Winston, Inc., 1967), p. 6.

[49]*Ibid.,* pp. 36-37.

[50]*Ibid.,* p. 225.

[51]*Ibid.,* p. 181.

techniques of leadership (of management). Machiavelli frequently mentioned kings and princes (the type who usually inherited their power) who failed as rulers because their basic personality lacked the charismatic aura of a great leader. The inference was that some individuals, regardless of training, will always lack the necessary personal attributes to become capable leaders.

A prince (or manager) should by his example seek to inspire his people to greater achievement. Especially should he attempt to raise the spirit of his people when the state is being assaulted by enemies. In time of siege the people can be roused by the intangible leadership qualities of their prince as they make preparations for combat and defense.[52] Sounding somewhat like a human relations adviser, Machiavelli instructs the prince to ". . . pay attention to all the groups, mingle with them from time to time, and give them an example of his humanity and munificence, always upholding, however, the majesty of his dignity, which must never be allowed to fail in anything whatsoever."[53]

To be a good manager, a prince should offer rewards and other incentives to those persons who would improve the city and the state. He should encourage the citizenry to pursue their professions and callings to the best of their abilities by guaranteeing that they will not be unjustly deprived of their goods.[54]

A good prince must also be a wise observer of events and people, able to use both to his advantage. Not in an underhanded way but, like most successful managers, he should learn to take advantage of an opportunity when it arises. Also he should be able to sense the trends of the times and to adapt.[55] He should be sagacious enough to distinguish between those nobles who are loyal to him and those who pursue only their own ends. He must be able to recognize both and use them to advantage.[56]

4. Will to survive. One of the primary objectives of any organization, Machiavelli realized, must be its own survival. Government bureaus, ecclesiastical groups, and corporations all seek self-perpetuation. He therefore counseled that, like the Romans, a prince should be constantly on the alert for disorders in order to stamp them out while they can still be remedied. When the survival of his kingdom is at stake, a prince is justified in taking cruel measures and dropping all pretensions of virtue if necessary, and in breaking faith when the reasons that made him bind himself no longer exist.[57]

Machiavelli set forth management precepts for the successful operation of a *state,* not for a chain of stores. But in his principles of reliance on consent, cohesiveness, leadership, and will to survive, we find one of the first published pronouncements of fundamentals basic to all organized endeavors. Perhaps his

[52]*Ibid.,* p. 41.
[53]*Ibid.,* p. 85.
[54]*Ibid.*
[55]*Ibid.,* p. 14.
[56]*Ibid.,* p. 37.
[57]*Ibid.,* p. 64.

major contribution of interest to management scholars is that he overtly identified management as a concept, for it was *management* that the princes (or managers) would have to apply effectively if they were to survive.

SUMMARY

The medieval period serves as a bridge between antiquity and the age of awakening known as the Renaissance. Although organized in a feudal structure, man began to take significant steps in his thinking about organization and management.

Alfarabi in the 900s in effect set forth a job description for a state ruler. In 1100 Ghazali counseled the king on how he should act and the traits he should develop to be a good manager.

Venice, the caldron of economic exchange, developed early forms of business enterprise, and her arsenal in particular gives us an excellent picture of the state of managerial awareness, thinking, and practices of the period.

Sir Thomas More contributed utopian ideas for the management of an ideal society. Machiavelli, on the other hand, gave us a clear insight into the machinations of young prince-managers and distilled the thinking of the time into four managerial principles: (1) reliance on managerial consent, (2) cohesiveness, (3) leadership, and (4) will to survive.

From the viewpoint of management thought, the period is not especially noteworthy, but it is of interest to the management scholar because it affords insight into the first real system of managerial practice and into the thinking of the early management elite.

3

A MANAGERIAL
AWAKENING

It has been said that few ideas are ever really new. Certainly this applies in great measure to the management of the 1700s. Few management ideas were applied in this era that could not be traced to an earlier time. Some techniques were rediscovered, others were borrowed, but no new ideas were developed. The contribution of this period to management history was one of extended application, and the refinement of existing or known techniques and principles. It was not, as we shall see, a period of innovation.

Prior to 1700 most manufacturing utilized limited capital and uneducated workers on a small scale. The emerging technical developments of this period, however, provided a new opportunity for the application of some of the then newer managerial skills as well as an incentive for the application of others. Although the advances were small compared with those that followed, they served as the basic foundation for greater strides in the 1800s.

Up to this point we have reviewed some of man's managerial practices from the dawn of history through the 1600s, with illustrations drawn from various disciplines. By the beginning of the 1700s, however, a series of happenings had had a real impact on managerial practices. Among the more important of these occurrences were the growth in cities, the application of the principle of specialization, the extended use of the printing press, and the beginnings of the industrial revolution.

ORGANIZING FOR PRODUCTION

The period between 1700 and 1785 spotlights the English industrial revolution during which a new generation of managers developed with their own concepts and techniques emerging on every hand. It was during this short span of years that England changed dramatically from a nation of rural yeomanry to the workshop of the world—the first nation to successfully make the transition from a rural-agrarian to an industrial-commercial society.

Probably the most important innovations during this period were the changes in the basic *organization of production*. Although gradual and overlapping to a great extent, these changes can best be considered chronologically and in order of the impact which each new stage had on the whole.

Domestic System

The system predominant in most of the Western world during the early eighteenth century was the domestic system—the basic stage of a materially productive civilization. When people begin planting and fabricating to fill their needs instead of picking and hunting for what they use, the most important elements of this system are present. When specialization develops to the point that an individual, instead of supplying just his own needs, produces one or more types of goods for sale or barter, then the domestic system is in full bloom. Usually organized on a family basis, this system commonly existed in conjunction with a farm where the labor was provided by the farmer and his family. In fabricating textiles under the domestic system, for example, the family owned a spinning wheel (or later a jenny) or a loom. They bought their raw materials and sold their finished products at the local fair for whatever price they could get.

This system persisted for a great while because of two important factors: the smallness of the capital investment required to enter into such an enterprise and the decentralization of population. Lacking an efficient transportation system at the time, very few large markets were readily available; and without large markets, large capital investments were seldom undertaken.

Under the domestic system, there was little opportunity and even less incentive to develop or adapt sophisticated managerial techniques. In fact, the management function of planning does not seem to have developed noticeably under either the domestic system or its successor, the putting-out system. Without explicit planning, and under conditions of essentially pure competition, the market took over most of this function implicitly. The cottager saved his money until he could buy or make the equipment that would allow him to produce an industrial product, and the state of the market for the various possible products must have greatly influenced his choice of equipment. Once committed, the small size of his or his employer's working capital would control his supply of raw material in accordance with price fluctuations in the market, and his output was altered accordingly.

Although the effect of the market adds some interest to the planning function as it then existed, by and large the management functions were handled on an informal, unsophisticated basis. The organization involved was typically the family, which was small enough not to invite the invention or adaptation of sophisticated planning techniques or control methods.

Educational barriers, too, impeded the development of managerial skills. A working man of this period was considered well educated indeed if he could do simple addition and subtraction and stumble through his *Book of Common Prayer.* Thus, the managerial concepts previously expounded in other parts of the world would have been beyond his reach even if books had been available to him.

Putting-out System

The next stage, the putting-out system, was a logical evolution from the domestic system. At the rural fairs it became common for entrepreneurs to act as brokers, contracting for families' entire outputs at fixed prices. It was not a very great jump from that point to the practice of providing the worker with raw materials and paying him what amounted to a bargained piece rate for the finished product. This is the central point which differentiates the putting-out system from its predecessor, the domestic system. Many historians ignore this distinction, which may of course be a minor one in terms of general economic history. But in terms of management history, this point is most important, since it marks the worker's change in status from an independent manufacturer to an employee.

The putting-out system developed as a result of several factors. For one thing, dealers who contracted to sell large lots of goods needed control over their sources of supply to avoid defaulting on their obligations. Another major factor was the introduction into certain parts of the manufacturing process of more efficient tools of production, thus causing an imbalance in production. In textiles, for example, the spinning jenny enabled one spinner to outdo the best efforts of a dozen spinners using the spinning wheel. The net result was that raw materials were in short supply, while surpluses of spun thread appeared. The spinners, in an effort to control their sources of supply and to assure sales of their finished products, turned to the merchants who were putting out goods to be spun.

Other than the implications already noted, the only management function to receive much attention under this system was materials control. The piece rates paid to workers under the putting-out system were not notably high, and hard-pressed workers were not above withholding materials and selling them on the sly. Although the merchants realized what was going on, they could not prove it because they lacked objective standards of material usage, and they lost control of the material when they gave it to the artisan. To protect themselves from such practices, the merchants appealed for laws and were successful in having them passed. Kietz says, "Since fraud on the part of the workers, taking the form of stealing raw materials entrusted to them, was common, extraordinary rights of inspection, search, and punishment were made available to the manufacturer."[1] Yet despite these rigorous laws and rights, the practice of stealing was too widespread to be stopped by statute. The result of this failure appears to be one of the major factors that contributed to the breakdown of the putting-out system and to the rise of the factory system.

Factory System

Although the desire to supervise workers and materials was sufficient to cause the introduction of factories in some instances, the factory system as we know it did not come into being until the introduction of power-driven machinery. Power-driven machinery greatly increased productivity, but at the same time it raised capital requirements and capital costs. Few individuals, however, could buy and install the machinery in their home. This meant in effect that instead of the machinery going to the worker's home, the workers had to go to the machinery's home—the factory. If these factors do not seem sufficient, there was also the added motive of controlling capital costs by maximizing utilization, which could only be accomplished at a reasonable cost by centralizing the machines so that machines and men could be supervised in groups rather than singly. In addition, power sources, whether steam or water, were usually adequate to operate a number of machines with belts and jackshafts. Thus, from a technical standpoint, we can say that the factory system was brought about by the introduction of expensive power-driven machinery; but from a managerial standpoint the deciding factor must have been the desire for control of men, materials, and machinery. And with the growth in manufacture under one roof came a concentration of men, materials, and machines, creating problems of control and coordination that focused attention on the functions and practices of the manager.

Management under the factory system was characterized by strict military control and organization. The owners were classified as merchant manufacturers, and they were more interested in selling their product than in developing a basic system of good management. Necessity, however, forced their attention to some of the more obvious managerial concepts and practices. And out of this attention grew some of the generally accepted managerial concepts.

[1] Frederick C. Dietz, *An Economic History of England,* (New York: Henry Holt and Co., 1942), p. 289.

EARLY MANAGERIAL PRACTICES AND CONCEPTS

The introduction of the factory system effected some improvement in materials control by preventing or at least minimizing theft, a primary aim. Quality control, however, was little if any improved over the previous systems. Products continued to be made from nonstandardized materials using non-standardized methods, thereby resulting in products of variable quality. The only real standards used were measures of dimensions, weight, and in some instances, purity. The most common form of quality control was the inspection of the product by the purchaser, under the common law rule of *caveat emptor*.

At this time the concept of *production control* was in a primitive state. One important principle, however, was known and clearly understood: A man who receives a piece rate is likely to outproduce a man who receives a day wage. Needless to say, piece rates were set as low as factory owners could set them and still obtain an adequate work force, no attention being paid to standard methods or to the objective control techniques. Production control in this era, therefore, consisted mainly of low piece rates and hard-driving supervision.

Financial control was perhaps the best-developed aspect of early managerial control probably because most of the factory owners came from England's prosperous merchant class who had adopted the best accounting and financial control techniques from Italy and other countries with which they frequently traded. Although more advanced techniques of production control, for example, existed at the Arsenal of Venice, these and similar methods would not have the appeal to English merchants whose business consisted only of buying, shipping, and selling. Finance was their kingdom, and they quickly picked up techniques such as double-entry bookkeeping to improve their reign. The essential grasp of the control value of the new bookkeeping system is seen in English print as early as 1716 when Thomas Watts, a teacher of accountancy in London, wrote in defense of double-entry bookkeeping, ". . . we have such a Relation and mutual Dependence of Accounts, and a perpetual Balance of all, that Nothing can be afterwards plac'd in the Books with dishonest or unfair Design; nor any Error made in the Progress left uncorrected."[2] Thus we see that Watts recognized the antitheft value of the system as well as its value in protecting against inaccuracy and ineptitude. The standard established is a continual balance of the debit and credit columns, and any deviation from this standard is the basis for taking corrective action.

Adam Smith also spoke of *control* in his *Wealth of Nations* when he stated that for a person to be truly controlled he must be held accountable for his performance to someone over whom he would be unable to exert any significant

[2]Thomas Watts, *An Essay on the Proper Method for Forming the Man of Business 1716* (Boston: The Krell Library of Business and Economics, 1946), p. 21.

influence. In fact, Smith moved from the factory to the college classroom when, deploring the irresponsibility of university professors, he went on to say, "If the authority to which he is subject resides in the body corporate, the college, or university, of which he himself is a member, and in which the greater part of the other members are, like himself, persons who either are, or ought to be teachers; they are likely to make a common cause, to be all very indulgent to one another, and every man to consent that his neighbor may neglect his duty, provided he himself is allowed to neglect his own."[3]

During the eighteenth century, the value of careful and explicit *planning* began to be recognized. Although factory owners did not seem to realize the extent to which planning could be utilized, and did not attempt to plan the minutiae of plant and office operations as is often done today, at least two planning techniques were successfully used in this period which remain among the most productive: plant location and payback computations.

As early as 1759 we find clear evidence of *location planning* in the Carron Ironworks in Scotland, where "everything, even the site, was planned with a view to the greatest efficiencies of production and transportation in the smelting and casting of iron."[4] Thus, planning was beginning to replace haphazard growth, and while the Carron studies were undoubtedly not carried out in either the sophisticated manner or the detail to which we are now accustomed, at least some of the most essential points of plant planning were considered.

Adam Smith, recognizing the need for *payback computations,* outlined a method for their application in machine acquisition and replacement in his *Wealth of Nations.* His explanation was that "when any expensive machine is erected, the extraordinary work to be performed by it before it is worn out, it must be expected, will replace the capital laid out upon it, with at least the ordinary profits."[5] And he defines ordinary profits as being double the prevailing rate of interest.

The managerial function of *direction* began to assume some importance with the advent of the factory system. Under the two earlier systems, direction had been largely unnecessary or ignored, but ". . . the sinking of capital in costly machinery made it seem in the interest of employers to work that machinery as continuously as possible,"[6] and this required supervision—a concept that was gaining ground. In fact, the success of some of the more astute manufacturers was attributed to ". . . a practical acquaintance with the details of manufactures, personal superintendence, and industry."[7]

[3]Adam Smith, *An Inquiry into the Nature and Causes of the Wealth of Nations* (London: A. Strahan and T. Cadell, 1793), III, 153.

[4]Dietz, *op. cit.,* p. 341.

[5]Smith, *op. cit.* I, 154.

[6]Sir William Ashley, *The Economic Organization of England* (London: Longmans, Green & Co. Ltd., 1922), p. 161.

[7]William Cunningham, *The Growth of English Industry and Commerce in Modern Times* (London: Cambridge University Press, 1903), p. 619.

The function of the supervisor purports to have been to insure the execution of standard orders, but his real *raison d'etre* was to drive the last possible bit of production out of his workers.

SIR JAMES STEUART

It has been said that if one looks long enough all the important *macro*economic and *micro*economic principles can be discerned in Sir James Steuart's *An Inquiry into the Principles of Political Economy*. Published in 1767, nine years prior to Adam Smith's *Wealth of Nations*, Steuart's book was written from the viewpoint of the statesman, and his work consisted of principles for a statesman or manager to follow in the administration of the political economy of a country.

Writing on the source of authority, he said, ". . . insofar as it is a question of the law of nature, I do not find the question so very difficult. All authority is in proportion to the dependency, and must vary according to circumstances. . . . Arbitrary power can never be delegated; for if it be arbitrary, it may be turned against the monarch as well as the subject."[8]

Steuart was quite aware of the problems inherent in the manufacture of goods, and in his references to dexterity acquired from repetitive functions he predates Adam Smith's division of labor concept. In the following paragraph, for example, Steuart catches the spirit of scientific management and incentive wage programs. He foresees by over a century the heart of work methods and incentive wages, and parallels Frederick W. Taylor's equal division of work between management and labor:

In the first supposition, it is the head of the Master which conducts the labor of the slave, and turns it toward ingenuity; in the second, every head is at work, and every hand is improving in dexterity. Where hands therefore are principally necessary, the slaves have the advantage; where heads are principally necessary, the advantage lies in favor of the free. Set a man to labour at so much a day, he will go on at a regular rate, and never seek to improve his method; let him be hired by the piece, he will find a thousand expedients to extend his industry. . . . From this I account for the difference between the progress of industry in ancient and modern times.[9]

Automation also existed as a threat in Steuart's day as is indicated by his answer to the question: "Is the introduction of machines into manufactures prejudicial to the interest of a state?" In his answer he points out that while a

[8]Sir James Steuart, *An Inquiry into the Principles of Political Economy* (London: A. Millar & T. Cadell, 1767), pp. 240-43.
[9]*Ibid.*, p. 192.

few workers may be temporarily unemployed, machines will create many more jobs than they will destroy—and that the disengaged workers will soon be reengaged in a healthier economy.[10]

ADAM SMITH

Adam Smith is another economist who showed great insight into the evolving management functions. Specifically, Smith laid great stress on division of labor and its concomitant benefits, thereby predating by a century the subsequent emphasis on breaking a job or task into its basic component parts.

To many people, Adam Smith and economics are synonymous. His *Wealth of Nations,* published in 1776, places him among the intellectuals of the modern world. His liberal thinking formed the basis for the laissez faire doctrine as we know it today, and his contributions to management throught are voluminous. Smith's discussion of the division of labor in the first three chapters of *Wealth of Nations* is so well known as to need no comment. He illustrates the outcome of the division of labor by the following description of manufacturing pins:

> A workman not educated to this business (which the division of labor has rendered a distinct trade), nor acquainted with the use of the machinery employed in it (to the invention of which the same division of labor has probably given occasion), could scarce, perhaps, with his utmost industry, make one pin in a day, and certainly could not make twenty. But in the way in which this business is carried on, not only the whole work is a particular trade, but it is divided into a number of branches, of which the greater part are likewise particular trades. One man draws out the wire, another straights it, and a third cuts it, a fourth points it, a fifth grinds it at the top for receiving the head; to make the head requires two or three distinct operations; to put it on is a peculiar business, to whiten the pins is another; it is even a trade by itself to put them into the paper; and the important business of making a pin is, in this manner, divided into eighteen distinct operations, which, in some manufactories, are all performed by distinct hands, though in others the same man will sometimes perform two or three of them. I have seen a small manufactory of this kind where ten men only were employed, and where some of them consequently performed two or three distinct operations. But though they were very poor, and therefore but indifferently accommodated with the necessary machinery, they could, when they exerted themselves, make among them about twelve pounds of pins a day.[11]

Continuing his comments, he gives three reasons for the increased output due to this division of labor:

[10]*Ibid.,* p. 119.
[11]Smith, *op. cit.,* I, 7-8.

This great increase of the quantity of work, which in consequence of the division of labour, the same number of people are capable of performing, is owing to three different circumstances; first, to the increased dexterity in every particular workman; secondly, to the saving of time which is commonly lost in passing from one species of work to another; and lastly, to the invention of a great number of machines which facilitate and abridge labour, and enable one man to do the work of many.[12]

Many critics of Adam Smith imply that he had a different meaning in mind when he referred to "division of labor." In their opinion Smith meant that laborers should specialize with respect to product rather than function. Further, they indicate that Smith meant artisan manufacture. There is, however, ample evidence that Smith was referring to division of functions in manufacture. He states clearly: "In every improved society, the farmer is generally nothing but a farmer; the manufacturer, nothing but a manufacturer. The labour, too, which is necessary to produce any one complete manufacture, is almost always divided among a great number of hands."[13]

In summary, we can say that Adam Smith wrote about many of the central problems and concepts of management. His idea about the division of labor is fundamental to modern work simplification and time study, and extends also into such areas as production simplification. His emphasis on the relation between specialization and technology closely parallels the theories of Charles Babbage and other pioneers of management whom we shall discuss later.

RICHARD ARKWRIGHT

The backbone of the industrial revolution in England in the eighteenth century was the emerging cotton industry. It has generally been conceded that one man, more than any other, provided the managerial know-how that greatly accelerated the advent of large-scale enterprise in this key industry. While John Kay, John Wyatt, Lewis Paul, and James Hargreaves provided the inventive genius in the cotton textile industry, Richard Arkwright (regardless of the legitimacy of his claims to the water frame patents) provided the managerial techniques for the successful coordination of men, money, materials, and machines in a large-scale production. As a result of Arkwright's centralizing all the various activities requisite to the continuous production of cotton textiles under one factory roof, the need arose for greater attention to coordination and control of the interrelated activities. Cooke-Taylor in his *Introduction to a History of the Factory System* underscored this development when he said:

[12]*Ibid.*, pp. 11-12.
[13]*Ibid.*, p. 9.

"Further the use of machinery was accomplished by a greater division of labour, and therefore a greater cooperation was requisite to bring all the processes of production into harmony and under central superintendence."[14]

Thus, with the application of heavy power-driven machinery, cooperation and coordination of the production processes became of paramount importance. Arkwright is repeatedly characterized by his ability to organize, coordinate, and plan. His selection of plant sites, too, shows acute foresight and planning. Mantoux points out that this extraordinary capitalist ". . . personified the new type of the great manufacturer, neither an engineer nor a merchant, but adding to the main characteristic of both, qualifications peculiar to himself: those of a founder of great concerns, an organizer of production and a leader of men."[15] Here are evident most of the characteristics of modern managers. In addition, we also recognize that Arkwright was the developer and practitioner of concepts in personnel management. For example, while the working day for most factories was fourteen or more hours, Arkwright never allowed his workers to exceed twelve hours. This fact does not imply that strict discipline was not maintained, but it is generally conceded that he was fair.

Arkwright, then, provided a model of advanced management applications for his contemporaries. His contributions of continuous production, plant site planning, coordination of machines, materials, men, and capital, factory discipline, and division of labor mark him as a pioneer in the use of efficient management principles. If he had written a principles book on good management practice he would probably rank as one of the true leaders in the field. Why, we might ask ourselves, did not he or some other industrialist of the period do so? The answer, it seems, is that they were too busy coping with the new problems evolving from large-scale production to be bothered with advancing a formalized, written analysis of correct managerial principles. Instead, the responsibility for writing and theorizing about management and managerial practices and principles was left to the theoreticians and economists. Early economists, however, such as Richard Cantillon and the Physiocrats, laid stress on the application of efficient managerial practices to agriculture but not to manufacturing. This emphasis constituted the chief reform measure of the Physiocratic school in the mid-1800s.

A TRANSITION PHASE

By the latter part of the 1700s the birth pangs of the industrial revolution had begun to subside; the new technology was emerging, with increased emphasis on its refinement by the application of analysis and study—scientific

[14]R. W. Cooke-Taylor, *Introduction to a History of the Factory System* (London: Longmans, Green & Co. Ltd., 1924), p. 423.

[15]Paul Mantoux, *The Industrial Revolution in the Eighteenth Century* (London: Jonathan Cape Limited, 1961), p. 233.

management. This is not to say that the scientific outlook had not been promulgated before this time. On the contrary, Sir Francis Bacon, Richard Petty, John Locke, Newton, and others had already provided a scientific vehicle upon which the manager could begin to build his discipline. In fact, the scientific approach had been slowly developing throughout the 1600s and 1700s and had already made its presence felt both in literature and in application. Thus it was inevitable that some hardy pioneers should attempt to provide scientific principles for the management of man, materials, money, and capital. These men were the leaders of the day, the avant-garde of management. They made careful, rational decisions; they kept accurate and orderly books; they reacted to events and information quickly and cogently, with finesse and expertise. These were the men who ushered in the application of scientific principles of management between the years 1785 and 1835.

EARLY SCIENTIFIC MANAGEMENT: THE RENAISSANCE OF APPLICATION

Soho Foundry

One of the first complete applications of scientific management to manufacturing occurred in Great Britain at the Soho Engineering Foundry of Boulton, Watt, and Company in 1800. In this plant we find concrete evidences of market research and forecasting, planned site location, machine layout study in terms of needed work flow, established production standards, production planning, standardized components, cost control applications, cost accounting, employee training, work study and incentives, and an employee welfare program.

Boulton, Watt, and Sons was originally formed by Matthew Boulton and James Watt to manufacture Watt's steam engine. In 1800 their two sons, inheriting management responsibilities, changed the name and instituted the practices indicated above. Interchangeable mechanisms were developed to a high degree of perfection ". . . and from the great experience of the proprietors, they have applied the power of steam to the boring of cylinders, pumps, to drilling, to turning, to blowing their smelting furnaces, and to whatever tends to abridge human labour and obtain accuracy, for by a superiority of their tools they are enabled to obtain expedition and perfection in a higher degree than heretofore."[16] When demand necessitated factory expansion, detailed plans were made regarding factory layout, size, and location of power sources. As a source of power, several different sizes of engines were used, with the cost of acquiring and operating each engine estimated.

[16]Erick Roll, *An Early Experiment in Industrial Organization* (London: Longmans, Green & Co. Ltd., 1930), p. 169.

One modern concept employed by these early managers was product forecasting and production planning. To aid in this endeavor, agents on the continent informed the home office of events affecting demand for engines, and based upon this information sales were forecast and future production was scheduled.

When the plans for building Soho's new factory were completed, they included complete lists of materials based on definite and preconceived plans of what the factory should be. So detailed were the plans that a primer was printed outlining operations performed and machines required in the production process. The normal practice of the time was that workmen would bear the expense of purchasing and maintaining their tools, but at the new Boulton and Watt factory "current repairs of tools and grinding them to be borne by the borer and new tools to be provided at our expense."[17]

The new management calculated speeds for each machine and adjusted these speeds to the type of work performed, thereby predating some of Frederick W. Taylor's work by almost a century. Detailed plans for work flow or routing were also put into effect. The production processes for each particular article were divided into a lengthy series of minor operations, indicating a very high degree of division of labor. Each worker had a fixed standard job; workers were classified by skills: fitters, turners, borers, patternmakers, and general laborers. All of this, of course, reflected the "new" science of work organization and management—the state of managerial thought at the time.

We can note several important facts from the foregoing: (1) extensive use was made of detailed operating plans; (2) the methods employed in planning were scientific, problems were broken into elements, and statistical data were gathered from which inferences were drawn; and (3) the production processes were organized on the basis of machine and worker.

Soho managers were concerned over the comparative advantages of piece rates over set wages, as indicated by the order "Query if it would not be better to persuade Joseph Horton to undertake the work by the pound?"[18] Piece rates were, of course, in operation for some classes of workers; fitters, for instance, were paid by the number of nozzles installed, with a standard number for basic wage. Control, of course, was one of management's main reasons for considering piece rates: "he will by no means be fit to be left to himself, except he has piecework—for I know he has made very long hours—generally nine or ten days per week when the work might have been done without overtime."[19] However, the Soho management applied piece rates only to those articles that were standardized and easily classified into groups. In its efforts to apply piece rates or to pay by results, Soho's managers measured and standardized the time for each operation, again predating Babbage, Taylor, and Gilbreth. Evidence shows

[17]*Ibid.*, p. 172.
[18]*Ibid.*, p. 191.
[19]*Ibid.*, p. 192.

clearly that work experiments took place before piece rates were set. Further, management realized that a switch to piece rates from an hourly rate would cause men to work faster. The men, therefore, were paid a time wage for the standard which equaled their previous output plus an incentive pay for output beyond the standard.

At Soho Foundry the men engaged in group work were hired for a weekly wage. The group foreman, however, was hired on a piece rate basis on the theory that since he was the one to benefit from increased output it would be to his interest to speed up the work.

With many piece rates at Soho it was found that the time it took to make different-size items varied more nearly in proportion to the diameter of the part than to any other factor. A formula was therefore developed to express this relationship and was used for setting standards and piece rates—an example of management's use of standard data a century ahead of other firms. Soho managers, however, took great pains to make the system simple and easily understood by the workers. In all, three wages scales were used: (1) a flat piece rate for each article, (2) a piece rate varying according to size or diameter, and (3) a piece rate varying with the horsepower of the engine for fitting working gears.

The employee's physical well-being was more carefully considered at Soho than in other contemporary industries in England. Boulton's attitude concerning the importance of labor and the rationale behind this concept is expressed as follows: "As the Smith cannot do without his striker, so neither can the Master do without his Workmen. Let each perform his part well and do their duty in that state which it hath pleased God to call them, and this they will find to be the true rational ground of equality."[20] Boulton improved morale by providing special entertainment for his employees on occasion. Likewise, he paid overtime for all work over a certain number of hours per day. That he also recognized that working environment is important to productive output is illustrated by the fact that the foundry walls were whitewashed to counteract the darkness and dirt normally existing in foundries.

Houses, too, were built for the workers, and part of their wage was in the form of rent for these homes. At the Christmas season, presents were given to employees and their families, and wage raises were announced at this time. Boulton also established a mutual insurance society for the employees' benefit. "Still further to increase the attachment of the Workmen to Soho and keep together his school of skilled industry as he called it, Boulton instituted a Mutual Assurance Society in connection with the works."[21] This was probably the first instance of an insurance society founded by a manufacturer for all workmen employed. This society was self-administered except that Boulton retained final

[20]*Ibid.*, p. 222.
[21]*Ibid.*, p. 226.

authority. Employee contributions were based on earnings, with benefits varying according to the employee's contributions. To insure fairness, an independent accountant was employed to audit the fund each year.

The foundry also maintained a very detailed accounting system. Single-entry cost records were maintained on raw material; a time book was kept for the various processes, with labor charges indicated; a departmental cost ledger was kept; and a finished goods inventory ledger was maintained. Indirect labor charges were kept, but no information is available as to how this charge was allocated to jobs. We do know, however, that management used these records to detect waste and inefficiency, to compute workers' wages per job; to compute the cost of each engine, to compute the results of changes in production, and to determine new wage rates based on results.

Thus, we see that Soho was truly a pioneer plant with its scientific works design, its subdivision and specialization of labor in conformity with the greater use of machinery, its more effective methods of wage payment, and its better system of record keeping and cost accounting. Today's typical managerial problems were in evidence then, and there is no reason for us to assume that the degree of common sense required to solve them was any less 170-odd years ago than it is today, even though management was not then systematized into a science. Without question, the Soho factory was a century ahead of its time.

New Lanark

In Scotland at this time was a place called New Lanark. Here, also, was living proof that the typical squalor and degradation of industrial life was not inevitable. At New Lanark stood rows of workers' homes with two rooms in each house; the garbage was piled neatly in the streets instead of being strewn about. In the factory a little cube of wood was hung over each employee, with a color painted on each side denoting, according to shade from light to dark, the different grades of deportment: white for excellent; yellow, good; blue, indifferent; black, bad.

No children under age ten were employed in the factories at New Lanark. Children that were employed toiled only 10 3/4 hours and were not punished! The factory manager's door stood open and anyone could complain to him about any rule or regulation; also every worker could inspect the deportment book and could appeal if he felt he had been unjustly rated.

Children under ten attended school taught by ladies who had been instructed that no child's question was ever to go unanswered, that no child was bad without reason, that punishment was never to be inflicted, and that children would learn faster from the power of example than from admonition!

The crowning glory of this experiment was that New Lanark was highly profitable! It was not an exercise in philanthropy, but an opportunity to test out theories which Robert Owen had evolved for the advancement of humanity as a whole. Owen was the man who showed England that industrialism need not be built on cheap and brutally abused labor; he paved the way for factory legislation by putting his principles into effect and proving they would work.

"Man is the creature of circumstances"[22] was Owen's philosophy, and he appreciated the vital part played by the human factor in industry. He was decades ahead of his time in proposing that at least as much attention be paid to the welfare of vital human machines as to inanimate machines.[23] Believing that the volume and the quality of a worker's output were influenced by environment both on and off the job, his labor policies were paternalistic, attracting wide attention but little imitation.

In a speech before a group of factory owners Owen stated, "Your living machines may be easily trained and directed to procure a large increase of pecuniary gain. Money spent on employees might give a 50 to 100 per cent return as opposed to a 15 per cent return on machinery. The economy of living machinery is to keep it neat and clean, treat it with kindness that its mental movements might not experience too much irritating friction."[24]

In general, Owen devoted himself to management as a profession. Under his direction, houses and streets were built, the minimum working age for children was raised, working hours were decreased, meal facilities were provided, schooling was introduced, and evening recreation centers were opened to meet the problems of leisure. Robert Owen might easily be called the father of modern personnel management.

Interchangeable Parts

Contrary to general thought the manufacture of interchangeble parts did not begin with the establishment of Eli Whitney's Hamden Rock Hill Mill in New Haven. W. F. Durfee points to many examples of interchangeable parts manufacture prior to the implementation of Whitney's approach—printing type, for example. In addition to the Durfee citation, Thomas Jefferson in his letters from France to John Jay precisely described a *manufacture de Versailles* which anticipated Whitney's whole interchangeable parts idea. In 1785 Jefferson wrote of Leblanc's approach:

> An improvement is made here in the Construction of muskets, which it may be interesting to Congress to know. . . . It consists in the making of every part of them so exactly alike, that what belongs to any one, may be used for every other musket in the magazine.[25]

[22]Robert L. Heilbroner, *The Worldly Philosophers* (New York: Simon and Schuster, Inc., 1953), p. 108.

[23]Harwood F. Merrill, ed. *Classics in Management* (New York: American Management Association, 1960), p. 13.

[24]*Ibid.*, p. 33.

[25]Thomas Jefferson to John Jay, May 30, 1785, in W. F. Durfee, *The History and Modern Development of the Art of Interchangeable Construction in Mechanismm (Journal of the Franklin Institute*, CXXXVII, No. 2 [February 1894], 122).

Jefferson even described the exact experiment conducted by Whitney some time later, but the experiment this time was conducted by Leblanc:

> ...He presented me the parts of fifty locks, taken to pieces, and arranged in compartments. I put several together myself, taking pieces at hazard as they came to hand, and they fitted in the most perfect manner. The advantage of this when arms are out of repair are evident.[26]

The technological and management implications of this early application of large-scale interchangeable parts manufacture are many. Such manufacture indicates, for example, a high level of technological know-how and an advanced knowledge of tooling. It points to an early and sophisticated application in manufacture of division of labor by operation, as well as a development of excellent methods of quality control. Other implications are materials and product routing, a pioneering use of dies and jigs, and finally, the exercise of modern production management techniques.

The Beginning of the American System

Up to this time the development and application of scientific management production techniques had taken place predominantly in England. Now, however, the seeds for the American system of manufacture were sown. This system, fathered by Eli Whitney, laid the groundwork upon which the early pioneers of scientific management built their discipline.

Greatly disappointed by the monetary results of his efforts with the cotton gin, Whitney turned to the prospect of more profitably manufacturing muskets for the government. Constance Greene describes the trials of Whitney in his attempts to meet government contracts. The whole scheme of inter-changeable parts manufacture was the result of a plan developed by Whitney, and his confidence in his plan is reflected in a letter to Oliver Wolcott, secretary of the treasury:

> My general plan of arrangement is good. My confidence in it increases in proportion as the execution advances. I have about sixty men engaged and a prospect of being able to procure such number as I may want. I am persuaded that I can do the work well. . . . I might have made 500 stands of arms by this time but they would have cost me 15 dollars apiece and would not have been such that it could not readily have been enlarged with advantage and it would have taken me six months to make another 500.[27]

Whitney also recognized the part that scientific method would play in his manufacture, as indicated in a letter to Wolcott written in 1799:

[26]*Ibid.*

[27]Constance McL. Greene, *Eli Whitney and the Birth of American Technology* (Boston: Little, Brown and Company, 1956), p. 115.

I am fully sensible that Actual Experiment is the only true touchstone of theories, the only infallible criterion by which we can discriminate between the theories formed on principle and the chimerical projects of a vague imagination. . . . So far as I have brought my projects to this test I have had the satisfaction to find them to fully answer my expectations.[28]

Whitney also developed an extensive cost accounting system in which ". . . every component, every process, carried its own dollar-and-cents cost."[29] Quality control of a sort was used in Whitney's Mill Rock Factory, where the inspector tested the ramrods by throwing them forcibly down a musket barrel and any rod that did not ring he rejected as defective.

Finally, Whitney recognized the principle of span of management when he reported: ". . . I find it vain to think of employing a great number of hands in erecting the works and making the tools—unless I can actually be present in many places at the same time—I must not only tell the workmen but must show them how every part is to be done . . ."[30]

Throughout a long and successful career, Whitney invented many of the modern machines that made large-scale enterprises possible. Of particular interest is the milling machine, which is the foundation of most modern factories.

SUMMARY

In retrospect, the 1700s were ripe for the introduction of an improvement in manufacturing techniques and the development of a new approach to management. The industrial revolution brought with it a breakdown in the provincialism of management concepts, and with these broadened horizons, managers began to look for ways to improve both manufacturing and management.

Two prime examples of this new approach to management are found in Boulton and Watt's Soho Foundry and Robert Owen's New Lanark Mill. Here for all to see was the embodiment of all the new concepts of the time. And most important—the ideas were sound, the companies were successful, and profits accrued.

With this genesis of bold ideas, it is no wonder that even greater strides were taken by subsequent leaders and writers who applied their own inventive genius to move from these early attempts into an era presaging the advent of true scientific management.

[28]*Ibid.*, p. 117.
[29]*Ibid.*
[30]*Ibid.*, p. 122.

4

EARLY MANAGEMENT
WRITERS

Compared with the two preceding centuries, the 1800s brought forth a veritable wealth of literature on management. Economists perceived of and wrote about managerial concepts, the functions of management, and the applications of management theory. Smith and Turgot saw the separation of ownership and management as well as the rise of a managerial class. And foreseeing this rise, the economists of the time wrote about this new species—the manager—discussing his functions, his duties, and his place in the new order. A brief look at some of their writings, therefore, should disclose the emphasis they placed on the emerging managers and management thought.

THE CLASSICAL ECONOMISTS

Before outlining their concepts of management, many classical economists began by describing the sort of person that would make a good manager. Samuel P. Newman, for example, wrote in 1835:

> There is . . . needed to constitute a good undertaker, a combination of qualities, rarely found united in the same individual. He should possess an unusual share of foresight and calculation, that his plans may be well

laid. He must also exhibit perseverance and constancy of purpose in carrying his plans into execution. Often too he is called upon to superintend and direct the efforts of others, and to execute this office well, he needs both discretion and decision of character. There is required also, to conduct some branches of production successfully, much knowledge, both of the state of the world generally, and of the details of particular employments and pursuits.[1]

This is assuredly an impressive set of qualifications to add to Adam Smith's simple list of "order, economy, and attention"![2] J. S. Mill, however, adds two important qualifications to the list: fidelity and zeal; while Alfred Marshall suggests self-reliance and promptness as worthy virtues for the well-qualified manager.

Moving into the concepts of management, many of the economists of this period distinguished between the functions of a manager and the functions of the organization. Each one, however, seemed to place special emphasis on some particular function. Turgot,[3] for example, was concerned primarily with direction and control, while Say[4] was struck with the importance of planning. Bowker,[5] on the other hand, felt that organizing and directing were a manager's chief functions. Of all these writers, Newman alone appeared to have the sharpest focus when he wrote that a manager's functions are "planning, arranging, and conducting the different processes of production."[6] Laughlin writing at the close of the century about the duties of management said, "The manager who selects the site of the factory, controls the finances, buys materials and sells the goods; who deals with the workmen, alloting their tasks, and classifying their labor; who watches the market, knowing when to sell and when to withhold his goods; who can find out satisfactorily what purchasers really want, and adapts the character of his goods to these wants . . . is a rare man."[7] These writings represent virtually the first attempts to express the functions of management as an emerging theory. In doing so, these writers laid the groundwork, as it were, for Fayol and others who were to follow half a century later.

[1] Samuel P. Newman, *Elements of Political Economy* (Andover: Gould and Newman, 1835), p. 283.

[2] Adam Smith, *An Inquiry into the Nature and Causes of the Wealth of Nations* (London: A. Strahan and T. Cadell, 1793), II, 119.

[3] See Anne Robert Jacques Turgot, *Reflections on the Formation and the Distribution of Riches* (New York: The Macmillan Company, 1922, first published in 1770), p. 18.

[4] Jean Baptiste Say, *Catechism of Political Economy,* trans. John Richter (Philadelphia: M. Carey & Son, May 17, 1817), p. 21.

[5] R. R. Bowker, *Economics for the People* (New York: Harper & Bros., 1886), pp. 153ff.

[6] Newman, *Elements of Political Economy,* p. 51.

[7] J. Lawrence Laughlin, *The Elements of Political Economy* (New York: American Book Company, 1896), p. 53.

We normally think of motion and time study as an innovation of the Taylor-Gilbreth era, perhaps somewhat presaged by Babbage. Adam Smith, however, essentially devoted the first chapter of his *Wealth of Nations* to observations similar to Babbage's. Moreover, six years before Babbage, James Mill suggested motion and time study as a separate activity when he wrote:

It is found that the agency of man can be traced to very simple elements. He does nothing but produce motion. . . . An operation, which we perform slowly at first, is performed with greater and greater rapidity by repetition . . . the repetition, upon which the greatest celerity depends, must be frequent. It is not therefore compatible with a great number of different operations. The man, who would perform one, or a few operations, with the greatest possible rapidity, must confine himself to one or a few. Of the operations, therefore, conducive to the production of the commodities desired by man, if any one confines himself to a small number, he will perform them with much more rapidity, but, what is often of the highest consequence, with greater correctness and precision.

A certain immense aggregate of operations is subservient to the production of the commodities useful and agreeable to man. It is of the highest importance that this aggregate should be divided into portions, consisting, each, of as small a number of operations as possible in order that every operation may be the more quickly and perfectly performed. . . .

If the immense aggregate of the operations which are subservient to the complicated accommodations, required in an artificial and opulent state of society, were to be divided, under circumstances the best calculated for breaking it down into those small groups of operations, which afford the greatest aid to the productive powers of labour, the most perfect philosophical analysis of the subject would be the first operation to be performed; the next would be an equally perfect philosophical synthesis.

In order to know what is to be done with a vast aggregate of materials, existing in forms, ill adapted to the ends which are to be obtained, it is necessary to contemplate the aggregate in its elements; to resolve it unto those elements, and carefully and comprehensively to pass them under review. This is the analytical operation.

When we have the full knowledge of the elements, which we are to combine, as means, towards our ends, and when we have an equally perfect knowledge of the ends, it then remains that we proceed to form those combinations, by which the ends will be most advantageously produced. This is the synthetical operation.

It is well known, that neither of these operations has as yet been performed, in order to obtain the best division and distribution of labour. It is equally certain, that this division is still in a most imperfect state. As far as it has been performed, it has been performed practically, as they call it; that is, in a great degree, accidentally; as the fortuitous discoveries of individuals, engaged in particular branches, enabled them to perceive that in these branches a particular advantage was to be gained. Such improvements must have always been founded on some very narrow view; an analysis and synthesis, certainly; but including a small number of elements, and these but imperfectly understood. Improvements, founded upon narrow views, are almost always equally confined in their application. There is no generalization . . . because a narrow view discovers no relations between the things which it embraces and the things which it excludes.[8]

And there we have it—the first recorded conceptual treatment of analyzing and synthesizing human motions. The very fact that it was recorded is an indication of its rising importance to the economy of the time and the level of managerial sophistication then in existence.

The economists of this period were apparently split on the subject of whether ownership and management could successfully be separated. Adam Smith[9] assures us that it was common in his day, at least in profitable times, and Turgot[10] gives us the same implication. Ricardo,[11] on the other hand, assures us that capital, not management skill, is the controlling factor, and this implies that a hired manager would be useless.

Managerial Functions and Principles

Of the five generally recognized functions of management (planning, organizing, staffing, directing, and controlling), several economists seem to consider *planning* the most important, Marshall among them. Laughlin gives the reasoning behind this when he says:

> He who controls a large capital actively engaged in production can never remain at a standstill; he must be full of new ideas; he must have power to initiate new schemes for the extension of his market; he must have judgment to adopt new inventions, and yet not be deceived as to their value and efficiency.[12]

The only portion of the *staffing* function to which the economists paid any attention was training. Though none of them were enthusiastic about training, de Laveleye felt that ". . . it is the duty of the employers of labour . . . to come to the aid of the dispossessed workmen by instructing them."[13] Marshall's comment on its profitability was that "Whoever may incur the expense of investing capital in developing the abilities of the workman, those

---

[8]James Mill, *Elements of Political Economy,* (3rd ed. (London: Baldwin, Cradock, and Joy, 1826), pp. 11-15.

[9]Smith, *op. cit.,* I, 147.

[10]Turgot, *Reflections on the Formation and Distribution of Riches,* p. 18.

[11]David Ricardo, *The Principles of Political Economy and Taxation* (New York: E. P. Dutton & Co., Inc., 1960, first published in 1817), p. 119.

[12]Laughlin, *Elements of Political Economy,* p. 223.

[13]Emile de Laveleye, *The Elements of Political Economy,* trans. Alfred W. Pollard (New York: G. P. Putnam's Sons, 1884), p. 96.

abilities will be the property of the workman himself; and thus the virtue of those who have aided him must remain for the greater part of its own reward."[14]

Along this same line, de Laveleye joined other nineteenth century economists in a plea for good business education, noting that "the first care, however, of a government should be to create institutions that will serve as training schools for good industrial managers."[15]

The *organizing* function was conceived very broadly by these men, with one of the most interesting concepts of organization given by van Buren Denslow:

> It is through the subserviency of the employer to the public, followed up by the subserviency of each employe to his or her own employer, that the entire force of employes may be held to the work of satisfying a public want. This is organization in industry.[16]

The span of control concept was barely mentioned by Walker and Denslow; however, the unity of command principle received more attention from Bowen and Bowker, with Bowen throwing especially sharp barbs at committees: "Committees of management are proverbially negligent or meddlesome, inharmonious and unsuccessful: one executive head, and a very able one, is an essential prerequisite of success in any large undertaking."[17] Marshall noted that even at the bottom level of an organization, split responsibility was unwise, pointing out that "a machine is not so well cared for when two men share the responsibility of keeping it in order, as when one man has the whole management of it."[18]

In the beginning the economists were mostly concerned with *control* to prevent theft, but quickly seemed to have turned to the idea of control to prevent waste—in fact, much sooner than did most managers or management theorists. This is not to say that they forgot theft, for as J. S. Mill said in 1848:

> All the labour now expended in watching that they (English workmen) fulfill their engagement, or in verifying that they have fulfilled it, is so much withdrawn from the real business of production, to be devoted to a subsidiary function rendered needful not by the necessity of things, but by the dishonesty of men.[19]

[14]Alfred Marshall, *Elements of Economics of Industry* (London: Macmillan & Co. Ltd., 1932, first published in 1892), p. 272.

[15]De Laveleye, *Elements of Political Economy*, p. 116.

[16]Van Buren Denslow, *Principles of the Economic Philosophy of Society, Government and Industry* (New York: Cassell & Co. Ltd., 1868), p. 183.

[17]Francis Bowen, *American Political Economy* (New York: Charles Scribner's Sons, 1870), p. 124.

[18]Marshall, *Elements of Economics of Industry*, p. 353.

[19]John Stuart Mill, *Principles of Political Economy*, ed. Sir W. J. Ashley (London: Longmans, Green & Co. Ltd., 1926), p. 111.

The best control—they still reasoned—was the master's eye!

Mill, additionally, was concerned with a systematic approach to control primarily out of distrust for the corporate form of organization. This, incidentally, appears to be the earliest reference to a control *system*. Mill put it this way:

> In the management of a great capital and great transactions, especially when the managers have not much interest in it of their own, small sums are apt to be counted for next to nothing; they never seem worth the care and trouble which it costs to attend to them, and the credit of liberality and openhandedness is cheaply bought by a disregard of such trifling considerations. But small profits and small expenses often repeated amount to great gains and losses: and of this a large capitalist is often a sufficiently good calculator to be practically aware; and to arrange his business on a *system* which, if enforced by a sufficiently vigilant superintendence, precludes the possibility of the habitual waste otherwise incident to a great business. But the managers of a joint stock concern seldom devote themselves sufficiently to the work to enforce unremittingly, even if introduced, through every detail of the business, a really economical *system*.[20] [Emphasis mine.]

If there is one topic on which all the early economists agree, it is the principle of *specialization* or *division of labor*. Almost all treated it at such length that no specific references should be necessary on the general concept. It is, however, important to note that they treated the subject on three separate levels. International trade was usually considered as an outgrowth of the territorial division of labor. The specialization of companies might be called the organizational division of labor. And the specialization of individuals in their work could be called the trade division of labor. The latter, of course, fades into the concept of motion and time study previously mentioned.

Wage Payment

On motivation and incentives the good Reverend Malthus, *inter alia,* felt that a day's work was a day's work; any laborer was interchangeable with any other. De Laveleye, however, disagreed. He insisted that the following descending scale of efficiency held true:

1. Those who keep for themselves all they produce.
2. Those who have a share in the profits.
3. Those paid according to the work done.
4. Those paid according to the time they are supposed to be working.
5. Slaves, the produce of whose labours belongs to their masters.[21]

---

[20]*Ibid.,* p. 140.
[21]De Laveleye, *Elements of Political Economy*, pp. 59-60.

Most economists in the 1800s, agreeing with de Laveleye, felt that piecework where applicable was the answer to low labor productivity, even though some of them were concerned, as was Smith, that "workmen . . . , when they are liberally paid by the piece, are very apt to overwork themselves, and to ruin their health and constitution in a few years."[22]

In reply to this fear, however, Mill was quick to point out that piecework was not the only incentive system that both management and labor could respond to. He added:

> It must be further remarked that it is not a necessary consequence of joint stock management, that the persons employed whether in superior or subordinate offices, should be paid wholly by fixed salaries. There are modes of connecting more or less intimately the interest of the employes with the pecuniary success of the concern. There is a long series of intermediate positions, between working wholly on one's own account, and working by the day, week, or year for an invariable payment.[23]

Automation

As we have seen, automation is not so entirely a modern concern as we often think. In the 1830s it was feared that man might be superseded by machines. Even Aristotle had noted over three hundred years before Christ that "if a tool could anticipate and execute the workman's orders, if the shuttle could transverse the woof of its own accord, art would have no more need of labourers, or masters of slaves."[24]

Samuel Newman, however, had his doubts that automation could ever become complete:

> The supposition is sometimes made, that machinery is introduced, so as entirely to supersede the labors of man; and it is asked, whether, in this case, the resulting effects would be advantageous.
>
> I answer, that the supposition is an impossibility. . . . It does not follow, that men need be idle, or that their condition would not be improved. . . . In proportion as men are set free from the necessity of toil in the supply of their animal wants, they will have both leisure and inclination to engage in the labor of the mind.[25]

Economists' Contributions

The importance of these and similar writings by economists is perhaps obvious to the student of management thought. These men were the *educated*

[22]Smith, *op. cit.,* I, 124.
[23]Mill, *Principles of Political Economy,* p. 141.
[24]As quoted by De Laveleye, *op. cit.,* p. 92.
[25]Newman, *Elements of Political Economy,* pp. 79-80.

and *learned scholars* of the time whose ideas were valued by their contemporaries. The importance of their writings is, therefore, threefold. First, they established the concept that management was a separate entity—an entity worth studying and understanding. Second, the very fact that they wrote about management indicated its new elevation and importance to the firm and the economy—important enough for them to conceptualize about it and spend time analyzing it. Finally, their writings about management spurred further *thinking* and *writing* on the subject among scholars and managers where the capacity for each was greatest.

This is not to say, however, that the economists had the entire field to themselves, Other early writers included doctors, industrialists, teachers, engineers, and military leaders. Examples from some of these will illustrate their views on the newly emerging managerial concepts.

OTHER WRITERS

Carl von Clausewitz

Carl von Clausewitz (1780-1831) was a Prussian general who wrote extensively on war and the management of large armies in war. Entering military service at twelve, Clausewitz encountered the rigid discipline of the Prussian army at an early age and considered such discipline a requisite for any organization. Although Clausewitz was never in charge of a large-scale military operation, his writings[26] discussed thoroughly the many considerations of a person in such a position.

Though principally concerned with the management of armies in war, Clausewitz considered his concepts applicable to the management of any large organization, stating that business was simply a form of human competition greatly resembling war.

Clausewitz prescribed careful planning as a necessity in managing a large organization, with the first requisite being to define one's objective. He also emphasized that all decisions must be based on probability, not on logical necessity, as commonly believed at the time. Of course, his idea of probability was not as detailed as our current statistical probability, but the theory of trying to prepare best for what might happen is the same.

Out of all his enunciations, perhaps Clausewitz's major contribution to management was that managers should accept uncertainty and should act on the basis of thorough analysis and planning designed to minimize this uncertainty. Foreshadowing Taylor, Clausewitz advocated decisions based on science rather than hunch, and management based on analysis rather than intuition.

---

[26]See in particular Carl von Clausewitz, *On War* (New York: Barnes & Noble, Inc., n.d.) and *Principles of War* (Harrisburg: Military Service Publishing Company, 1832).

Charles Dupin

Charles Dupin, nineteenth century French engineer, wrote extensively on industry, work, and the welfare of workers. Often he spoke before the Academy of Sciences of the Royal Institute of France on these subjects as well as on more purely academic pursuits in the fields of engineering and mathematics.

From 1816 to 1820 Dupin made a study of the English navy in an effort to discover the bases of the efficiency of that organization which the French should adopt to build a strong navy. The principles of management that Dupin recognized and wanted copied from the British navy pertained to personnel management and human relations.

Dupin also advocated integrity in management—specifically, the prompt payment of debts and honoring engagements and agreements. Though these ideas do not seem novel today, Dupin's consideration of integrity and honor in 1820 represents one of the first enunciations of the concept as a factor in effective leadership and management.

As an engineer, Dupin's contribution was largely in the development of scientific, mechanized production in the early nineteenth century; yet his writings on management show greater concern with human factors such as personnel and employee welfare than with the more technical aspects of production.[27]

Charles Babbage

Perhaps Charles Babbage is currently best known for his pioneering work in the development of the first digital computer. In addition to this, however, he was a mathematician, a scientist, and an author. His best-known work, *On the Economy of Machinery and Manufactures,* first appeared in 1832, and all three thousand copies printed sold out in less than two months. A second edition appeared five months later, and by 1835 a fourth edition had been published in London. In the United States his 1832 edition was published and *Mechanics Magazine* (New York) reproduced it, starting in 1833, in serial form.[28]

Charles Babbage, more than any other author during this period, contributed to the initiation and development of the scientific approach to the study of management. He was conscious that principles of organization were applicable to every field where coordination of human effort was essential to the attainment of some common purpose. Babbage was primarily concerned not with designing or making machines, but with their use and the organization of human beings for that purpose.

[27]See Charles Dupin, *Discours sur le sort des ouvriers* (Paris: Bachelier, Libraire, 1831).

[28]Raymond Villers, *Dynamic Management in Industry* (Englewood Cliffs, N.J.: Prentice-Hall, Inc., 1960), p. 17.

In the preface to *On the Economy of Machinery and Manufactures* Babbage writes, "Having been induced during the last ten years to visit a considerable number of workshops and factories both in England and on the continent for the purpose of endeavoring to make myself acquainted with the various resources of mechanical art, I was insensibly led to apply to them those principles of generalization to which my other pursuits has naturally given rise."[29] It is interesting to compare this passage with a similar passage from Frederick Taylor's *Principles of Scientific Management,* published in 1913:

"When men whose education has given them the habit of generalizing and everywhere looking for laws, find themselves confronted with a multitude of problems, such as exist in every trade, and which have a great similarity one to another, it is inevitable that they should try to gather these problems into logical groups, and then search for some general laws or rules to guide them in their solution."[30]

In general, Babbage recommended that data obtained as a result of rigid investigation should be utilized in managing an enterprise. He also indicated that management should find out the number of times each operation was repeated each hour; that work should be divided into mental and physical efforts, that the precise cost for every process should be determined; and that the worker should be paid a bonus in proportion to his own efficiency and the success of the business. Babbage emphasized the importance of division of labor, indicating that greater profit could be made by specializing, that the time required to learn a certain process could be cut considerably, and that the skill acquired in that process could be increased by division of labor. Babbage put it this way:

"That the master manufacturer, by dividing the work to be executed into different processes, each requiring different degrees of skill and force, can purchase exactly the precise quantity of both which is necessary for each process; whereas, if the whole work were executed by one workman, that person must possess sufficient skill to perform the most difficult, and sufficient strength to execute the most laborious of the operations into which the art is divided."[31]

In the area of time study Babbage again preceded Taylor when he stated:

"If the observer stands with his watch in his hand before a person heading a pin, the workman will almost certainly increase his speed, and the estimate will be too large. A much better average will result from inquiring what quantity is considered a fair day's work. When this cannot be ascertained, the number of operations performed in a given time may frequently be counted when the workman is quite unconscious that any person is observing him. Thus the sound

---

[29]Charles Babbage, *On the Economy of Machinery and Manufactures* (London: Charles Knight, 1832), p. v.

[30]Frederick W. Taylor, *Principles of Scientific Management* (New York: Harper & Bros., 1913), p. 103.

[31]Babbage, *op. cit.,* p. 173.

made by . . . a loom may enable the observer to count the number of strokes per minute . . . though he is outside the building. . . ."[32]

Babbage also emphasized the importance of balance in processes and the principle of optimum size of the manufacturing unit for each class of product. There are not many areas that Babbage did not touch upon, as the following proposals by him indicate:

1. Analyze manufacturing processes and cost.
2. Use time study techniques.
3. Use printed standard forms for investigation.
4. Use the comparative method of studying business practices.
5. Study the effects of various tints of paper and colors of ink to determine which is least fatiguing to the eye.
6. Determine how best to frame questions.
7. Determine demand from statistics based on income.
8. Centralize the production processes for economy.
9. Inaugurate research and development.
10. Study factory location relative to the proximity of raw materials, considering whether the raw material gained weight or lost weight relative to the finished product.
11. Use a beneficial suggestion system because "every person connected with it should derive more advantage from applying any improvement he might discover."[33]

Obviously, Charles Babbage was an astute observer, a precise reporter of manufacturing practices, a generator of ideas, and the harbinger of the new scientific management which was to follow.

W. S. Jevons

W. S. Jevons was born in Liverpool in 1835. At fifteen he attended University College School. Upon his graduation, he worked briefly at assaying and meteorology but gave these up to obtain a more diversified education. He began to study mathematics, philosophy, and political economy at University School, receiving the gold medal in the first two. In 1865 he was appointed lecturer at Queens' College.

Jevons brought into the development of English economic thought more of the spirit and discipline of pure science than any predecessor. He was no moral philosopher or retired businessman or social reformer. He was a social scientist who specialized in economic questions for the sake of ascertaining the laws that govern them. His principal work, *The Theory of Political Economy*, first published in 1871, contains some interesting passages on the intensity of labor and fatigue:

[32]*Ibid.*, p. 132.
[33]*Ibid.*, p. 250.

Let us take such a simple kind of work as digging. A spade may be made of any size, and if the same number of strokes be made in the hour, the requisite exertion will vary nearly as the cube of the length of the blade. If the spade be small, the fatigue will be slight, but the work done will also be slight. A very large spade, on the other hand, will do a great quantity of work at each stroke, but the fatigue will be so great the labourer cannot long continue at his work. Accordingly, a certain medium-sized spade is adopted, which does not overtax a labourer and prevent him doing a full day's work, but enables him to accomplish as much as possible. The size of a spade should depend partly upon the tenacity and weight of the material, and partly upon the strength of the labourer. It may be observed that, in excavating stiff clay, navvies use a small spade; for ordinary garden purposes a larger spade is employed; for shovelling loose sand or coals a broad capacious shovel is used, and still a larger instrument is employed for removing corn, malt, or any loose light powder.[34]

Taylor was also concerned with the science of shoveling, and it is interesting to note that these concepts about work-study were in print shortly before Taylor started his experiments. Jevons, writing about the most favorable work loads and fatigue, concludes with a reference to marching and a hint at future development in time and motion study:

In different cases of muscular exertion we shall find different problems to solve. The most advantageous rate of marching will greatly depend upon whether the loss of time or the fatigue is the most important. To march at the rate of four miles an hour would soon occasion enormous fatigue and could only be resorted to under circumstances of great urgency. The distance passed over would bear a much higher ratio to the fatigue at the rate of three, or even two and a half miles an hour. But, if the speed were still further reduced, a loss of strength would again arise, owing to that expended in merely sustaining the body, as distinguished from that of moving it forward. The Economics of Labour will constantly involve questions of this kind. . . . In a regular and constant employment the greatest result will always be gained by such a rate as allows a workman each day, or each week at the most, to recover all fatigue and recommence with an undiminished store of energy.[35]

Jevons, again predating Taylor, called for cooperation between labor and management. He went further than Taylor, however, when he advocated industrial partnerships, including profit sharing and ownership of stock by employees. To him this represented a method of settling differences and eliminating union strife.

This, then, was Jevons's influence: a scholar of prestige who sought to ascertain the basic laws that govern men and the management of men in their labors. He was concerned with a scientific and systematic analysis of work, and

[34]W. S. Jevons, *The Theory of Political Economy* (New York: The Macmillan Company, 1888), p. 204.
[35]*Ibid.*, p. 208.

in his search for basic laws governing work performance and fatigue, he anticipated Frederick W. Taylor.

SUMMARY

In reviewing these early writings about management, we note one feature common to most of them: They were firm oriented. Adam Smith and his successors centered their comments around the firm, the manager's job in meeting demand, the role of planning to achieve economical operations as well as supply customer demand, and so on. This, of course, is not unexpected in an emerging industrial economy. As we shall see, however, the emphasis shifts as the economy matures.

Early nineteenth century writers dealt principally with fundamentals. No unified theory of management was developed, but they did recognize and understand the functions of management and often discussed many of management's interesting and little-recognized aspects. The important fact about these writers, however, is not what they said, but that they made a beginning. They started thinking and writing about management and managers from many approaches. Their writings along with those of the economists served to reinforce the growing idea of management's importance to the developing firm and at the same time encouraged other scholars to analyze further this emerging concept.

5

A PRELUDE
TO SCIENTIFIC MANAGEMENT

During the second half of the nineteenth century a new industrial era began in America, brought about primarily by the expansion of mechanical industries and by the abolition of slave labor.

Capital as we know it was not yet in existence. Our modern form of capital was not determined until the introduction in 1862 of the limited liability joint-stock company, an association of individuals which had some of the features of both a partnership and a corporation. It resembled a corporation in that shares of stock were transferable, its existence was not affected by the death of a member, and its management was in the hands of elected directors. It was like a partnership, however, in that each shareholder was personally liable for all the company's debts and the relationships between members were governed by the general law of partnership.

The introduction of joint-stock companies in the economy provided for a separation of the capitalist from the employer and a division between capital and management. Owners were not shareholders, and employers were, in the main, salaried managers. As a result of these changes, large business organizations were built up by financiers such as Jay Gould, J. P. Morgan, and Cornelius Vanderbilt, and these organizations had a definite influence on the development of the American economy throughout the nineteenth century.

During this period America's most dramatic enterprise, the railroads, grew in importance and stature. Rail lines were extended, new territories were opened, and competition for business was keen. After this initial period of expansion, however, the managers began to consolidate their holdings in order to operate more efficiently for greater profits. One example of this type of operation was the New York Central, consolidated by Cornelius Vanderbilt when he merged the competing railroads from New York City to Albany and from Albany to Buffalo.

HENRY POOR

The managers of these consolidations soon discovered that the administration of the large railroad organizations posed a completely new set of problems from those encountered in their smaller enterprises. As if to answer these problems, Henry Poor, editor of the *American Railroad Journal* (1849 to 1862), appeared on the scene to establish basic managerial principles for large business organizations.

Fundamentally, Poor argued that the railroad managers needed to be guided by only three principles: organization, communication, and information—with organization, or the careful division of work, the most fundamental of all. He proposed that a railroad's organization should be designed to insure that each man's time was fully utilized and the railroad's equipment was kept in service as fully as possible. By communication Poor had in mind a reporting system which would keep management informed of the operations, and the information principle was described as analyzing reports to improve operations.[1]

DANIEL C. McCALLUM

Daniel C. McCallum, superintendent of the Erie Railroad from 1854 to 1857, worked closely with Henry Poor and was one of the first men to make practical use of Poor's management recommendations.

Born in Scotland in 1815, McCallum was self-educated with the exception of a few years of elementary education in Rochester, New York. Despite this handicap, however, McCallum's alert mind and vivid imagination found solutions to managerial inefficiencies which were plaguing the railroads at that time.

Basically, the problem was one of control. Most railroad managers at that time felt that large railroads were too dispersed physically to be capable of close supervision. They therefore saw the larger railroad complexes as necessarily inefficient and incapable of profitable operations. McCallum felt otherwise. He believed that effective operation could result from precise and well-defined rules

[1]Ernest Dale, *The Great Organizers* (New York: McGraw-Hill Book Company, 1960), p. 19.

or codes for operation. In navy terms, he believed in running a taut ship, and this is precisely what he did upon taking over the Erie in 1854.

As one would expect, his regimentation did not go too well with the engineers, and they struck for ten days after McCallum assumed charge.[2] Essentially, McCallum's managerial approach to running the Erie was one of system, common sense, reports, and control. He instigated job descriptions, made promotions on the basis of merit, and insisted that those in charge of specific operations were both responsible and accountable for their successes and failures. In other words, he applied in 1854 what we would today regard as routine. What was a totally new and comprehensive approach for the railroads at that time, we recognize as simply including a logical delegation of authority, the exaction of responsibility, and control through a system of prompt reports.

After getting his system in operation, McCallum developed an organization chart for the railroad (one of the first), a treelike structure showing the president and the board as a central portion, with the five major divisions of the company shown as branches of the tree.[3]

After he left the Erie in 1857, McCallum's genius for organization and management did not go unemployed. The secretary of war, Edwin M. Stanton, made him director and superintendent of all United States railroads in February 1862, with the power to seize and operate any railroad necessary for the successful culmination of the war effort. As with the Erie, McCallum distinguished himself in his new job through his superior managerial proficiency. Under his management 160 cars a day were sent over 360 miles of single track to supply Sherman's Atlanta campaign employing one hundred thousand men and sixty thousand animals. In this role, McCallum ended his illustrious and unique managerial career.[4]

Like the railroads, industrial enterprises were also growing in size, and with the advent of new markets, they soon grew to match the railroads in complexity. During the last three decades of the nineteenth century managers of these fast-growing complexes began to realize that they, too, had problems in management, and this realization along with the complexity they faced ushered in the beginning of the movement for scientific management.

THE SCIENTIFIC MANAGEMENT MOVEMENT

In their quest for solutions, the managers of these industrial complexes began discussing their problems and reading papers before associations such as the American Society of Mechanical Engineers. The first real management publications during this era were few, and these were published almost

[2]"Big Business Takes the Management Track," *Business Week,* April 30, 1966, p. 104.
[3]*Ibid.,* p. 106.
[4]*Ibid.*

exclusively in engineering journals. A list of these early publications on management prepared by the New York Public Library in 1917, for instance, showed no American titles to 1881; eleven titles in the seventeen years from 1881 through 1897; and six titles in the three years from 1897 through 1899.[5]

Examining these early titles we find that one of the first management problems concerned wages and wage systems. This problem, emphasized by the industrial revolution, was one of labor efficiency. Sensing that large organizations were losing their power of direct supervision, managers were seeking incentives as a substitute. One of the first practitioners of this new management concept was Henry R. Towne.

HENRY R. TOWNE

President of the Yale and Towne Manufacturing Company for forty-eight years, Henry R. Towne was instrumental in establishing modern management methods in his company's shops. The editors of *Industrial Management, The Engineering Magazine* claimed that Henry R. Towne was unquestionably the pioneer of scientific management; that as early as 1870 Towne began the systematic application of efficient management methods; and that his paper, "The Engineer as an Economist," delivered to the American Society of Mechanical Engineers in 1886, probably inspired Frederick W. Taylor to devote his life's work to scientific management.[6]

In his paper Towne emphasized that shop management was equal in importance to engineering management in the efficient direction of an enterprise. Recognizing that information on shop management did exist but that there was no established vehicle for exchanging and disseminating this knowledge, Towne pleaded for the recognition of a science of management with its own literature, journals, and associations. Only through such exchange, he emphasized, could entrepreneurs benefit from the experience of others.

In a second paper, "Gain Sharing," published in 1896, he contended that profit sharing was neither an equitable adjustment nor a correct solution to an economic problem. The gain that one department could make through its increased efforts could be lost in another. Hence, he advocated the determination of the cost for each element of production. Then, what the employees of one department gained could be returned to them according to their merit. For this reason he called his plan *gain-sharing* rather than profit sharing.

Towne's plan guaranteed a definite wage rate to each employee, with the gain that each department made above the scientifically determined standard

[5]Henry C. Metcalf, *Scientific Foundations of Business Administration* (Baltimore: The Williams and Wilkins Co. 1926), p. 196.

[6]*Industrial Management, The Engineering Magazine*, LXI (1921), 232.

split fifty-fifty between employer and employee. Towne realized that this determined cost should be fixed after a study of three to five years to prevent rate cutting.

In his third paper, "Evolution of Industrial Management," written in 1921, Towne contrasted the status of scientific management in 1886 and in 1921, noting particularly the establishment of industrial management courses in technical colleges and universities and crediting F. W. Taylor as the apostle of the scientific movement.

Without doubt, Henry R. Towne's main contribution to management is that he set the climate and atmosphere for the later application of scientific methods. Of lesser importance was his plan of gain-sharing as a system of wage payment.

HENRY METCALFE

While Towne was developing his ideas at Yale and Towne, Captain Henry Metcalfe was exploring the management labyrinth at the Frankford Arsenal.

Upon taking over the managerial reins there, Metcalfe soon discovered that the traditional methods of organization and control used by industry were both wasteful and ineffective. His solution was the development in 1881 of a system of control which was so complete and thorough that even years after he left, the Arsenal continued its use. Both Frederick W. Taylor and the American Management Association recognized Metcalfe's managerial genius—Taylor, by acknowledging his debt to Metcalfe for some of his ideas, and the American Management Association by pointing out the practicality of Metcalfe's system for use even today.

In 1885, four years after Metcalfe introduced his system, his book, *The Cost of Manufactures and the Administration of Workshops, Public and Private,* was published by John Wiley & Sons. The book was hailed as a pioneer work in the area of management science.

Like McCallum's, the Metcalfe theory of management was based on system and control. He visualized and insisted that all authority should emanate from a given source, with a flow back to that source of detailed information concerning expenditures and accomplishments. This is not to say that Metcalfe was a generator of records and reports. On the contrary, he disposed of all except the most important and needed reports and even eliminated thirteen different kinds of books and reports that had been in regular use at the Frankford Arsenal.

After being transferred to arsenals in Benicia, California, and Watervliet, New York, Metcalfe still continued to experiment in better managerial control techniques. He ended his career teaching at West Point.[7]

[7]"It Was All in the Cards," *Business Week,* December 25, 1965, pp. 74-75.

FREDERICK HALSEY

In 1891 Frederick Halsey read an important paper before the American Society of Mechanical Engineers outlining his ideas about wages.

Halsey fundamentally disagreed with Towne's profit-sharing ideas because he thought that profits arose from many sources other than worker production; that the lazy men benefited by the good work of industrious workers; that the increase in pay was received too long after it had been earned; and that it was not fair for workmen to share profits when they did not share losses. In addition, Halsey strongly disagreed with the prevailing practice of cutting piece rates when the worker was earning too much money.[8]

To overcome these weaknesses, Halsey's "premium plan" called for a determination of the normal time for completing a job, with a premium rate (about one-third of the normal pay rate) paid the employee for the time saved.

The plan guaranteed each worker a full day's pay plus the premium if his initiative warranted it. The rate setting was simpler than other wage rate plans inasmuch as no attempt was made to determine a worker's possible output. Instead, an employee's present output was taken as standard or normal. In other words, workers under the Halsey plan were allowed the same length of time they had been taking in the past as a standard. If they increased output, two-thirds of the gain went to the employer and one-third was given to the men, with security to management arising from the two-thirds portion of the gain.[9]

Halsey outlined other advantages of his system: Every workman was guaranteed a day rate regardless of output; some of the worker-management friction arising from incentive work was eliminated because the employee was paid a premium as soon as he began to produce more; and intricate time studies were not needed. Halsey did not believe that it was possible to find out exactly how fast a job could or should be accomplished, and on this belief he developed his widely heralded premium plan.

Many premium plans for wage payment have been set forth, but Halsey's is considered an original contribution to management for several reasons. It was, first of all, an attempt to ameliorate the antagonism between management and labor over wages; and it guaranteed a daily or hourly rate based on the worker's past performance plus a premium of one-half to one-third on any savings he made. Under Halsey's plan, therefore, a worker's earnings would not be excessive even if he doubled output, and the employer would not be tempted to cut the rate because he, like the worker, would gain from the additional output. Finally, it offered a positive improvement over Towne's plan in that the increase in

[8]Horace B. Drury, *Scientific Management* (New York: Columbia University Press, 1915), p. 43.
[9]*Ibid.*, p. 47.

output under Towne's plan provided a reward to the good and to the bad worker without distinction.

Hailed as a new concept in wage payment, Halsey's plan had a major influence in the United States and Great Britain, and along with Taylor's ideas on piece rates, it served as a model for many subsequent pay schemes. James Rowan's system of 1901, for example, was undoubtedly based on Halsey's.

Education for Management

In 1881 a new development appeared on the managerial horizon. Recognizing the need for managerial education, a Philadelphia financier and manufacturer, Joseph Wharton, gave one hundred thousand dollars to the University of Pennsylvania to establish a department where young men could get the education and training needed for careers in management. In Wharton's thinking, the colleges of that period were preparing only a few individuals (doctors, lawyers, and clerics) for their actual duties in life, and he believed something should be done to incorporate managerial education in the higher echelon. He wanted the new department at the University of Pennsylvania to incorporate a liberal business education into the total curriculum, covering such topics as the problems of strikes, principles of cooperation, business law, elocution, clearinghouse functions, causes of panics and money crises, and the nature of stocks and bonds, to name a few.

Thus the Wharton School was started—a new first in the continuum of management. For seventeen years it was the *only* such school, but in 1898 the Universities of Chicago and California established their business schools, and by 1911 a total of thirty such schools were in operation.[10]

SUMMARY

The latter part of the nineteenth century saw the beginnings of *scientific management*—even the first use of the term itself. As business continued to grow both in size and in number, multiple problems not previously faced by managers were encountered. Concern was expressed over these problems of bigness, and emphasis in thinking moved from the area of the firm to the area of things within the firm: processes, equipment location, layout, production techniques, incentive systems, and the like. Management was becoming "things" oriented instead of "firm" oriented as it had been in the past. People amassed in large groups pointed up problems of organization and efficiency, and these concerns, too, appeared in the literature.

Concern was also being expressed over the promulgation and exchange of

[10]"How Business Schools Began," *Business Week,* October 12, 1963, pp. 114-16.

ideas, with the need recognized for societies, publications, and meetings to exchange views. The ground swell of management as a separate entity was gathering momentum. And the shining light of this era was the recognition of management as a teachable curriculum in a leading university.

In just a few short years, the concept of management had moved successively from one of casual detachment to partial analysis to a concept, still somewhat nebulous, of a total body of knowledge affecting man's economic endeavors. A manager was recognized as a person of some esteem, and the subject matter of managerial principles had spread from industry to the classroom.

Management as a separate field had finally come into being.

6

SCIENTIFIC MANAGEMENT

At the close of the Civil War a new industrial climate began to descend upon American business. During the years between the end of the war and the turn of the century, for example, the West became more fully settled, industry expanded and tried to keep up with the population's appetite for more goods, and technological unemployment began to be felt.

During this period big business spawned a further separation between management and labor, and the growth of a managerial class in industry became apparent. It was during this era that management began to change from a day-to-day, brush-fire type of operation to a more all-inclusive, longer-run approach. Concepts of control, for example, were being generated to replace the visual effect of the boss. Leaders like Towne and Metcalfe began to develop and apply a unified system of management instead of the usual hit-or-miss one typically employed. Each act, each part, each problem was viewed in the new light of its relation to the other parts and to the whole.

Sensing this emergence, Towne, we saw, called for managers to form organizations, to publish journals, and to exchange their findings and views. It was a time of genesis in the totality aspect of management thought. Towne had called this new philosophy of management a management of science, of precision. In this generative air of managerial expectation Frederick Winslow Taylor emerged.

FREDERICK W. TAYLOR

As an almost unknown engineer from Philadelphia, Frederick W. Taylor rose from this milieu with a new and total concept of management. Instead of being whip men, managers, according to Taylor, would have to develop a new philosophy and approach to managing. They would have to change to a broader, more comprehensive view in order to see their job as incorporating the elements of planning, organizing, and controlling.

Taylor, of course, did not burst on the scene with these thoughts marshaled in a complete and mature thesis. His ideas were generated as he worked for various firms, starting in 1878 with the Midvale Steel Company. At Midvale he rose from patternmaker to chief engineer in 1884 at the age of twenty-eight.

During these years he first began to recognize some of the many shortcomings of factory operation which he subsequently referred to in his writings. He saw, for example, that management had no clear concept of worker-management responsibilities; that virtually no effective work standards were applied; that no incentive was used to improve labor's performance; that systematic soldiering existed on every hand; that managerial decisions were based on hunch, intuition, past experience, or rule-of-thumb evaluations; that virtually no overall studies were made to incorporate a total-flow concept of work among departments; that workers were ineptly placed at tasks for which they had little or no ability or aptitude; and, finally, that management apparently disregarded the obvious truth that excellence in performance and operation would mean a reward to both management and labor.

It was at this time, too, that he experienced the typical struggle between foremen and workers over the quantity of output. At first he attempted to employ the usual methods of the time—some persuasion and a lot of force—with the usual outcome of bitterness, resentment, and an air of division and struggle. Realizing that he could only direct their efforts if he knew more than his men about the technical aspects of their job, Taylor began a series of experiments which lasted for more than two decades.

He experimented with machine tools, speeds, metals, and the like. In fact, one line of his experiments conducted at the Bethlehem Steel Company led to the discovery of high-speed steel and revolutionized the art of cutting metals. Other experiments pertained to the way his men handled materials, machines, and tools—motion and time study—and led him to the development of a coordinated system of shop management. From this shop approach, he expanded his concepts to a philosophy which ultimately became known as *scientific management*.

Development of Taylor's Shop System

To understand the principles of management that Taylor subsequently enunciated, it may be well to review briefly the chronological steps involved in the development of his shop system. First, he wished to know how long it would and should take a machine or a workman to perform a given process, to fabricate a part, using specified materials and methods, under controlled conditions. Systematically, he explored the various ways he could arrive at this information and ultimately decided that stopwatch studies of various performances permitted the determination of a practical, relatively precise, and reliable standard of output. This enabled him to set feasible standards per man- or machine-hour, usually higher than the average of current performance.

Second, Taylor wanted to develop a uniform method of routine to prepare and direct the efforts of those responsible for establishing the conditions under which these standards could be set and met. With this objective in mind, he worked out such techniques as instruction cards, order-of-work cards, routing sequences, materials specifications, inventory control systems, and material-handling standards. By employing these and similar techniques, Taylor coordinated and organized the total operation of the shop to the point where working conditions, materials, and methods of work flow were standardized so as to make standards of worker performance possible and meaningful.

Third, Taylor recognized the need for a method by which he could ascertain which man would be best for which job, considering his initial skill and his potential for learning. Fourth, with this degree of skill and careful placement of workers. Taylor saw the need for equally good supervision of an employee and his working conditions. From this need he developed his concepts of functional foremanship, with specialists employed in every phase of supervision to insure excellence of operation. Finally, he wanted to relieve the foreman of his whip-persuasion role and offer the workers the incentive of higher pay that would result from the increased productivity his shop system would provide.

Taylor's Papers

In 1886 Taylor joined the American Society of Mechanical Engineers and heard Henry R. Towne read his paper "The Engineer as an Economist." This paper had a profound impact on Taylor, since it probably first directed his attention to management as something separate from and in addition to innate executive ability and asserted that management must also include a composite collection, marshaling, and analysis of all facts and accounts (wages, supplies, expenses) pertaining to or having any effect on the economy of production and thereby the cost of the product. Here was a man speaking Taylor's language—who painted with a broader brush and included *all* facets of a firm, not just shop operations!

During the remainder of the nineteenth century, other managers presented papers which dealt with narrower aspects of management than Towne's—particularly popular being methods of wage payment.

One of the outstanding papers in this category was Frederick W. Taylor's "A Piece Rate System" wherein he described the system of management that he had developed, indicating that it contained principles that must be used in any system of wage payment where differential reward was offered. To his disappointment, however, the title and emphasis of his paper focused attention on the differential piece rate and neglected his concepts about management.

In 1903, therefore, he again appeared before the society and presented his second paper, "Shop Management," which focused attention on his philosophy of management rather than on wage payment. In essence, what Taylor was trying to say in "Shop Management" was that:

1. The objective of good management was to pay high wages and have low unit production costs.
2. To achieve this objective management had to apply scientific methods of research and experiment to its overall problem in order to formulate principles and standard processes which would allow for control of the manufacturing operations.
3. Employees had to be scientifically placed on jobs where materials and working conditions were scientifically selected so that standards could be met.
4. Employees should be scientifically and precisely trained to improve their skill in so performing a job that the standard output could be met.
5. An air of close and friendly cooperation would have to be cultivated between management and workers to insure the continuance of this psychological environment that would make possible the application of the other principles he had mentioned.

The audience, however, again failed to grasp the true significance of his contribution.

Taylor's Concept of Management

Taylor's philosophy of management was much deeper than a surface examination of his principles would lead one to suppose. After studying his various writings and his life's work, it would appear reasonable to state that Taylor's major thesis was that the maximum good for all society can come only through the cooperation of management and labor in the application of scientific methods to all common endeavors. He genuinely believed that man started with a given amount of natural resources and that his only means of utilizing these was through the application of human effort. Further, he saw that the greater the effort, the greater man's wealth. To maximize output with a given level of effort, Taylor felt that the scientific method had to be applied to worker selection, job determination, creation of proper environment, and so on, to determine properly the task for each man. If under these conditions the worker achieved a level of excellence in output, he was to be rewarded; if standard output was not achieved, he was to be penalized. Realizing that these concepts were contrary to actual practice in many instances, Taylor called for a mental revolution on the part of both labor and management so that they might understand these principles and cooperate in the spirit of work harmony in order to improve their respective lots—attaining higher wages for labor and increased output at lower costs for management.

Taylor frequently stated that management was negligent in performing its functions—that in actuality it placed the burden of methods and output on labor, disclaiming any immediate responsibility for itself. Taylor declared this was wrong. Management should do the work for which it was best suited— planning, organizing, controlling, determining methods, and the like—and not push it off on labor's shoulders. He estimated that over 50 per cent of labor's work should be assumed by management, thus incurring a highly centralized planning function with specialized (functional) foremen. Only through this total application, Taylor felt, could the best interests of employer and employee be served. Under these conditions of harmonious cooperation, emphasis would be on increasing the whole and not on the relative size of one's particular share, with a resultant increase in production, sales, job opportunities, wages, profit, and general well-being. With the enunciation of these ideas, Taylor had obviously moved from the shadow of the shop into the light of Towne's torch on the total function of management.

Principles of Management. To put these ideas succinctly for public consumption, Taylor simply stated:

First: Develop a science for each element of a man's work, which replaces the old rule-of-thumb method.

Second: Scientifically select and then train, teach, and develop the workman, whereas in the past he chose his own work and trained himself as best he could.

Third: Heartily cooperate with the men so as to insure all of the work being done in accordance with the principles of the science which has been developed.

Fourth: There is an almost equal division of the work and the responsibility between the management and the workmen. The management take over all work for which they are better fitted than the workmen, while in the past almost all of the work and the greater part of the responsibility were thrown upon the men.[1]

[1] Frederick W. Taylor, *Principles of Scientific Management* (New York: Harper & Bros., 1911), pp. 36-37.

Taylor stated, moreover, that the *combination* of these four great principles of management constituted *scientific* management, which was more conceptual and philosophical than mechanical. He warned against confusing the mechanisms of management with the philosophy of scientific management, and he listed the following as some of the mechanisms:

> Time study, with the implements and methods for properly making it.
>
> Functional or divided foremanship and its superiority to the old-fashioned single foreman.
>
> The standardization of all tools and implements used in the trades, and also of the acts or movements of workmen for each class of work.
>
> The desirability of a planning room or department.
>
> The "exception principle" in management.
>
> The use of slide-rules and similar time-saving implements.
>
> Instruction cards for the workman.
>
> The task idea in management, accompanied by a large bonus for the successful performance of the task.
>
> The "differential rate."
>
> Mnemonic systems for classifying manufactured products as well as implements used in manufacturing.
>
> A routing system.
>
> Modern cost system, etc., etc.[2]

AWAKENING INTEREST IN SCIENTIFIC MANAGEMENT

The ramifications of Taylor's ideas, the impact that these concepts could make and have made on man's economic well-being, are truly staggering. Reviewing the management innovations he propounded at the turn of the century one is astounded at the exhaustive thoroughness of his program. Some regard him as the father of all present-day management. Whatever role we may ascribe to him, he was without dispute a perfectionist and a master in his work, possessed with piercing insight and comprehension of the role of management.

Despite all this, however, Taylor's audience at the 1903 meeting of the American Society of Mechanical Engineers failed to grasp and appreciate the significance of his concepts. In 1911 at an Interstate Commerce Commission hearing on the efficiency of railroads, and at a subsequent investigation by a special House of Representatives Committee on the effects of Taylor's system at Watertown Arsenal, the public was more interested in the sensational testimony than in the concepts of sceintific management.

[2]*Ibid.*, pp. 129-30.

But, *from this point on,* the public was aware of scientific management. Interest and discussion were sustained and widespread among managers—not only in the United States but in France, Italy, Germany, Holland, Russia, and Japan.

This sudden upsurge of interest in scientific management could be explained as an idea meeting a need. Management was hungry for an answer to its problems, and this appeared to be a body of logical and practical principles incorporated in a comprehensive system of management techniques. For a decade now, management's interest in self-improvement had grown, spurred on by conventions and papers such as those previously discussed. The outgrowth of this interest was a series of techniques for cost gathering, cost allocation, control systems, control forms, and the like—each making existing managerial practices more precise but not seriously modifying them to any degree.

As might be expected, all this led to the appearance of a series of articles and books on the subject of management. But it was not until after the hearings of the Eastern Rate Case in 1911 that Taylor's ideas became widely known. The testimony to the effectiveness of Taylor's system appealed to the intellect of the serious students and practitioners of management, and the concepts generated by the term *scientific management* appealed to everyone. Taylor's ideas were starting to bear fruit. His concepts had arrived—although the bloom faded quickly for some as a result of the House investigation.

For the serious student of management, however, these hearings did much to promulgate Taylor's ideas. They gave Taylor another chance to expound his ideas of scientific management. One part of his testimony is particularly appealing for its statement of what scientific management is *not:*

> Scientific management is not any efficiency device, not a device of any kind for securing efficiency; nor is it any bunch or group of efficiency devices. It is not a new system of figuring costs; it is not a new scheme of paying men; it is not a piecework system; it is not a bonus system; it is not a watch on a man and writing things down about him; it is not time study; it is not motion study nor an analysis of the movements of men; it is not the printing and ruling and unloading of a ton or two of blanks on a set of men and saying, "Here's your system; go use it." It is not divided foremanship or functional foremanship; it is not any of the devices which the average man calls to mind when scientific management is spoken of. The average man thinks of one or more of these things when he hears the words "scientific management" mentioned, but scientific management is not any of these devices. I am not sneering at cost-keeping systems, at time study, at functional foremanship, nor at any new and improved scheme of paying men, nor at any efficiency devices, if they are really devices that make for efficiency. I believe in them; but what I am emphasizing is that these devices in whole or in part are not scientific management; they are useful adjuncts to scientific management, so are they also useful adjuncts of other systems of management.
>
> Now in its essence, scientific management involves a complete

mental revolution on the part of the workingman engaged in any particular establishment or industry—a complete mental revolution on the part of these men as to their duties toward their work, toward their fellow men, and toward their employers. And it involves the equally complete mental revolution on the part of those on the management's side—the foreman, the superintendent, the owner of the business, the board of directors—a complete mental revolution on their part as to their duties toward their fellow workers in the management, toward their workmen, and toward all of their daily problems. And without this complete mental revolution on both sides scientific management does not exist.

That is the essence of scientific management, this great mental revolution.[3]

If all these concepts seem obvious, routine, orthodox, and traditional in managerial practice, we must remember that at the turn of the century they were truly avant-garde—so new, in fact, that one could class them as revolutionary. Many of Taylor's ideas, of course, had been suggested previously. Babbage, among others, had traveled much the same road. But Taylor's genius lay in his assimilation, conceptualization, and application of these ideas as a unified approach to effective management.

IMPACT OF SCIENTIFIC MANAGEMENT

One obvious contribution of scientific management was the overall improvement in factory management. And as soon as it opened the way for improvements in the shop, it pushed into sales, general administration, and other facets of an enterprise. It brought about a more effective utilization of equipment, labor, and materials. It spurred the development of more accurate controls, routing, and planning. For labor, it resulted in better placement, more opportunities for advancement, higher wages, better working conditions, proper work hours, and a broadening of the scope of individual initiative through increased job opportunities and incentive applications.

For management, it has pointed the way to a more effective organization, a more reliable product, a better work force, a better understood customer, an improved corporate image, and a more effective profit position. We could name still more, but these serve to indicate the grand scale of the total impact. These effects, of course, grew from the *system* of scientific management that Taylor developed, and it is this *system* that is so important—not the ephemeral day-to-day operating mechanics that so often we confuse with the concepts.

If nothing else, Taylor firmly planted the concept of *research* in place of rule of thumb. And the newer management has continued to experiment and

[3]Frederick W. Taylor, *Scientific Management* (New York: Harper & Bros., 1947), pp. 26-27.

look for the new as a basic element in a sound managerial approach. He also championed the use of *standards* in every phase of management, always driving hard the need for standards of consistency as a prelude to high standards of operation and product quality.

A third impact—for many years overlooked and neglected—was the systematic *planning* that was necessary for any visible improvement. For years many individuals confused the mechanics with the system, failing to see that these were only the evidences of the planning aspect of his system. Taylor gave to management the collective concept of *control*—control as a sensing mechanism to maintain established procedures, standards, conditions, and the like, necessary for the effective and total operation of the system.

And finally, Taylor introduced the principle of *cooperation,* pointing out that only through mutual understanding and cooperation could the basic needs and desires of both management and labor be met.

Upon these five concepts Taylor emphasized that management should be founded. And these five principles—*research, standards, planning, control,* and *cooperation*—form the solid basis of virtually every successful venture.

AIMS OF SCIENTIFIC MANAGEMENT

Scientific management, according to its early proponents, had clear objectives; but it was left to the Taylor Society in its early days to enunciate the thirteen aims of scientific management:

1. To gauge industrial tendencies and the market in order thereby to regularize operations in a manner which will conserve the investment, sustain the enterprise as an employing agency and assure continuous operation and employment;
2. To assure the employee not only continuous operating and employment by correct gauging of the market, but also to assure by planned and balanced operations a continuous earning opportunity while on the payroll;
3. To earn through a waste-saving management and processing technique, a larger income from a given expenditure of human and material energies, which shall be shared through increased wages and profits by workers and management;
4. To make possible a higher standard of living as a result of increased income to workers;
5. To assure a happier home and social life to workers through removal, by increase of income, of many of the disagreeable and worrying factors in the total situation;
6. To assure healthful as well as individually and socially agreeable conditions of work;
7. To assure the highest opportunity for individual capacity through scientific methods of work analysis and of selection, training, assignment, transfer and promotion of workers;

8. To assure by training and instructional foremanship the opportunity for workers to develop new and higher capacities, and eligibility for promotion to higher positions;
9. To develop self-confidence and self-respect among workers through opportunity afforded for understanding of one's own work specifically, and of plans and methods of work generally;
10. To develop self-expression and self-realization among workers through the stimulative influence of an atmosphere of research and valuation, through understanding of plans and methods, and through the freedom of horizontal as well as vertical contacts afforded by functional organization;
11. To build character through the proper conduct of work;
12. To promote justice through the elimination of discriminations in wage rates and elsewhere;
13. To eliminate factors of the environment which are irritating and the causes of frictions, and to promote common understandings, tolerances and the spirit of team work.[4]

These aims have been a basic and integral part of the concepts of scientific management from its early days. Not always overtly stated, they were nevertheless present—each depending upon the application of the *system* of management for its realization as a viable achievement.

NEW VIEWS GENERATED
BY SCIENTIFIC MANAGEMENT

Early frontier conditions of opportunism and plenty set the tone for managerial thinking at the turn of the century and provided for the managerial quagmire in which Taylor found himself. His new system of management employing scientific principles promoted many new attitudes that offered sharp contrasts to those existing at the time.

Scientific management, for example, called for *conservation,* not waste. Management became aware gradually, of course, that they were wasting the facilities of production and that one way to be more effective as a manager in compensating for the narrowing profit margin was to eliminate these wastes in effort, materials, time, and the like. As the idea grew, it spread into many areas and influenced the development of the still broader idea of social waste.

By its very nature, scientific management promoted an air of *investigation.* It called for research into all avenues of endeavor to determine—scientifically— which would be best for the particular case under consideration. This approach to problem solving was not typical of the times. Research, investigation, and analysis were largely foreign to the vocabulary of the average business leader. Problem solving consisted mainly in following someone else's action—imitation.

[4]*Scientific Management in American Industry,* ed. H. S. Person (New York: Harper & Bros., 1929), pp. 16-17.

Or, if imitation were not the apparent solution, the path of least resistance or the obvious way open would suffice.

In dealing with labor, scientific management ushered in a new era. It viewed management and labor as a team that, working together, could excel the best endeavors of either individually. It promoted and called for a new look of harmonious and wholehearted *cooperation* in place of the old tendency toward rugged individualism, which had characterized the early settler.

Finally, under the influence of individualism and the accepted practice of arbitrary and sudden change, management had tended to be revolutionary in its decisions—often ill considered from an overall point of view. Scientific management, with its emphasis on planning, use of standards, research, and cooperative endeavor, encouraged management to reach conclusions after research, to use the laws of the situation instead of individual guess and intuition. In a word, it promoted careful consideration that would make for gradual *evolutionary* changes as opposed to the abrupt revolutionary practices frequently employed.

These "new views," though radical then, are commonplace today and are accepted as standards for excellent practice. And this acceptance in itself is indicative of the total effect of scientific management. It was, indeed, a concept twenty to thirty years ahead of its time.

FRANK B. AND LILLIAN M. GILBRETH

No discussion of scientific management would be complete without Frank Bunker and Lillian Moller Gilbreth. Whenever these names are mentioned one immediately thinks of the Gilbreths' pioneering efforts—their work and refinements in the field of motion study laid the entire foundation for our modern applications of job simplification, meaningful work standards, and incentive wage plans.

Born in 1868, Frank B. Gilbreth, despite having passed the M.I.T. entrance examinations, decided to enter the contracting business, starting as an apprentice bricklayer with the firm of Whidden and Company. Gilbreth quickly noted that the men teaching him to lay bricks used three different sets of motions: one set to *teach* a person to lay bricks, a second set to work at a *slow* pace, and a third to work at a *fast* pace. Observing these and other variations in the motion patterns used by bricklayers in their work, Gilbreth wondered which set of motions was the best and most efficient.

His interest aroused, Gilbreth studied the motions used by the men in relation to the work and tools used, and he developed an improved method. In laying exterior brick, for example, he reduced the number of motions from 18 to 4½ per brick laid, and on interior brick he reduced the motions from 18 to 2, resulting in an increase of from 120 to 350 bricks per man-hour! He also developed a new way to stack bricks that eliminated the motions normally required by the bricklayer for examining a brick to determine its best surface. He developed an adjustable stand that eliminated the bending normally required to pick up a brick; and he prescribed a precise consistency for mortar which would allow bricks to be laid without extra tapping on the brick with the trowel. By thus studying and analyzing the motion of workers scientifically, Gilbreth developed a more efficient and less time-consuming method of laying bricks—and unwittingly started on a lifetime search for the "one best way" of performing any given task.

In 1904 Gilbreth married Lillian Moller who had a unique background in psychology and management, and the two embarked on a quest for better work methods.

In the course of their studies the Gilbreths invented and used many devices and techniques. They were among the first to use motion-picture films to analyze and improve motion sequences. Though he could study the film and analyze the motions employed, Gilbreth was unable to determine how long a motion took because the early cameras did not run at a constant speed, most of them being hand cranked.

To overcome this handicap, Gilbreth invented the microchronometer, a clock with a large sweeping hand, capable of recording time to 1/2000 of a minute. With this clock placed in the field of work study being photographed, Gilbreth could analyze each motion from the film and could determine how long its performance required. Even today, unless a camera equipped with a constant-speed electric motor is employed, we still use Gilbreth's microchronometer in photographing and studying motion patterns.

Using these films, the Gilbreths constructed three-dimensional wire models of motions, to permit better study and analysis. To outline more clearly a motion sequence on film, a small lighted electric bulb was attached to the employee's hand, and time exposures were made. The resulting film, called a *cyclegraph* by Gilbreth, showed as tracings of light the motion pattern employed in performing a given task. Speed and direction of movement, however, could not be determined from these solid lines of light on the film. Gilbreth therefore added an interrupter to the circuit which caused the bulb to flash on and off. By this device, which he named a *chronocyclegraph*, Gilbreth could determine the acceleration, deceleration, and direction of movement by the increasing or decreasing length of the dash and the direction of the "tail" formed by the moving light.

In their study of hand motions, the Gilbreths found that classifications generally used, such as "move hand," were too broad for detailed analysis. Gilbreth accordingly refined hand motions into seventeen basic or fundamental motions—for example, "grasp," "transport loaded," "hold"—which he termed *therbligs* ("Gilbreth" spelled backwards with the *th* transposed).

To record process and flow patterns used in a work situation, the Gilbreths developed the process chart and the flow diagram, both widely used today.

Moving from the area of motions, the Gilbreths developed the "white list" card system on personnel—a forerunner of current merit-rating systems. They emphasized written instructions to avoid confusion and misunderstanding. They also worked on simplifying the English alphabet, the typewriter keyboard, and. spelling. They urged that the principles of management and motion analysis could effectively be applied to the huge untapped area of self-management. They started a search into the area of fatigue and its impact on health and productivity that continues today.

And thus the list goes on. Considering Gilbreth's intense interest and study of the field of motions, it is no wonder that he is known today as the father of motion study. But his fame did not come until many years after his death in 1924.

Gilbreth's Contribution

Gilbreth should not be regarded solely as a motion-study man, any more than Taylor should be regarded simply as a stopwatch man. Like Taylor, Gilbreth's perspective far exceeded the bounds of the work place. His interest lay in the development of man to his fullest potential through effective training, work methods, improved environments and tools, and a healthy psychological outlook. He was, in a word, interested in improving the totality of man and his environment. His was a unique contribution to the state and the art of management. He applied science to a new dimension of work. He provided a practical application of the new science of management, thereby enhancing its possibilities of acceptance and success. And through his exhaustive work, better motion patterns could be developed on which to build sound incentive pay plans.

Even more than this, however, the Gilbreths' legacy to the development of management thought is the inculcation in the minds of managers that any and every thing should be questioned as to its feasibility and applicability, and that even the new should be discarded if an improvement is in the offing. It is a legacy of the questioning frame of mind, the quest for a better way.

7

EARLY TWENTIETH CENTURY CONCEPTS

Following the emergence of the concepts indicated in the preceding chapter and the publication of Frederick W. Taylor's ideas about scientific management, a number of associates, contemporaries, and followers of Taylor's doctrine appeared to promulgate their versions of the new science of management. Among them were outstanding educators such as Harlow S. Person, Hugo Munsterberg, and Walter Dill Scott, associates of Taylor such as Henry L. Gantt, consultants such as Harrington Emerson, and industrial independents such as Henri Fayol. Each of these men added a new dimension to the new corpus of managerial concepts, each of them contributed to the totality of thought, and each of them lent further support and prestige to the movement.

In this chapter we shall examine the work and contributions to the development of managerial thought by these and other writers.

HENRY L. GANTT

If one had to choose one word to describe Henry L. Gantt and his impact on management, it would be *humanistic*.

Gantt was a contemporary and a protégé of Frederick W. Taylor, but it was not until 1887 when he joined Taylor in his experiments at Midvale Steel

Works that he became inbued with Taylor's concepts and ideals. He differed from Taylor, however, in his special sympathy for the underprivileged and in his compulsion to measure democracy by the opportunity it offered all men. It was from these two influences that his two concepts of humanism and task-and-bonus grew. Of course his ideas did not spring forth overnight but developed over a fourteen-year association with Taylor.

In 1901 Gantt brought out his task-and-bonus wage system. It was based on Taylor's differential piece-rate system but was, in Gantt's words, "as far as possible removed from the old-fashioned method of fixing piece rates from records of the total time it has taken to do a job."[1] Instead, the time allowed for the job was based upon standard shop conditions and a first-class performance. Thus, if an employee accomplished his task for the day, he received a bonus in addition to his regular day rate. If he did not finish the task, he received only the day rate but was not penalized. This differed from Taylor's piece rate which did not pay guaranteed wages for substandard performance; and Taylor's system paid by the piece for above-average workers, whereas Gantt's more humanistic system was geared to the employee's day-wage rate.

With the introduction of Gantt's system, production often more than doubled. This convinced Gantt that his concern for the worker and his morale was one of the most important factors in administrative practices—that the human element was the most important in all problems of management.

In addition to this area, Gantt developed the "daily balance chart," now known as the Gantt Chart. In simple terms, the chart shows output on one axis with units of time on the other. Nothing could be simpler, yet at the time nothing of its kind could have been more revolutionary in the area of production control.

In his later years Gantt was sometimes referred to as the apostle of industrial peace because of his standing plea for wider recognition of the human factor in management, and for recognizing that financial incentives are only one of many that influence employee behavior.[2]

Contributions

Henry L. Gantt made four discernible contributions to the existing concepts of management. The one most easily recalled was the idea of a straight-line chart to portray and measure an activity by the amount of time needed to perform it. We know it today as the Gantt Chart, a device used by management to compare actual to planned performance.

Out of his passion for a more humanitarian approach to management came

---

[1] Henry L. Gantt, "A Bonus System for Rewarding Labor," *Transactions of the American Society of Mechanical Engineers,* XXIII (1901), 373.

[2] L. Urwick, ed., *The Golden Book of Management* (London: Newman Neame Limited, 1956), pp. 89-91.

Gantt's second contribution, the task-and-bonus plan for remunerating workers. Unlike Taylor's differential piece-rate system, Gantt's plan guaranteed a day wage for output less than standard, offered a bonus in addition to the day wage for achieving standard, and rewarded the worker for production above standard. Under his plan workers could earn a living while learning to increase their efficiency.

In 1908 Gantt presented his "Training Workmen in Habits of Industry and Cooperation" to the American Society of Mechanical Engineers. In this paper we find his third contribution: a policy of instructing workers rather than driving them. It was here that Gantt introduced what might be termed "the psychology of employee relations," with the idea that management had a responsibility to teach and train workers to become more skilled, form better work habits, lose less time, and become more reliable. Gantt, like many other pioneers in management, was ahead of his time. It was not until after World War I that management in general acceded that training was a managerial responsibility.

Finally, Gantt pleaded that emphasis be placed on service rather than on profits. Feeling that only by having service as its ultimate goal could our business system stand, Gantt did more to introduce the concept of industrial responsibility than any prior individual.

There is no question that Henry L. Gantt was one of the great contributors to the development of management thought. Through his contributions were more in the nature of refinements rather than fundamental concepts, they have made scientific management more meaningful to a larger number of Taylor devotees.

HUGO MUNSTERBERG

Born in Danzig, Germany, on June 1, 1863, Hugo Munsterberg earned the Ph.D degree in psychology at the University of Leipzig in 1885 and the M.D. degree at the University of Heidelberg two years later. He was only twenty-nine years old when he took charge of the psychological laboratory as professor of experimental psychology at Harvard University. Despite this lofty position, Munsterberg was frequently the author of not scholarly dissertations but sensational features written in a popular style appearing in local papers and magazines. These articles along with subsequent publications brought psychology—particularly the psychological aspects of management—to the attention of industrialists.

Early in his career Dr. Munsterberg had proposed the use of psychology for practical purposes, and in 1910 he and his students began research dealing with the application of psychology to industry. The outcome of this work was his pioneering book published in 1913, *Psychology and Industrial Efficiency,* which made a strong plea for more science in management, particularly for better understanding and application of psychology.

After paying tribute in his book to Frederick W. Taylor as the brilliant originator of scientific management, Munsterberg proposed that the role of psychologists in industry should be (1) to help find the men best fitted for the work; (2) to determine under what psychological conditions the greatest output per man could be achieved; and (3) to produce the influences on the human mind desired in the interest of management. As he expressed it, ". . . we ask how to find the best possible work, and how to secure the best possible effects."[3] In addition, Munsterberg believed in industrial research and experimentation. It was through his experiments in developing tests for the selection of streetcar drivers that Munsterberg ushered in the beginning of vocational guidance along scientific lines in industry.

A frequent guest at major industrial complexes, Munsterberg in turn received numerous businessmen who came to consult with him at Harvard.[4] As a result of his and Walter Dill Scott's efforts and writing, industrial psychology was well established by 1920 as one of the most important aspects of the new science of management.

WALTER DILL SCOTT

Walter Dill Scott, a noted American educator, taught at Northwestern University from 1901 to 1920 and then served as president for the following nineteen years. During World War I he devised the system adopted by the army for classifying personnel and testing officer candidates, and for this work he was awarded the Distinguished Service Medal. Scott is perhaps best known today as a pioneer in business psychology encompassing the areas of advertising and personnel management.

At Northwestern University, Scott taught psychology and advertising, and like Munsterberg, he also studied in Germany under Wilhelm Wundt. In 1901 he set up a psychological laboratory at Northwestern, and in 1902 he began his work in business by studying the psychology of advertising. In Scott's mind the human factor had too long been neglected by management in that the proper selection and supervision of employees had not kept pace with technological improvements. Because of poor personnel practices, Scott reasoned, the average worker performed at a considerably lower level of efficiency than was normal. Scott was particularly concerned with employee attitudes and motivation in production and how suggestions could influence their behavior.

In the March 1910 to October 1911 issues of *System* magazine (now *Business Week),* a series of articles by Scott appeared under the title, *The*

---

[3]Hugo Munsterberg, *Psychology and Industrial Efficiency* (New York: Houghton Mifflin Company, 1913), p. 24.

[4]For an interesting treatment of Munsterberg, see "Measuring Minds for the Job," *Business Week,* January 29, 1966, pp. 60-63.

Psychology of Business.[5] These articles, based on actual business cases, represent one of the earliest applications of the principles of psychology to motivation and productivity in industry. Scott's emphasis differed from Munsterberg's, however, in that he was mainly concerned with the importance of attitudes in motivation and productivity, while Munsterberg's emphasis was on managers and their application of psychology to industrial efficiency. Both men, of course, dealt with the same overall problem but approached it through different facets of the science of psychology. However, through their efforts and zeal in applying psychology to management, industrial psychology emerged firmly as one of the more important aspects of the science of management.

In addition to these early articles, Scott published two other works of major importance. In his *Psychology of Advertising in Theory and Practice* (1921), he made a comprehensive study of the proper advertising to appeal psychologically to the reader. Systematically he outlined the psychological concepts that could be applied to the appeal of the printed work, including perception, imagery, idea association, memory, emotion, suggestion, and illusion. He consistently and constantly stressed the value of emotional appeal in advertising.

Influencing Men in Business: The Psychology of Argument and Suggestion, published in 1923, was Scott's third publication in the area of psychology. This time, however, he was concerned with persuasion in the business arena in a more general sense than just the printed advertisement. His thesis was that there are generally two methods of persuasion—argument and suggestion—the latter being equally effective as logical reasoning and in some situations, if properly employed, even more effective.

In summary, Scott brought his background of psychology to the area of personnel, stressing that the employee is both a social and an economic entity possessing different characteristics in various work situations. He also applied the fundamentals of psychology to business methods. Through his efforts and insights, the psychological facet of management was further rounded out.

HARRINGTON EMERSON

Harrington Emerson, a Presbyterian minister's son from Trenton, New Jersey, is probably best remembered as the expert witness for Brandeis in 1910 who stated that the United States railroads could save one million dollars per day if they would adopt scientific management principles in their operation. It was also Emerson who first used the term *efficiency engineering* to describe his brand of consulting. In fact, he pushed the concept of efficiency to such a

[5]This series was reprinted in 1969 by the Bureau of Business Research, University of Texas, as *Studies in Personnel and Management No. 21,* under the direction of Professor Edmund C. Lynch.

magnitude that today he is frequently referred to as the "high priest of efficiency."

Emerson's concept of efficiency was simple: conservation—the elimination of "wanton, wicked waste." To him this included waste in government, waste that was robbing and depleting our natural resources, and waste in the efficiency of men and machines in our industrial sector.

In 1911 the Engineering Magazine Company published Emerson's book *Efficiency as a Basis for Operation and Wages,* and in 1913 his expanded concepts were published as *The Twelve Principles of Efficiency,* his best known and most popular work. The major thesis in his *Principles* was that *ideas*—not land, labor, and capital—create wealth; that *ideas employing the tools* of land, labor, and capital generate wealth. To explain this further, he set forth twelve principles of efficiency upon which management should rest—principles that we may regard as commonplace, but were new for his time.

Emerson's Principles

The first five of Emerson's principles of efficiency relate to interpersonal relations, particularly between employer and employee; the remaining seven principles relate mainly to methodology or systems in management.

1. *Clearly defined ideal*—know what you are attempting to accomplish. Eliminate vagueness, uncertainty, and aimlessness characteristic of a great many undertakings.
2. *Common sense*—a supernal common sense that enables one to differentiate between woods and trees. This is a common sense that strives for knowledge and seeks advice from every quarter, unconfined in any position yet maintaining dignity of balance.
3. *Competent counsel*—actively seeking advice from competent individuals.
4. *Discipline*—adherence to rules; strict obedience. The function of this principle is to bring about allegiance to and observance of the remaining eleven principles.
5. *Fair deal*—justice and fairness.
6. *Reliable, immediate, adequate, and permanent records*—a call for facts upon which to base decisions.
7. *Dispatching*—scientific planning through which each small function is performed so as to serve to unify the whole and enable the organization to reach its end objective.
8. *Standards and schedules*—a method and time for performing tasks.
9. *Standardized conditions*—uniformity of environment.
10. *Standardized operations*—uniformity of method.
11. *Written standard-practice instructions*—systematically and accurately reducing practice to writing. [This was Emerson's legal codification for industrial practice.]
12. *Efficiency reward*—reward for successful execution of a given task.

Contributions

Though Emerson was in correspondence with Taylor from 1903 on, he was not an associate or a disciple of Taylor's. He was an independent who developed during the years when scientific management was trying to get established. We can see much in Emerson's ideas that harken back to Taylor, but we also see his focus on the managerial problem of *organization and the objectives of a firm.* He was an advocate of counsel, of a strong staff, and pointed to the military for lessons in this respect.

He developed the term *efficiency engineer* and was one of America's first consultants, thus bringing emphasis to the staff principle. His was the first attempt at codifying a set of principles to guide management, and this attempt, along with the soundness of his principles, served to reemphasize the growing awareness of the distinct nature and universality of management.

HARLOW STAFFORD PERSON

Harlow Stafford Person, for the greater part of his productive life, probably came closer to being "Mr. Management" than any other man in the country.

The new concept of scientific management was still in its infancy when, at the ripe old age of twenty-seven, Person joined the Amos Tuck School at Dartmouth in 1902 as an instructor in commerce and industry. Nine years later, as dean of the Tuck School, Dr. Person organized the first scientific management conference in the United States, giving widespread academic recognition to Taylor and his methods for the first time.

As one of the leaders in the management movement, Dr. Person was for a number of years director of the Taylor Society (formerly known as The Society to Promote the Science of Management). As an educator, he encouraged widespread discussions of the new science of management, and even insisted on labor's joining management in assessing the possible value of proposed industrial changes. In all probability, through his writing and leadership the word was spread that scientific management was not dedicated to the stopwatch and speedup, but rather to the purposive and scientific determination of effective ways to accomplish given tasks.

Person's contribution was to give scientific management a new academic respectability and to help dissipate the idea that scientific management was an offshoot of the stopwatch dedicated to the speedup.[6]

[6]"Organizing a Profession," *Business Week,* March 21, 1964, pp. 87-88.

HENRI FAYOL

Fayolism, the earliest comprehensive statement of a general theory of management, has had an interesting history.

First published in France in 1916, Henri Fayol's *Administration industrielle et générale* was virtually ignored in the United States until published here in 1949 as *General and Industrial Management*. While Taylor's methods were being avidly sought and studied by European executives, American pioneers of scientific management ignored Fayol, the French pioneer, and regarded scientific management as an American invention. Even now many managerial authorities are just discovering that the French had a name for it—that they viewed the practice of management as something distinct from finance, production, distribution, and other typical business functions. Fayolism was a French brand of new managerial thinking.

Although Fayol's ideas were developed about the turn of the century, they have a contemporary ring. Consider, for example:

> The question of centralization or decentralization is simply a matter of proportion—finding the optimum degree for the particular firm.
>
> Each employee intentionally or unintentionally puts something of himself into his work. He does not operate merely as a cog in a machine.
>
> The scalar chain is the chain of supervisors ranging from the top to the bottom ranks.
>
> For order to prevail, there must be an appointed place for every employee and he should be in his appointed place.
>
> Dividing enemy forces is clever, but dividing one's own team is a grave error.

Fayol's Career

Henri Fayol is without doubt the most distinguished European in the field of management thought. Born in 1841 of a French bourgeois family, Fayol was appointed engineer of the Commentry mine pits of the S. A. Commentry-Fourchambault in 1860, and by 1888 he had risen to the position of managing director of the mining firm. When he took charge the company was on the verge of bankruptcy; when he retired in 1918 its financial position was impregnable.[7]

Fayol attributed his success not to his own personal capacities, but to his system of management which he emphasized could be both taught and learned. In fact, isolating and analyzing the concepts and principles of management constitute Fayol's original and unique contribution to the continuum of

[7]L. Urwick, *The Golden Book of Management*, p. 21.

management thought. He opened the door to the development of the functional school of thought and breathed clarity into the muddled thinking on the nature of top management.

Though they differed in approach, Fayol and Taylor were working on the same problem—Taylor from the shop up, and Fayol from the board of directors down. Taylor's approach to management dealt with specifics of job analysis, employees' motions, and time standards; while Fayol viewed management as a teachable theory dealing with planning, organizing, commanding, coordinating, and controlling.

Through the application and testing of his ideas at Comambault (as the mining company was known), Fayol was ready in 1914 to release for press his ideas on the overall theory of management.[8] But the war interfered, and it was not until 1916 that his now famous *Administration industrielle et générale* appeared in the Bulletin de la Société de l'Industrie Minérale and was subsequently published in English as a book in 1929.

Unfortunately for Fayol, this delayed publication caused his ideas to take a back seat to Taylor's concepts which were sweeping France and Europe at the time. The French were, in fact, much taken by the speed and efficiency of American troops in building docks, setting up roads, establishing lines of communication, and the like; they branded all this efficiency as Taylorism. So intrigued were they with Taylor's principles that Georges Clemenceau, then French minister of war, ordered all plants under his control to study and apply Taylor's scientific management.[9] Taylor's cause was also helped by Charles de Fréminville and Henry-Louis Le Châtelier, both of whom devoted the influence of their great reputations to further the teachings of Taylor in France.

Time, however, was on Fayol's side. With the publication of his book, French executives began to analyze their operations in its new light. Here was a man of experience who spoke their language, recognized their problems, and presented his ideas in a neat theory that added perception rather than confusion to their thinking.

Thus Fayol's theory gained success both in industry and in other fields, for Fayol maintained strongly that any valid theory of management could not be limited to business but must be equally applicable to all forms of human endeavor.

Concepts of Management

Fayol observed that management was an activity common to all human undertakings, whether in the home, business, or government. He noted further that all these undertakings required some degree of planning, organizing,

[8]"Discoveries from Looking Inward," *Business Week*, June 6, 1964, p. 152.
[9]*Ibid.*,

commanding, coordinating, and controlling. Since management was all-pervasive, Fayol reasoned that a general knowledge of it would benefit everyone and it should therefore be taught in schools and universities. This, naturally, brought him to a consideration of what subject matter should be taught. At that time, of course, there was no comprehensive theory of management that would be acceptable in academic circles. To answer this need, he presented his own theory which could serve as a model for instruction.

Fayol began by dividing the total industrial undertaking into six separate activities:

1. Technical (production, manufacture, adaption)
2. Commercial (buying, selling, exchange)
3. Financial (search for and optimum use of capital)
4. Security (protection of property and persons)
5. Accounting (stocktaking, balance sheets, costs, statistics)
6. Managerial (planning, organizing, commanding, coordinating, controlling)

Indicating that the last of these—the *managerial* activity—was by far the most important and deserved the most attention, Fayol developed this aspect further. He indicated that all management activity is made up of five components: *planning, organizing, commanding, coordinating,* and *controlling,* and elaborated on each as follows.

Planning consisted of examining the future and drawing up a plan of action.

Organizing consisted of building up a dual structure (human and material) to achieve the undertaking. Further, Fayol indicated that the organizer (manager) had sixteen managerial duties to perform:

1. Insure that the plan is judiciously prepared and strictly carried out.
2. See that the human and material organization is consistent with the objective, resources, and requirements of the concern.
3. Set up a single, competent energetic building authority.
4. Harmonize activities and coordinate efforts.
5. Formulate clear, distinct, precise decisions.
6. Arrange for efficient selection of personnel—each department must be headed by a competent, energetic man, each employee must be in that place where he can render greatest service.
7. Define duties clearly.
8. Encourage a liking for initiative and responsibility.
9. Have fair and suitable recompense for services rendered.
10. Make use of sanctions against faults and errors.
11. See to the maintenance of discipline.
12. Insure that individual interests are subordinated to the general interest.
13. Pay special attention to the unity of command.
14. Supervise both material and human order.
15. Have everything under control.
16. Fight against excess of regulations, red tape and paper control.

Commanding consisted of maintaining activity among the personnel of the organization. Speaking of the manager who commands, Fayol added that he should:

1. Have a thorough knowledge of his personnel.
2. Eliminate the incompetent.
3. Be well versed in the agreements binding the business and its employees.
4. Set a good example.
5. Conduct periodic audits of the organization and use summarized charts to further this. Fayol heavily emphasized organization charts.
6. Bring together his chief assistants by means of conferences, at which units of direction and focusing of effort are provided for.[10]

Coordinating consisted of binding together, unifying, and harmonizing all activity and effort.

Controlling consisted of seeing that everything was accomplished in conformity with the established plan and command.

Finally, Fayol completes his network of managerial theory by stating that to be effective, management should be founded upon and observe the following fourteen principles:

1. Division of work (specialization belongs to the natural order).
2. Authority and responsibility (responsibility is a corollary with authority).
3. Discipline (discipline is what leaders make it).
4. Unity of command (men cannot bear dual command).
5. Unity of direction (one head and one plan for a group of activities having the same objectives).
6. Subordination of individual interest to the general interest.
7. Remuneration (fair, rewarding of effort, reasonable).
8. Centralization (centralization belongs to the natural order).
9. Scalar chain (line of authority, gang-plank principle).
10. Order (a place for everyone and everyone in his place).
11. Equity (results from combination of kindliness and justice).
12. Stability of tenure of personnel (prosperous firms are stable).
13. Initiative (great source of strength for business).
14. Esprit de corps (union is strength).[11]

Most of these principles need little elaboration, except number four: unity of command. Fayol was most emphatic about this principle, stating that each individual, whether manager or laborer, should have one and only one boss. In

---

[10]Henri Fayol, *General and Industrial Management* (London: Sir Isaac Pitman & Sons Ltd., 1949), p. 97.

[11]*Ibid.*, pp. 19-20.

fact, he took Taylor to task for his idea of functional foremanship, whereby each worker might have as many as eight bosses.

Fayol's theory of management is, as was previously indicated, the first complete theory to be presented. It incorporated proven principles, elements, procedures, and techniques—all based on his practical experience. The close similarity between his theory and current thinking is sufficient evidence of its applicability and true value.

Contributions

Fayol's *General and Industrial Management* was a singular and significant contribution to management thought in that it presented three revolutionary aspects highly important to the development of management:

1. The concept that management as a separate body of knowledge is applicable to all forms of group activity—the universality of management.
2. A first complete and comprehensive theory of management which could be applied to all endeavors.
3. The concept of teaching and developing management curricula in colleges and universities.

Fayol viewed the organization as an abstract or a legal entity that grew out of and was directed by a rational system of rules and authority. To Fayol, the enterprise justified its existence by meeting its primary objective of providing value in the form of goods or services to consumers. Attaining this objective permitted the organization to reward its contributors (employees, managers, etc.) for their contributions.

In Fayol's scheme, the work of an administrator involved five facets: planning, organizing, commanding, coordinating, and controlling. Planning effort was described largely in terms of decision making, goal setting, developing policy, and allocating functions to organizational components. Fayol thus reasoned that planning led to organizing, because to allocate functions management would of necessity have to identify and properly arrange (i.e., organize) the units or components of the undertaking.

In a similar manner, Fayol linked commanding, coordinating, and controlling. He reasoned that once an enterprise was organized, its employees would need commands (communications) from the manager to know what and how to perform; that their actions and functions required managerial coordination to bind and harmonize their efforts; and finally, that the manager would of necessity have to control their activities to be sure they conformed with the original plan.

In evaluating Fayol's work, one cannot help being impressed by this type of logical thinking and foresight. He applied the lessons of experience to the needs of the future, and the result was a philosophy of management which seems almost contemporary. His broad comprehension of the planning function was unique at the time. He conceived of all departments and all functions of the business operating under a carefully developed, comprehensive plan. He even went so far as to discuss in some detail his ten-year forecasts. Yet today, nearly a half-century after the publication of Fayol's treatise, most companies still do not have any comprehensive plan for forecasting.

His influence on the thinking in France and in many other European countries has surely been equal to that of Frederick W. Taylor in the United States. The work of these two brilliant men was complementary, though they differed completely in their approach. Taylor concerned himself primarily with the worker level and the technical aspects of production, emphasizing the importance of technical ability in management. Fayol, on the other hand, concentrated on management from the top down, emphasizing managerial ability and the application of sound management principles and techniques to all organizations.

Without question, both were extraordinary men, far ahead of their time. It is highly doubtful that either one was understood or fully appreciated by his contemporaries. Taylor, however, could probably be characterized as more of a philosopher at heart than was Fayol. Though Taylor's philosophy grew from his early experiments with techniques, his philosophy was basic to all his teachings, his writings, his life's work—everything he stood for. Fayol, though also a philosopher, did not have the almost religious zeal exhibited by Taylor. Taylor strikes us as a man fired by a cause, while Fayol emerges as a man possessing a managerial mission in life. Both were giants; both were pioneers. Modern management thought owes a tremendous debt to each.

SUMMARY

The six men we have studied in this chapter each made significant contributions to the embryonic science of management. Reviewing them briefly in the table on page 116 may help fix each individual and his work more clearly in our minds.

As we have seen, each of these men lived during the formative years of management and made a significant impact on the developing thoughts of the time. Modern management thought is further indebted to these men for the creation of a healthy managerial image and an environment for its growth. Management's subsequent growth and position is due in no small part to the vision and efforts of these men to promote its dissemination, and to the prestige that each lent to the developing science and study of the function of management.

SIX MAJOR CONTRIBUTORS

Individual	*Contributions*
Henry L. Gantt	1. *Gantt Chart.* 2. *Humanitarianism in employee treatment and pay.* 3. *Teaching and training employees.* 4. *Service as an objective.*
Hugo Munsterberg	1. *Creation of field of industrial psychology.* 2. *Initiation of system of tests and measurements of psychological differences between employees.*
Walter Dill Scott	1. *Application of psychology to employee motivation and productivity.* 2. *Application of psychology to advertising and personnel management.*
Harrington Emerson	1. *Broader focus on the organization structure and its importance.* 2. *Emphasis on the objectives of a firm and their relation to organization.* 3. *Emphasis on use of experts: staff, consultants, and the like.* 4. *Twelve principles of efficiency.*
Harlow S. Person	1. *Academic recognition to scientific management.* 2. *Emphasis on total scope of management, lifting it from a movement dedicated to the stopwatch and speedup.*
Henri Fayol	1. *Concept of universality of management.* 2. *First comprehensive theory of management.* 3. *Need for teaching management in schools and colleges.*

8

MINOR WRITERS
AND CRITICS

After the first wave of publications concerning the work and ideas of such pioneers as Taylor, Gantt, Gilbreth, and Fayol, a veritable league of converts arose to champion the cause of the new science of management and to instruct in its application. Unlike the innovators, these men worked more in the area of interpreting, evaluating, and applying scientific management than in developing managerial principles and guides. They expanded concepts, improved techniques, and generated some new but relatively minor ideas.

Though these were field workers who labored in the periphery, nonetheless their part in firmly establishing scientific management was critically important for mass understanding and application. In this chapter we want to look at the work and contributions of some who were typical of this secondary wave of enthusiasts.

ALEXANDER H. CHURCH

Alexander Hamilton Church, a consultant and a specialist in costing systems, published his first work, *The Proper Distribution of Expense Burden,* as a series of articles in *The Engineering Magazine* in 1901, and later as a book in

1916. These articles are regarded by many as a reference work in accounting literature both in the United States and in Great Britain.

Church's improvements in the machine-rate method for allocating overhead expenses along with his pointing a way to the technique of standard costs were a major contribution to the development of managerial cost concepts.

It was in his 1914 book, however, *The Science and Practice of Management,* that Church collected the disconnected ideas represented by the elements of scientific management and reduced them to regulative principles of management.

In this work Church conceived of two fundamental instruments of management: analysis and synthesis. In *analysis* he saw such things as cost accounting, time study, motion study, the exact study of routing of produce, layout of machines, and planning; while *synthesis* served to combine the functions of administration in such a way that their cooperation produced some useful result. Church, presenting a functional approach for analyzing management, saw in administration a synthesis of five organic functions:

1. *Design,* (which originates), prescribed in advance the shapes, sizes, and properties, and set up standards with respect to product.
2. *Equipment,* which provided physical conditions for production.
3. *Control,* which specified duties and supervised the daily performance of these duties.
4. *Comparison,* which concerned itself with setting up, measuring, recording, and comparing standards.
5. *Operation,* which concerned itself with the transformation of material into new forms in conformance with *design.*

In addition to this functional concept of management, Church evolved what he termed the *universal laws of effort* which, if properly applied to the organic functions of management, would be important aids to practical administration. He defined these laws as:

1. Experience must be systematically accumulated, standardized, and applied.
2. Effort must be economically regulated:
   a. It must be divided.
   b. It must be coordinated.
   c. It must be conserved.
   d. It must be remunerated.
3. Personal effectiveness must be promoted:
   a. Good physical conditions and environment must be maintained.
   b. The vocation, task or duty should be analyzed to determine the special human faculty concerned.
   c. These should be applied to determine in what degree candidates possess special faculty.
   d. Habit should be formed on standardized bases, old or new.
   e. Esprit de corps must be fostered.
   f. Incentive must be proportioned to effort expected.[1]

[1] Alexander Hamilton Church, *The Science and Practice of Management* (New York: *The Engineering Magazine* Co. 1914, p. 111.

These laws of effort (perhaps laws of *labor* would be a better term) are quite perceptive considering the emphasis and thinking that prevailed at the time.

Here for the first time in the United States is an attempt to conceive of the entire managerial function. Fayol, of course, published his French treatise in 1916. But it was Church who, as an American writer, attempted to explain the totality of the managerial concept and to relate each of its components to the whole. Through his efforts, a first "total conceptual model" of management was presented from which more sophisticated departures could be made. In Church, as in Fayol, we see the emphasis on the parts and the whole, and the interrelatedness of all facets of an undertaking.

HUGO DIEMER

A self-made man, Hugo Diemer rose to an important position in the American management movement mainly through his publications. As a professor and as an active engineer in industry, he was the author of dozens of articles and books dealing primarily with management principles and foremanship. Diemer is probably best remembered for his pioneering textbook, *Factory Organization and Administration,* first published in 1910.[2] An immediate success, the book showed the interrelation and universal application of management principles. In his later career, Professor Diemer was again in the vanguard of management thinking through his books on foremanship. In addition to his writings, Hugo Diemer aided the recognition and growth of the science of management through his lectures, his public speeches, and his consultation with leading public and private institutions.

JOHN C. DUNCAN

John C. Duncan, a professor of accounting at the University of Illinois, published his *Principles of Industrial Management* in 1911.[3] Although the ideas in his book were not new, the book itself was original. Along with Diemer's, this was one of the first textbooks on industrial management. Somewhat more theoretical than Diemer's book, Duncan's *Principles of Industrial Management* showed that he recognized the existence of a body of knowledge that could and should be included in a college-level curriculum. He saw the need for enlightened management in industry; but more than this, he saw the need for the mass education of students in this developing field of management.

[2]Hugo Diemer, *Factory Organization and Administration* (New York: McGraw-Hill Book Company, 1910).

[3]John C. Duncan, *The Principles of Industrial Management* (New York: D. Appleton and Company, 1911).

Prior management thinkers, of course, had pointed out the need for a general education. Duncan, however, assembled and organized the prevalent current practices in a concise, well-written manner so that an understanding of them could be gained in an academic rather than in a practical environment. This meant that a young man interested in business learned about it in theory instead of serving an apprenticeship and at the same time made normal progress in his general studies.

In design, Duncan's book took a form widely used today in many texts. The chapters were substantially equal in length and were organized in the common outline form, with headings and subheadings; illustrations, charts, and exhibits were provided as supplemental matter; and an index appeared at the end for easy reference.

The contents, briefly, covered the problems of where and how a plant should be built; what form of power was best; the extent to which integration, concentration, and specialization should be employed; the type of internal organization to use; how to handle the labor force; materials handling; and finally, how to determine the efficiency of equipment.

Although the material covered in Duncan's book may be of interest, we should not forget that his real contributions were recognizing the need for such a text, devising the best way to present the subject matter, and lending the prestige of his name and profession to further the study of the emerging practice of management.

LOUIS D. BRANDEIS

Louis D. Brandeis must stand as one of the truly unselfish men in management history. He may well have contributed more to the people of the United States—through voluntary donations of time, energy, money, and ability—than he is commonly given credit for, probably because of his modesty and refusal to accept public commendation. Nevertheless, his belief in industrial democracy and his uncommon concern for the man in the street marked him as a humanitarian of the highest order.

A successful Boston lawyer prior to his appointment in 1916 to the Supreme Court, Brandeis combined a tremendous background in law with a storehouse of knowledge of business and finance. His way of operating was practical: he would choose a problem, study it extensively, propose a better solution, communicate his idea to the public, and let the weight of public opinion force the adoption of his new and better system. Brandeis never openly attacked the old methods, preferring always to expose the weaknesses to public view by the clarity of his own proposal.

Brandeis made his most important contribution to management thought in 1911 when he argued before the Interstate Commerce Commission against the proposed rate hikes of the railroad trusts. His contention was that the railroads were wrong in claiming that no additional economies of operation existed. His skillful brief showed that by using the principles of scientific management, the railroads could save one million dollars a day, thus eliminating the need for any increases in the rate structure. This case, by drawing nationwide attention to Brandeis's presentation, made efficiency a national idea and did more to publicize the effects of scientific management than any other single event.

JAMES HARTNESS

James Hartness, born in 1861 in Schenectady, New York, grew up in a machine shop and acquired all his training there, his formal education consisting only of grammar school. A prolific inventor of machinery, he became president of the Jones and Lamson Machine Company which under his leadership rose to the top of the tool-building industry. During his career he took out 119 United States patents, his most important invention being the flat turret lathe.

In 1913 he was elected president of the American Society of Mechanical Engineers; in 1924, president of the American Engineering Council; and in 1920, governor of Vermont.

In 1912 Hartness published his only book, *The Human Factor in Works Management.* In it he expressed three of his basic ideas: (1) that many of the features of the new approach to management were too mechanistic; (2) that many of the new efficiency engineers were completely ignoring human nature; and (3) that the problem of increasing efficiency included psychology as well as engineering and economics.

Of course, the Gilbreths and Henry L. Gantt had already written about this matter, but *The Human Factor in Works Management* had peculiar significance because it was written by the president of a large and successful manufacturing company. Here was a statement by a well-known executive stressing that the new scientific management would be almost useless if human nature and habit were ignored.

Refuting the argument that specialization degrades the worker by restricting his range of operations, Hartness stated that a manager should "... see to it that each man's work in the world is the best that is available for him. And when he is in that position to see to it that he is given every facility for improvement of which he is capable."[4]

Recognizing that habit sets up automaticity and relieves the mind from repetitious detail, thus freeing it for other more useful things, Hartness stated that on jobs that did not furnish mental nourishment, the mind should be occupied with some form of study or interest, such as music, so that it would not wander when work was monotonous.

---

[4]James Hartness, *The Human Factor in Works Management* (New York: McGraw-Hill Book Company, 1912), p. 32.

Speaking on machine design, Hartness proposed that machines should be designed to utilize man's habits as much as possible—that the machine designer should become acquainted with the men who would use the machine. Throughout his book he stresses the necessity of management's centering its thought and effort on *men*, in addition to the usual methods and machines.

Hartness's importance to the development of management thought is his emphasis—a layman's—on the necessity of considering human nature and habit. He understood the advantages of specialization and standardization and was one of the leaders in putting these principles into use. But with them he employed to the fullest all of his ideas about human nature and habit.

MEYER BLOOMFIELD

Meyer Bloomfield, a lawyer and a social worker, was one of the pioneers in the early 1920s who recognized the need in industry for a well-rounded employee-human relations approach in the form of a personnel department. Hugo Diemer, a professor of industrial engineering at Pennsylvania State College, suggested in his 1910 book that the labor function in business was important enough to warrant the specialization of hiring workers, paying wages, and maintaining employee efficiency records.[5] By 1913 Bloomfield had carried it a step further. He viewed the handling of men as a new concept requiring special training, vision, a spirit of justice, the capacity to cooperate, and insight into the workers' needs and desires. Bloomfield's all-comprehensive approach was a new dimension in the managerial arena, and in many management circles leaders frequently heard talk of the new profession of handling men. Here, then, were emerging the first comprehensive ideas about personnel management.

Why, we might ask ourselves, was this important concept overlooked? In all probability the answer lies in the economics of the situation. Labor costs due to inefficiency were not as quickly seen or as easily measured as other costs of production. Emphasis, therefore, was being placed on technology. The supply of immigrant and native labor far exceeded the demand, and management, therefore, saw no reason to pay particular attention to conserving a plentiful resource. World War I, however, with its sharply increased production demands, changed this picture and caused managers to examine in more detail this new approach to human resource management. This was particularly true in those firms where scientific management principles had successfully been applied.

In the May 1916 issue of *The Annals,* the first comprehensive writing on the subject appeared as a series of articles edited by Bloomfield and Joseph H. Willits. The series, containing articles by leading educators as well as by employment managers (Willits himself was teaching at the Wharton School), was

---

[5]Diemer, *Factory Organization and Administration,* p. 242.

indicative of the new status of this innovative concept about employee relations. In 1917 Bloomfield began editing a new section of the *Industrial Management* magazine, "The Employment Manager's Department."

None of this is to suggest immediate acceptance of Bloomfield's new approach to employment management. By 1919 there were only about seven hundred employment departments in the entire United States, and of these Paul Douglas estimated that not over fifty were performing comprehensive, well-rounded services.[6] But the concept of a total approach to human relations had made a strong foothold in management's thinking. And to Meyer Bloomfield we owe a debt as the founder of the movement and the promoter of personnel management.[7]

ROBERT F. HOXIE

Robert Franklin Hoxie, an associate professor of political economy at the University of Chicago, wrote two books during his career—*Scientific Management and Labor* in 1915 and *Trade Unionism in the United States* in 1917.

Hoxie's principal contribution to the development of management was his probing and questioning the fundamentals of scientific management. His was probably one of the first published criticisms of the scientific management movement. As a teacher and scholar, Hoxie wanted his students and the public to question the validity of F. W. Taylor's assumptions, his basic criticism being centered around labor's relation to scientific management.

Hoxie saw scientific management as an attempt through accurate industrial analysis to discover and put into operation the objective facts and laws that underlie true efficiency in production, using motion and time study. But though the basic elements of scientific management might be justified with regard to its mechanical objectives, once the conception was broadened and the human element entered the situation, he believed motion and time studies could not be used.

Furthermore, in Hoxie's opinion there was insufficient scientific basis for scientific management because there was nothing in the system capable of preventing violations of its own standards in matters pertaining to human conditions and relations. He felt that inasmuch as scientific management concerned itself wholly with production, it was unfair in setting standards and in fixing wage rates; that in spirit and essence it was a cunningly devised

---

[6]Paul H. Douglas, "Plant Administration of Labor," *Journal of Political Economy*, July 1919, p. 551.

[7]Much of the material in this section was adapted from Edmund C. Lynch, *Meyer Bloomfield and Employment Management, Studies in Personnel and Management No. 22*, Bureau of Business Research, University of Texas, 1970.

speeding-up and sweating system; that it intensified the modern tendency toward task specialization; that it condemned the worker to the monotony of routine; that it tended to deprive the worker of his job-oriented thought and initiative, and even his trade; that it destroyed his individuality and inventive genius; that it lessened the continuity and certainty of employment; and finally, that it was incompatible with, and destructive of, collective gargaining.

The entire second half of Hoxie's *Scientific Management and Labor* is devoted to a thorough castigation of scientific management. The major point he made was that there was an essential incompatibility between the basic ideals of scientific management and those of trade unionism. He believed that scientific management could function successfully only on the basis of constant and indefinite change of industrial conditions; while on the other hand, trade unionism could function successfully only through the maintenance of a fixed industrial situation and condition. The unions had to retain their status quo. Hoxie feared the extinction of craft conditions in the United States, and that the philosophy of scientific management would spell doom for unionism as it then existed.

Here for the first time, we have an example of outright disdain for scientific management and its principles. If for no other reason, Hoxie should be remembered because he caused men to reexamine their faith in the new science of management and to stand foursquare in their beliefs in its efficacy and value to society. His scorching derision of the movement probably did more to anchor it more firmly than his approbation would have.

HORACE B. DRURY

Horace Bookwalter Drury was an instructor of economics and sociology at Ohio State University. In 1915 he wrote a *History and Criticism of Scientific Management*.

The first part of his book dealt with the evolution and history of scientific management, while the second half, like Hoxie's, was a critical review of it. He approached his subject in the same manner as Hoxie, criticizing scientific management and its harmful effects on labor. On the whole, however, and in contrast to Hoxie, his criticism was favorable toward scientific management. He believed that there was a large amount of good in the system and that it was still in its formative period.

Disagreeing with Hoxie on one major point, Drury thought that scientific management represented a shift of managerial thought from machines to men. He saw scientific management as a study of man, of his nature, and of his ideals. He felt that scientific management was based upon the principle that cheerful workmen were more profitable than sullen ones and that the individual was a more satisfactory unit of study and administration than groups.

Drury, along with Hoxie, was one of the first to publish criticisms of a system that was hailed by many to be of prime value to society. And, interesting to note, both of these criticisms came from men in the academic rather than in the business sector.

ORDWAY TEAD

Ordway Tead, an educator, an editor, an administrator, and a popular college lecturer, has written prolifically since 1918 on the subjects of management and education. His earlier writings dealt primarily with the behavioral aspects of human nature, while his more recent works have explored how these ideas apply to the creative process in management.

In all his writings, Tead dealt with people—how and why they behave as they do, how to influence their behavior, and how to organize them so that their behavior achieves desired results. In *Instincts in Industry,* published in 1918, a study of working-class psychology, he attempted to show the relationship between the fears, ambitions, attitudes, and achievements of working people and the realities of human nature. His objective was to see if behavior in industry could become more intelligible in light of the existing understanding of psychological habits and predispositions. His conclusion was that instincts have as much to do in the long run with determining people's conduct as any other single factor.[8]

Tead's contribution is that he has applied psychology to industry to emphasize the importance and sacredness of the individual personality. This initial application of psychology to industry helped explain the conduct of the ordinary laborer, stressing the importance of his individual personality. In addition, Tead willingly gave of his time to spread his message of industrial democracy to colleges, public institutions, and groups throughout the country. He spoke and write in an easily understood manner to a wide audience on a subject that has in the past been considered the exclusive domain of the executive.

MORRIS L. COOKE

The writings and studies of Morris Llewellyn Cooke have greatly contributed to demonstrating the diverse applicability of scientific management principles and techniques in the nonindustrial as well as the industrial fields. As a management consulting engineers, Cooke applied scientific methodology to the problems of municipal management and to the study of university organization

[8]Ordway Tead, *Instincts in Industry* (New York: Houghton Mifflin Company, 1918), p. 5.

and operation. He was among the first individuals who realized the efficiency that could be achieved by proper application of science to industry, and he proceeded to apply these same managerial fundamentals to other forms of endeavor.

In his *Academic and Industrial Efficiency* (1910), Cooke studied the university as a business institution and found typical inefficiencies in university management: committee management was too prevalent, departments had too much autonomy, the department heads lacked real authority, and the university lacked a guage of efficiency.

In 1919 Cooke explored another area where scientific management could be used: municipal management. During his four years as director of public works in Philadelphia, from 1912 to 1916, Cooke was committed to set the example of proper administration by the application of the scientific method in management. He instituted new and efficient methods of complaint handling, financial planning, equipment replacement, personnel selection, inventory recording, subcontract letting, public relations, and standardization.

Cooke's major contribution was the systematic application of the methods of scientific management to the functions of municipal government and to university administration. Both of these applications undergirded the original universality concepts and served to emphasize in a practical way the viability and usefulness of the growing practice of scientific management.

CARL C. PARSONS

Carl C. Parsons wrote one book, *Office Organization and Management,* a broad and fundamental guide published in 1918.

Believing that the heart of efficiency in any business organization was its office, that the office's influence reached every department and every worker, that it was the means of securing final and complete accountability, and that its records, reports, and statistics furnished the manager with the facts necessary for intelligent decision making, Parsons wanted to see the scope of scientific management extended to the office.

Able to visualize the universal application of scientific management to all types of work, he recognized the need for its application in organizing the office, in properly selecting and training office employees, and in properly utilizing office machinery. Speaking of the need for layout techniques, he emphasized the proper layout for clerical work, with work flow based on the straight-line principle. In addition, he stressed that the office, like the factory, should have proper lighting, heating, and ventilation and that noise should be kept to a minimum.

WILLIAM H. LEFFINGWELL

Whereas Parsons recognized the *need* for scientific office management, it was left to William H. Leffingwell to *apply* the principles of the Taylor system to office work. Leffingwell was the first person to demonstrate that the principles of scientific management could be applied to the office with the same success they had enjoyed in the shop.

Although he and Parsons covered essentially the same ground, where Parsons recognized the desirability of, say, standard requisition forms, Leffingwell showed *how* to standardize them. His book, *Scientific Office Management,* published in 1917, was the forerunner of all modern studies in office management and pointed up the results of increased efficiency by the use of scientific methods. A careful and meticulous worker, he wrote about proper office layout, lighting, ventilation, and the like, and went into elaborate detail to analyze the proper storage bin, the best height for footrests, the proper size of cards for filing credit information, and the correct way to store stationery. He even took time and motion studies of typists, recorded head and manual movements, developed proper muscle exercises for the fingers, observed the time lost in erasing, and adjusted the height of the typist's table. He attempted to standardize dictation by getting each stenographer to use the same shorthand method so that the notes could be transcribed by any typist in the office. He also showed which unnecessary motions could be eliminated through the proper location of desks, telephones, files, pencil sharpeners, and the like.

In each application of scientific management to the office, Leffingwell made a careful analysis of the particular problems of the office concerned rather than give pat answers to some general problem.

HERFORD, HILDAGE, AND JENKINS

Shortly after Leffingwell's and Parson's books appeared in this country, a small book was published in England which set forth the then prevailing ideas on practically every phase of industrial management. The book, entitled *Outlines of Industrial Administration,* was written by R. O. Herford, H. T. Hildage, and H. G. Jenkins. Though not a major work, it is worthy of note because it represents the beginning in 1920 of a British comprehensive view of management.

In this book, H. T. Hildage listed the following as the proper considerations for planning plant location and layout:

(a) To decide which is the best district in which our factory or works, or as the Americans say, "our plant," is to be located.
(b) . . . to state our requirements as regards site, in size, shape, and topography, and to decide, of all available sites, which is the best.
(c) To decide, with the single view to the utility for the purpose under discussion, what are the best kinds of buildings to put upon the site as regards size, shape, type, and method of construction, and how they are to be lighted, heated, and supplied with power.
(d) To fix upon the positions of the machines within those buildings, having in view the receiving of the material into the building, the handling of it through all the various processes, and the delivery of the finished product.
(e) To decide in the same way how the buildings shall be placed on the site in order that the raw material may be conveniently and economically received, if necessary, put into stock, and handed from the receiving point or from the warehouse to the various manufacturing processes—and the finished product, in turn, conveniently and expeditiously sent away to the markets by road, railway, or water.
(f) Having made all these decisions and having obtained a plan that can be considered ideal, or approximately ideal, to get out a careful estimate of the cost of carrying it out and see how this estimate compares with the sum of money available—if it exceeds it, to decide whether the additional sum can be obtained or is worth while. If not, to decide what modification in the plan can be made with a view to bringing this cost within the sum available with a minimum loss of efficiency of working.[9]

Discussing personnel, R. O. Herford stated that no material factors could be made use of for production without the direction and manipulation of the human brain and hand. An organization, he said, was not a matter of numbers but of cooperative action on the part of a number of individuals, the first essential being that of a common goal or purpose. Emphasizing the importance of organization structure, Herford said that the duties of each individual must be clearly understood; that every man must know from whom to expect his work and to whom to send it; and that it was a good idea to draw up and display an organization chart.

A strong believer in delegating authority, Herford summarized his thoughts by saying, ". . . in a well-organized staff, the duties are divided among its members; the division must be recognized and understood and the responsibility given. The duties of each man must lie within a narrower field than that of his superior, and every key position must be safe-guarded by a possible substitute."[10]

Although these pronouncements are routine today, the book does mark the introduction in England of a comprehensive treatise on a system of management.

[9]R. O. Herford, H. T. Hildage, and H. G. Jenkins, *Outlines of Industrial Administration* (London: Sir Isaac Pitman & Sons Ltd., 1920), pp. 15-16.
[10]*Ibid.*, p. 87.

SUMMARY

In these fifteen men, whom we have labeled minor writers and critics, we continue to see new concepts added and old ideas strengthened through their efforts.

John Duncan and Hugo Diemer wrote the first texts on management, moving it foursquare into the classroom. Louis D. Brandeis popularized the scientific management idea and put the word *efficiency* on almost every tongue.

Ordway Tead reinforced the application of the behavioral aspects of human nature to the scientific study of individuals in industry. In addition, he probed the reasons behind industrial behavior, in light of the known psychological factors.

Alexander Hamilton Church collected many of the dissociate concepts of management and molded them into a set of regulative principles. Without providing a theory, his principles did broaden the horizon of management thought by pointing out possible relations between the parts and the whole.

Robert F. Hoxie, the first great critic of scientific management, challenged the proponents of the new science of management to reexamine their newfound concepts. Withstanding the test of critical evaluation, the advocates became strengthened in their beliefs and the science of management became more firmly and securely founded. Horace B. Drury, too, was a critic of scientific management, though much of his criticism was of a favorable nature.

Carl C. Parsons's writings pointed out the possibility of moving scientific management from the shop to clerical operations, the heart of the office. It remained, however, for William H. Leffingwell to demonstrate that scientific management could be applied in the office with the same success that it had found in the plant.

And, finally, Meyer Bloomfield founded and promoted the concept of personnel management.

Although by no means of the stature of Taylor or Fayol, these men played a needed role in the evolution and application of management thought. They expanded it in minor ways. They explored new applications. They popularized it. They nationalized it. And they nurtured it through its infancy by breathing into the young science the life-giving stamp of theoretical soundness and practical applicability.

9

THE MANAGERIAL
PHILOSOPHERS

As we have seen, the writings of Taylor, Gilbreth, Gantt, and their contemporaries brought new insights into the problems of business and gave new dimensions to management thought. As pragmatists, these men dealt with the everyday immediate problems that they saw: problems of human and material waste, problems of organization, problems of technology and production. In their systematic search for solutions they naturally turned to science and scientific methodology. They developed a science of motion study, a science of time study, a scientific approach to wage payment, scientific measures for control, and so on. This pragmatic approach and its "scientific" solutions gave a technique orientation to the emerging management thought of the day.

The men who figured prominently in this scientific management approach, however, were a decided cut above the old-school managers who determined procedures and made decisions on the basis of "what worked before should solve the problem now." This new breed of scientific managers emphasized "Let's investigate the facts and make our decisions in light of the findings." These men, symbolized by Taylor and his contemporaries, were perceptive to the facts at hand, especially as they applied to the processes of industry. They were hard-hitting practical men, who tackled the mountain of industrial problems on the basis of urgency: What is a fair day's work? How long should a worker require to do a given job? What is the best location for a plant? How should workers be supervised? What is the best way to select a worker for a job? These were the problems of the moment.

As a result of the efforts of these practitioners of scientific management, managerial reasoning changed from a this-is-the-way-we've-always-done-it approach to a what-is-the-best-way approach. These managers, we should emphasize, made the first major break with traditional decision making by advocating a management approach based on facts and scientific reasoning.

Hard on the heels of these men, however, another breed of managerial disturbers appeared bringing with them even newer and more challenging concepts, including a philosophical approach to managerial "oughtness." This new approach represented a further move from purely mechanistic thinking to the realm of values and value judgments. It posed new concepts of organization and applied new emphasis on group dynamics. These "new-look" managers viewed not only the problems of management but management's entire gamut of opportunities and *obligations*. All these new facets gave to management and management thought new meaning, depth, and stature.

In this chapter we will review the concepts of some of the new-wave managers and see what each contributed to the continuum of managerial thought.

OLIVER SHELDON

After graduating from Oxford and completing his military service, Oliver Sheldon settled down in York, England, for a lifetime's work at the Coca Works of Rowntree & Company, Limited, moving from personal assistant to B. S. Rowntree to a directorship on the general board of directors. During his tenure at Rowntree Sheldon developed the concepts that made him famous, the best expression of which can be found in his 1923 book, *The Philosophy of Management*.[1] In this book Sheldon departed from the milieu of everyday functions and attempted to meld social ehtics with the practicality of scientific management.

Basically, Sheldon concerned himself with the totality of management and its logical position in the community. As he put it:

> It is the belief that the direction of industry by that function broadly termed Management is a matter primarily of principles, both scientific and ethical, and only secondarily of the detail consequent upon the application of those principles that this book has come to be written. What follows, therefore, is not to be regarded as an exposition of any particular branch of management, but rather as an attempt to define the

[1] See Oliver Sheldon, *The Philosophy of Management* (London: Sir Isaac Pitman & Sons Ltd., 1923); published in New York by Pitman Publishing Corp., 1966.

purposes, the lines of growth, and the principles which shall govern the practice of Management as a whole.

. . . It is important, therefore, early in our consideration of Management in industry to insist that however scientific Management may become, and however much the full development of its powers may depend upon the use of the scientific method, its primary responsibility is social and communal.[2]

This was a novel direction for management. It stemmed from the industrial atmosphere that developed during World War I, which possessed a bigness, a newness of character that had not prevailed before. Profits, growth, unions, scientific management, and the awakening of the public to a more responsible social atmosphere all contributed toward increasing in number and complexity the problems facing management. Up to this time, the emphasis had been on the "things" of production. Sheldon now emphasized the ethics or "oughtness" and the human elements of industrial responsibility.

Based on the thesis that management's primary responsibility was service to the community, Sheldon developed a set of principles to serve as a guide that would satisfy both the scientific approach to production and management's social responsibility. Sheldon made it clear that the mechanics of production were secondary to the human element.

Sheldon's ideas about management's responsibility to the community grew out of four observations of the social scene: First, he observed an awakening of public interest in the inner workings of business and industrial affairs—evidently an outgrowth of the close cooperation demanded of industry and the community during wartime conditions. Second, he noted the growing desire, almost demand, of workers for more leisure time and for the opportunity for self-development. Third, the association of workers in larger groups such as trade unions, political clubs, and benevolent and religious societies was creating an atmosphere conducive to social change, including the emergence of pressure groups. Finally, there was emerging on all fronts the new spirit of inquiry and the scientific approach to solving industrial problems. In short, Sheldon was struck by the social awakening in England and recognized that it could have a significant impact on human relations in industry and on industrial statesmanship as a whole.

Essentially, Sheldon believed the problem of industry was to determine the proper balance between the "things of production" and the "humanity of production"—a balance between the scientific approach and social responsibility. Gantt had earlier recognized the problem but it devolved upon Sheldon to put it in a better perspective. ". . . Industry is not a mass of machines and technical processes; it is a body of men. It is not a complex of matter but a complex of

---

[2]Oliver Sheldon, *The Philosophy of Management* (New York: Pitman Publishing Corp., 1966), pp. xiv-xv.

humanity."[3] Surely this was a refreshing and perhaps disturbing breeze in the staid air of industrial thinking at that time!

Riding this dual approach of humanity and things, Sheldon developed the fundamentals of his managerial philosophy. Briefly stated, they are:

1. Industry exists to provide the commodities and services that are necessary for the good life of the community in the volume required.

2. Industrial management must be governed by principles based on the concept of service to the community.

3. Management as a part of industry is separate from capital and labor and is broken into three main parts: administration, management, and organization.

> *Administration* is the function of industry concerned in the determination of the corporate policy, the co-ordination of finance, production and distribution, the settlement of the compass of the organization, and the ultimate control of the executive.
>
> *Management* proper is the function in industry concerned in the execution of policy, within the limits set up by administration, and the employment of the organization for the particular objects set before it.
>
> *Organization* is the process of so combining the work which individuals or groups have to perform with the facilities necessary for its execution that the duties, so formed, provide the best channels for the efficient, systematic, positive, and co-ordinated application of the available effort.
>
> Organization is the formation of an effective machine; management, of an effective executive; administration, of an effective direction. Administration determines the organization; management uses it. Administration defines the goal; management strives towards it. Organization is the machine of management in its achievement of the ends determined by administration.[4]

4. Management while keeping industry on an economic basis must achieve the communal objectives for which it exists through the development of efficiency in both the human and the material elements of the factory.

5. This efficiency is to be developed by management through the use of science in management and the development of the human resources of industry.

6. Efficiency is dependent upon a structure of organization based on a detailed analysis of the work to be done and the facilities needed to do it.

7. The activities of management are divided into four functions. First, those concerned with the inception of manufacture, such as design and equipment. Second, the actual operation of manufacture. Third, those functions that facilitate the manufacture, which are transport, planning, comparison, and labor. Fourth, those functions necessary for the distribution of the product, such as sales planning and execution.

8. The use of scientific methods for the economical utilization of the

[3]*Ibid.*, p. 27.
[4]*Ibid.*, p. 32.

people and the things of the factory involves the following: first, the use of research and measurement in the activities that management undertakes or controls; second, the preparation and use of definitions for the makeup of each item of work; third, the determination of references and working standards for the justifiable and precise determination of desirable achievement; and fourth, the institution of these standards to insure the most economical methods of production and management.

9. The policy of responsibility to the community demands certain practices in regard to the human element of production. Associations of workers must be recognized as long as they are not detrimental to society, and their self-development toward the goal of service to the community should be facilitated. An effort should be made toward the promotion of individual and corporate effectiveness of effort through leadership and equitable discipline. In relation to the worker as an individual, the following rules should be followed: First, all the workers should share in deciding the conditions of work; second, the worker should receive a standard of living in keeping with the civilized community; third, the worker should have adequate leisure time for self-development; fourth, the worker should be secure from involuntary unemployment; fifth, the worker should share in industrial prosperity according to his contribution; sixth, a strict spirit of equity should be found in all relations between labor and management.

10. Through study and the development of standards, a "Science of Management," distinct from the science it uses and the techniques of an industry, can be formulated toward the end of forming a code to govern the conduct of industry.

Contribution

Sheldon provided several contributions to the progress of management, the most important being his philosophy, with its emphasis on management's social responsibility. This new philosophy focused attention on the various social aspects mentioned and eventually resulted in a reorientation of managerial thinking so that today we find modern management giving prime consideration to social responsibilities.

In addition, Sheldon did more than any prior individual to conceptualize management and promote it to a higher theoretical level. The genuine *philosophy* of management he developed through his writings and lectures clearly pointed out that management was a separate, distinct function in industry that revolved about a given set of principles which could be analyzed and studied. Thus Sheldon imbued management with a new dignity, moving it further from the materialistic to the conceptual.

Fayol, of course, moved in much the same direction as Sheldon. They agreed, for example, on the following points:

1. The evolution of management as a separate profession.
2. The need for a code or a set of rules to serve as a guide for good managerial practice.
3. The need for formalized management training, particularly at the university level.
4. The greater importance of managerial ability over technical ability in the higher echelons of management.
5. The importance of developing better leadership to secure the best cooperation from the workers.
6. The importance of conferences in coordinating the overall effort.
7. The need for unity of command.

Where Fayol and Sheldon disagreed as to the functions of management it was more a matter of interpretation than of intent.

With Sheldon's notable contribution—a philosophy of management—management attained prestige and professional status. Taylor developed the idea of scientific management; the Gilbreths made the transition between things and people, introducing psychology as a managerial tool; Fayol brought management study into the school curriculum. Now finally, Sheldon proclaimed a philosophy of management as a guide in its practice and evolution. In the few short years that separated these authors, management evolved from a role of high-class foreman to a dignified profession that used scientific knowledge to serve people in organized groups.

ELTON MAYO

Elton Mayo, a Harvard professor, born in Australia and trained in psychology, also worked in the realm of social factors and industrial relationships, but unlike Sheldon, his work was experimental rather than theoretical.

Between the years 1927 and 1947 Mayo conducted experiments at the Department of Industrial Research at Harvard. The program was started as a result of an investigation at Western Electric's Hawthorne Works financed by the Rockefeller Foundation to study attitudes and reactions of groups under varying conditions. The story is well known of how a study to determine the effects of illumination on output, sponsored by the National Research Council, found at Hawthorne that production rose when illumination was increased for the experimental group and likewise rose when no increase in illumination was provided the control group. To their consternation, production continued to rise in both groups even when illumination was decreased to a barest minimum for the experimental group.

A six-girl team started on their unique manufacturing career in April 1927. As the account goes, the conditions of work were changed one at a time to study their effects on production, some of these changes being rest periods of different length and number, shorter work days, shorter work weeks, soup or coffee at the morning coffee breaks, and so on. With each change the effect was consistent: output increased, and at the same time the girls felt less fatigued. Here was the proof Mayo needed to support his concept of the factors that influence industrial relationships.

Briefly stated, Mayo's idea was that logical factors were far less important than emotional factors in determining productive efficiency. Furthermore, of all the human factors influencing employee behavior the most powerful were those emanating from the worker's participation in social groups. Thus, Mayo concluded that work arrangements in addition to meeting the objective requirements of production must at the same time satisfy the employee's subjective requirement of social satisfaction at his work place. With this new emphasis on human relations the factory assumed a social dimension in addition to its economic aspect. This concept was embodied in Mayo's book, *The Human Problems of an Industrial Civilization,* published in 1933.

Within ten years, every practitioner in personnel management or human relations pointed to Mayo's work to support the contention that each individual's problems were so important to the effective operation of a firm that any manager worthy of the name must be concerned with personnel-human relations.[5]

The twenty-year research study that Mayo and his colleagues conducted was the most comprehensive study ever undertaken to evaluate the attitudes and reactions of a group of workers under shop conditions. He found that workers in a factory constituted a culture of their own that could be observed and analyzed. He found that to be effective, management must recognize that the work performed by individuals must satisfy their personal, subjective requirement of social satisfaction, as well as the company's requirement of productive output. This, Mayo emphasized, meant that management must assume a new role in its dealings with employees; it must develop a new concept of authority and right to command; and it must help foster a new social order based on the individual's cooperative attitude and the system of coordinative organization and communication developed by management. Henceforth, management would be based on the *sociological concept of group endeavor.*

As a result of Mayo's work, the industrial woods abound today with behavioral scientists, personnel counselors, industrial chaplains, sensitivity trainers, group dynamicists, sociogram analysts, nondirective interviewers, role-playing instructors, critical incident teachers, and industrial psychologists—each trying to satisfy management's demand for the creation of a work situation conducive to a maximum long-run productivity.

[5]"Workers Can Be a Team, Too," *Business Week,* May 25, 1963, pp. 49-50.

JAMES D. MOONEY

The name James D. Mooney is seldom mentioned in texts on management. Yet it was he who coauthored the 1931 classic on the nature and development of organization entitled *Onward Industry!*[6] Curiously, the title does not do justice to the contents. In 1926 Mooney conceived of the idea that the principles of organization employed by all great leaders throughout history must surely be the same; he therefore set out on a search of all available literature, reading sources on such leaders as Alexander the Great, Caesar, and Aristotle. What he found was that all sound organization structures, including the Catholic Church, are based on a system of superior-subordinate relationships arranged in a hierarchical fashion, which he called the scalar principle. His was a precise and classic treatment of the traditional managerial organization based on scalar processes, functional definitions of jobs, and fundamental coordination. He made no mention of the human side of organization or of its sociological aspects. His contribution was strictly one of a tight engineering approach to the age-old problem of harnessing human effort to achieve an objective.

Subsequent writers, however, have freely borrowed from Mooney's analysis and have used his concepts as a framework on which to hang more humanistic approaches to the managerial problem of organization.

MARY PARKER FOLLETT

Born in Boston in 1868, Mary Parker Follett attended Thayer Academy and Radcliffe College, concentrating on philosophy, law, and political science, with graduate work at Newham College in Cambridge, England, and additional study in Paris.

From the start of her social and educational work in 1891 to her death in 1933, Miss Follett attempted to establish a management philosophy based on the grounds that any enduring society, any productive society, must be founded upon a recognition of the motivating desires of the individual and the group.

Recognizing that a man on the job is motivated by the same forces that motivate his duties and pleasures away from the job, Miss Follett realized that the basic problem of any organization, business or otherwise, was the harmonizing and coordinating of group efforts to achieve the most efficient

[6]James D. Mooney and A. C. Reiley, *Onward Industry!* (New York: Harper & Bros., 1931).

effort toward completing a task. Drawing on her background in social work and philosophy, she showed that authority as an act of subordination was offensive to man's emotions and therefore could not serve as a good foundation for cooperative organization. Instead, she proposed an authority of function, whereby an individual has authority over his own job area.

Through her eyes, power, leadership, and authority became dynamic concepts—not heavy tools which only burdened administrators. She raised such thought-provoking questions as, "Is power power over or power with?" "Is authority a social status or an integrating force?" "Does it inhere in the environment—does it arise from the laws of the situation—or is it conferred from without and enforced from without?"

Speaking on leadership, Miss Follett said that it was not a matter of a dominating personality, but rather the ability of one who was able to secure an interpretation from within a group of the best concepts of the leader and the led. Agreeing with Fayol and Sheldon, she stressed education and the fact that leaders were not born only, but could be made through education in understanding group dynamics and human behavior.

In her view, coordination was the central core of management, and she called attention to four of its facets:

1. Coordination by direct contact with the people concerned.
2. Coordination that was a continuous process.
3. Coordination found in the initial stages of endeavor.
4. Coordination as a reciprocal relation of all aspects of a situation.

Miss Follett, harkening back to Machiavelli, pointed out that when the uses of physical force pass beyond a certain point, energies lessen and self-respect is lost; thus no community could long stand unless it was founded upon the consent of the governed.

As she moved about consulting with various industrial and political leaders, Mary Parker Follett recognized that a new principle of association was needed because men had not yet learned how to live together in harmony. This new principle she called the group concept, and prophesied that it would become the basis for our future industrial systems, the new approach to politics, and the foundation of international order. In many respects, hers was an early approach to the systems concept of management. She was, in effect, a prophet in the management wilderness, crying, as she put it, for "togetherness" and "group thinking."

Mary Parker Follett was a true management philosopher, a pioneer who helped span the gap between the mechanistic approach of Taylor and our contemporary approach emphasizing human behavior. More than any other individual, she is responsible for bridging the gap between scientific management and the group or systems approach to solving managerial problems.

CHESTER I. BARNARD

Chester I. Barnard has probably had a more profound impact on the thinking about the complex subject matter of human organization than has any other contributor to the continuum of management thought.

A man of divers talents, Barnard was president of the Bach Society of New Jersey, a sought-after lecturer, an accomplished pianist and improviser in the style of any classical composer; he also served as president of New Jersey Bell Telephone Company. He attended Mount Hermon Academy and entered Harvard in 1906, leaving three years later without a degree: he had no patience with college rules which required him to take a prerequisite to a course he had already passed with honors.

In June 1909 Barnard entered the employ of American Telephone & Telegraph as translator and engineer. In 1922 he joined Pennsylvania Bell Telephone where he got his first taste of general management. In 1927 he became president of Jersey Bell. From the early thirties to shortly before his death in 1961, Chester I. Barnard was deeply involved in analyzing the nature of contemporary management.

Inspired by the work of Sheldon, Mayo, Follett, and others, Barnard's forte lay in his logical analysis of organization structure and his application of sociological concepts to management. He is perhaps best known today through his 1938 publication, *The Functions of the Executive*.

Barnard's purpose in writing the book was twofold: to set forth a theory of cooperation and organization and to present a description of the executive process. Barnard described a formal organization as "that kind of cooperation among men that is conscious, deliberate, and purposeful."[7] He defined it further as "a system of consciously coordinated activities or forces of two or more persons"[8] and then indicated that the executive or executive capacity is the most strategic factor in organized or cooperative systems. This is his basic premise—that organization is a *system of consciously coordinated activities, in which the executive is the most strategic factor.* The reason that Barnard believed the executive to be of such vital importance to organization was because of his three functions:

1. To provide a system of communication for cooperative systems.
2. To promote the acquisition of the efforts needed for the operation of the system.
3. To formulate and define the objectives or purposes of the system.

[7] Chester I. Barnard, *The Functions of the Executive* (Cambridge: Harvard University Press, 1938), p. 4.
[8] *Ibid.*, p. 61.

Barnard repeatedly emphasized how important it was that the individual be induced to cooperate. This inducement could of course take the form of an order, but if so, it would be accepted as authoritative only if the individual (1) understood it, (2) believed it to be consistent with the purposes of the organization, (3) believed it to be compatible with his own personal interests, and (4) was able to comply with it.

From this brief account it is apparent that Barnard viewed organization from the vantage point of the social scientist. But he also brought to organization analysis the meticulous approach of the physical scientist.

Obviously, Barnard's treatment of management differed considerably from Taylor's. Taylor and his associates used the terms *scientific management* and *task management* interchangeably; they concentrated on improving the task efficiency of the individual. Fayol and Sheldon, moving to the totality concept of management, directed their analysis to the operational side—principles of management, managerial functions and responsibilities. Barnard, however, penetrated the subject more deeply, analyzing the kinds and qualities of forces at work and the manner of their interactions. He started with the individual, moved to cooperative organized endeavor, and ended with executive functions.

The Functions of the Executive is a highly significant work, a classic in the field. Written in a period following Mayo and his associates' efforts in the area of worker psychology, Barnard introduced social concepts into the analysis of managerial functions and processes. By painstaking scientific exploration he formulated a logical network of definitions and concepts, with heavy applications of sociology to the management of organizations.

JAMES BURNHAM

James Burnham, son of an executive vice-president of the Burlington Railroad, was educated at Princeton and at Oxford University in England and joined the staff of the Washington Square College of New York University as a professor in the Department of Philosophy.

In 1941 the book for which he is best known, *The Managerial Revolution,* appeared. Its thesis, in essence, was that capitalist society would be replaced by a managerial society—with managers taking over every position of importance, and with state ownership of the major instruments of production. This revolution, according to Burnham, would virtually eliminate the need for money, do away with mass unemployment, increase production, smooth out economic cycles, and so on.

Although many of Burnham's forecasts have long since been discredited, the book is of interest to scholars of management thought as a work by a recognized intellectual that placed tremendous confidence in the managerial function, even according it a cardinal position in a new society. This concept might be regarded as the ultimate recognition of management's emergence from a shop-boss concept to an astute controller of considerable segments of our national wealth. This marks a significant point in our history: the idea that management had evolved through the rigorous stages of prior philosophers and had reached a level of conceptual maturity where it could be considered for a role of national prominence. Burnham's thesis signaled this new maturity in management thought. And the publication and ensuing discussions of this 1941 work served to emphasize the public's recognition of the new science of management.

LYNDALL URWICK

The last individual to be considered in this group of managerial philosophers is an Englishman who majored in history at Oxford. He has authored, coauthored, and edited a number of significant books, but the one of major importance to students of management thought is his 1943 publication, *The Elements of Administration.*

Recognizing that the gap between the physical and the social sciences caused the science of management to remain imprecise, Urwick undertook in his book to demonstrate that the body of knowledge about management is sufficiently large to make it a more scientific, more unified field than was commonly supposed. To do this, he chose the works of several leading proponents of management—such as Fayol, Taylor, Follett, and Mooney—and systematically analyzed their thoughts, concepts, and principles. Using Fayol as a framework, he tabulated points of identity and similarity.

When one recognizes that these authors worked with little or no cross-fertilization of ideas, Urwick's thesis begins to take on real form. These various authors followed similar lines of inquiry and often developed principles which, though worded differently, were alike in many respects. Inasmuch as these closely related concepts developed from different cultures, different countries, and different professions, Urwick reasoned that a highly useful and reliable body of management knowledge already existed and needed correlation. This was his major contribution—to point out the existence of these similarities and to correlate them. In the process of doing so, Urwick aided in interpreting the ideas of many of these writers, placing them in proper perspective for subsequent readers, while at the same time imparting some of his own personal concepts.

Lyndall Urwick is not an innovator in the field of management in the sense that Fayol and Sheldon were. He has made a contribution, however, by his timely consolidation of the managerial principles developed by others. It sometimes happens that men who express the right theory at the right time make a greater contribution than the pioneer whose ideas were disregarded because they were decades ahead of their time. This is how Urwick has served the management continuum. His work crystallized the similar concepts that had been independently developed, thereby giving them more credence and serving to mold them into a system of managerial thought.

SUMMARY

Other writers might well be included in this group of managerial philosophers. More important than who should be included, however, is the fact that management has come of age as a philosophy of thought and action. Management theory has now matured to a point where managers may be conceived of as the new "proletariat"—come the managerial revolution!

Management thought has indeed been enlarged on by Sheldon, Mayo, Follett, Mooney, Burnham, and Barnard. And Urwick has solidified their concepts by pointing out the independence of their thinking, the interrelation of their analyses, and the similarity of their conclusions.

10

EMERGING SCHOOLS
OF MANAGEMENT THOUGHT

In preceding chapters we examined the writings and contributions of various management pioneers and saw their ideas evolve through time into one or more aspects of management theory. Each of these individuals, because of his peculiar background, introduced a new facet to the totality of management. Taylor, for example, brought a close scrutiny to the performance of shop work, as an outgrowth of his engineering education and his training in metalworking. Fayol, in contrast, brought an administrative and coordinative point of view to management's job, as a result of his administrative experiences with a mining company. Sheldon and Gantt, on the other hand, opened the new sphere of managerial responsibility with respect to the individual and his role in managerial efforts. And so on.

Because many of these individuals emphasized different aspects of management and gathered followers through the years, the state of management thought following World War II was somewhat of a maze. Many management scholars during the decade following the war therefore attempted through their writings to bring some semblance of order to the mass of theories that had grown up since Towne and Taylor. In this group, the first and probably the best critical analysis of the confusion in management theory was an article, "The Management Theory Jungle," by Professor Harold Koontz which first appeared in the July 1957 issue of the *Journal of the Academy of Management*. Since that time, articles by other scholars have attempted to add some new or clarifying perspectives. Even today the case is still not settled, but if we look back over the writings covered so far we can discern four clearly identifiable theories or schools of thought.

One stream of management thought that immediately comes to mind is the traditional or scientific school—sometimes called the classical school. Taylor and the Gilbreths belong to this school. A second stream of management thought is centered around individuals such as Mayo and Munsterberg and might be called the behavioral school. Still a third group might include those individuals who analyzed management by processes and functions. Names such as Fayol and Sheldon would fall here. Finally, for those who see in management a large amount of decision making based on quantitative analysis there is the quantitative school, which had its greatest growth during the years following World War II.

In this and the following chapter we will examine each of these schools in some detail to ascertain the state of management thought during the dynamic fifties and sixties. Before starting, however, it might help our understanding if we reviewed briefly the general economic conditions that existed at the beginning of the twentieth century.

BACKGROUND FOR AN EMERGING MANAGEMENT

At the turn of the century, the United States had been fairly well settled. The influx of immigrants had abated somewhat, but with a large and ever-growing market, industry continued to expand. Amalgamation, bigness, and larger concentrations of industry were the order of the day. Mechanization and invention were bywords of the time; the skills of labor were being replaced more and more by machines; the tools of the worker now became the tools of industry; the intimacy of the small shop was snuffed out in the smokestacks of big factories.

With the growing emphasis on output an individual came to the forefront, responsible for controlling and ordering the factors of production—the manager. His job was to extract the maximum efficiency from the human and the mechanical machines at any cost. What mattered was volume output, unit costs, product tolerances. Little or no attention was paid to the long-run effects of any given practice. The land of plenty was yielding its bounty and tomorrow was eons away.

In these surroundings managers developed as they could. With no training to guide them, each was left to his own devices. The relationship between management and labor was often confused. Without leadership experience, managers became dictatorial, abusive in the use of their increased authority. This is not surprising when we realize how little knowledge was available on the managerial functions and responsibilities.

The manager's relations with his employees were also muddled. Virtually all standards of output were subjectively established, with little or no thought given to systems of work or motion analysis. Matching an employee's talents with a job's demands was to a large extent accidental. Instead of being assigned to tasks in accordance with *determined* and *known* abilities, employees were haphazardly placed in accordance with the whim of the supervisor. Under these conditions, it is no wonder that workers did not respond with their best efforts. Add to this the lack of incentive reward for good job performance, and we can readily understand why the accepted norm of performance among the workers was one tempered by the "reasoning" of co-workers—in other words, systematic soldiering.

Without reliable standards of all types, managers were placed in the untenable position of establishing wages, determining promotions, and rewarding above-average performances all on the basis of guess, hunch, intuition, and past experience. Given these conditions, the workers were out to beat the system, and the managers were out to squeeze the last drop from the workers. It was neither a happy nor an efficient state of affairs, but at least it served to produce goods to fill the increasing demands of an expanding economy.

This was the economic picture that prevailed when a young engineer named Frederick W. Taylor started to develop a system of management which today is generally labeled traditional or scientific management.

TRADITIONAL SCHOOL: SCIENTIFIC MANAGEMENT

Traditional or scientific management evolved from the systematic observations of the things of production—research and analysis of shop operation. Although concerned with specific techniques such as motion study, time study, production planning and control, plant layout, wage incentives, personnel management, and human engineering—all centering on *efficiency* and *production*—it is nevertheless firmly grounded in theory. As the first body of management concepts it has served managers well and has provided a foundation upon which scholars can build and improve.

Frederick W. Taylor

In developing his brand of management, Taylor's approach was to study operations, determine the facts pertaining to the work situation, and from these observations develop principles. He looked upon management as the process of getting things done by people operating independently or in groups, and his approach to the managerial problem was a direct and simple one: define the problem, analyze the work situation in all its facets, apply measuring devices to all facets capable of being measured, experiment by holding all aspects of the job constant except one which would be varied, develop a guide or principle of management from the observations and study, and, finally, prove the validity of the principle by subsequent application.

Using this approach to studying work, Taylor left a veritable wealth of managerial information for subsequent practitioners. He is perhaps best known for his development of the use of stopwatch time studies to determine a standard of output that would constitute a fair day's work. Taylor's shoveling and pig-iron handling experiments, for example, are classics in the systematic study and analysis of problems.

Along with Maunsel White he developed high-speed steel, using the experimental approach previously described. Although the development of high-speed steel was of very real value to industry, our interest is more in the approach used than in the product obtained. Of similar interest to us is Taylor's twenty-six-year study dealing with the art of cutting metals. This project also provided a wealth of information that could be used by management in an operative sense.

Moving more into the conceptual realm, Taylor separated mental from manual work, laying great emphasis on the mental aspect of planning—what was to be done, how, by whom, how soon it was required, and when it could be completed. To achieve these planning ends, Taylor introduced the concept of functional specialists—what we might think of as the use of a staff organization.

His four principles of scientific management are legion by now. Briefly, Taylor said that workers should be scientifically selected, trained, and placed in work situations for which they are best suited mentally and physically. Second, work should be analyzed scientifically instead of by rule of thumb. Third, close cooperation should exist between those who plan the work and those who perform the work, so that all the work may be done in accordance with the principles developed by its scientific analysis. And last, management and labor should share equal responsibility—with each sector doing the work for which it is best fitted.

In his system of management Taylor favored the use of the exception principle, and he called for setting up a large daily task, with reward for meeting it and penalty for not achieving standard. Finally, Taylor advocated continued research and experiment to develop new paths for improvement in productive and managerial efficiency. All of this, he recognized, would make for high wage costs, but Taylor felt management should focus its attention on cost per unit of output rather than on labor cost; for even though total wages would increase, output would increase in greater proportion, thereby lowering unit costs. Taylor's object was to increase the output per worker, and to accomplish this he called for management to improve working conditions, reduce physical effort (and thereby fatigue), and allow each man to develop to his fullest potential.

As a man, Taylor was strong-willed, fair-minded, systematic, determined, and strict, with a strong sense of the Protestant ethic. He was at his weakest in writing and at his ablest in experimenting and doing.

That Taylor was catalytic in the development of the traditional management school cannot be denied. Many of his practices and principles, of course, were not new with him. We have already seen that men such as Babbage and Jevons had conceived of experiments like his many decades earlier. The time was ripe, however, for Taylor's doctrine, and if he had not propounded it, doubtless some other man would have come forward to lead in the scientific approach.

The Gilbreths

Closely associated in both work and time with Taylor, the Gilbreths (Frank and his wife, Lillian) were also original contributors to the traditional or scientific management school. They are best known for their development of rules of motion economy, in particular the basic hand motions which they named *therbligs*. With this analytic tool, standard motion sequences could be prescribed. Taylor was also interested in motion and time study. But while he was more concerned with *how long* it took to do a job, the Gilbreths were mainly concerned with the *motions* that were most effective. Consequently, the Taylor system increased output by stepping up the pace and by the systematic elimination of soldiering; the Gilbreth system increased output by eliminating wasted motions. These two systems applied together have formed a cornerstone of worker efficiency, which has survived all attacks and is firmly cemented in modern industry.

It is interesting to note that Mrs. Gilbreth introduced a behavioral concept when she called for the recognition of psychological factors and their importance to worker adjustment and productivity.

The Gilbreths, like Taylor, were shop oriented—that is, they were attuned to productivity increases. In addition, both were interested in developing a science of work and in spreading the new gospel by speaking and writing.

Other Contributors

Although Taylor and Gilbreth are acknowledged as the leaders, many others contributed to the debelopment of this school. Such early classical economists as Adam Smith, W. S. Jevons, and James Mill would fall in this camp. Charles Babbage, Boulton and Watt, and Robert Owen, too, with their systematic and analytical approach to shop management, laid out the fundamental concepts for many areas. Sir James Steuart caught the spirit of scientific management as early as 1767 when he wrote about division of work between mental and manual.

James Mill suggested motion and time study as a separate activity in 1826. In the 1850s Henry Poor enunciated his principles pertaining to the careful division of work and the effective utilization of men and equipment—principles put into effect by Daniel C. McCallum.

Many individuals claim that the earliest pioneer in the traditional school of management was Henry R. Towne with his scientific and systematic application of efficient methods in his plant as early as 1870.

In 1881 Henry Metcalfe introduced a comprehensive system of control at the Frankford Arsenal, a system so practical and efficient that thirty years later Taylor acknowledged his debt to it.

Harrington Emerson did more to popularize the philosophy of efficiency than any of his contemporaries. A strong advocate of Taylor's approach, Emerson's *Twelve Principles of Efficiency* (1919) clearly ties him to the traditional school: (1) clearly defined ideals, (2) common sense, (3) competent counsel, (4) discipline, (5) fair deal, (6) reliable records, (7) dispatching, (8) standards and schedules, (9) standardized conditions, (10) standard operations, (11) written standard instructions, and (12) efficiency control.

Harlow S. Person would also be included here, not so much for a conceptual contribution as for his leadership and help in proving that scientific management was not dedicated to the stopwatch and speedup.

Morris L. Cooke, though not an actual contributor to the traditional school, was instrumental in applying scientific management concepts to organizations other than business—particularly governmental and educational institutions. In 1940 he collaborated with Phillip Murray, then president of the CIO, to issue *Organized Labor and Production,* a book dealing with labor-management relations and scientific management.

Though none of these men can be ranked with Taylor and Gilbreth, their work is significant; and the combined efforts of all these contributors went into the body of thought known as the traditional or scientific school.

Writing about scientific management in 1954, Peter Drucker stated, "Altogether it may well be the most powerful as well as the most lasting contribution America has made to Western thought since the Federalist Papers. As long as industrial society endures, we shall never lose again the insight that human work can be studied systematically, can be analyzed, can be improved by work on its elementary parts."[1]

BEHAVIORAL SCHOOL

The behavioral school grew out of the early efforts of leaders such as Gantt and Munsterberg to recognize the centrality of the individual in any cooperative endeavor. They reasoned that inasmuch as managers get things done through people, the study of management must be centered around the workers and their interpersonal relations. The behaviorists concentrate on motivations, group dynamics, individual drives, group relations, and so on. The school is

[1]Peter Drucker, *The Practice of Management* (New York: Harper and Bros., 1954), p. 280.

eclectic and incorporates most social sciences, including psychology, sociology, social psychology, and anthropology. It ranges in scope from how to influence individual behavior to a detailed analysis of sociopsychological relationships. Centering on the human element, it is concerned on the one hand with understanding the relevant phenomena of intrapersonal and interpersonal relationships as they relate to work situations, and on the other hand with observing work groups as anthropological subcultures.

The origin of this school may be traced to 1879, when Wilhelm Wundt established at Leipzig a laboratory for the study of human behavior, the first major step in transforming psychology to an experimental science. It was at Leipzig that Dr. Hugo Munsterberg studied in 1885, but it was as a professor at Harvard in 1913 that he published *Psychology and Industrial Efficiency,* introducing the new field of industrial psychology.

Hugo Munsterberg

As a leader in Harvard's pioneering studies in experimental psychology, Munsterberg's work was eagerly devoured. He spoke and wrote on everything from temperance to job training, with popular articles in the *Ladies' Home Journal* and scholarly treatises in the most learned journals. At this time scientific management appeared on shaky ground because of a lack of intellectual pretense and the malapplications by would-be experts. Munsterberg, however, made a strong case in his book for more science in management. He created the field of industrial psychology, applying his laboratory techniques for measuring psychological differences between individuals to employees in on-the-job situations, and through this he opened a new facet of scientific management—the scientific study and explanation of individual differences. Here was the beginning of the human behavior school as an integrated part of scientific management. Munsterberg argued that industrial psychology and scientific management must join hands because both were proclaiming the same truth—that efficiency could never be achieved by excessive driving. Instead, it must come through scientific work analysis and the worker's adjustment of work and psyche so as to achieve an overflowing job and perfect inner harmony.

Henry L. Gantt

Gantt was both a contemporary and a protégé of Taylor's, and it is difficult to classify him in one school only. His charting concepts and bonus plan could easily place him with the traditionalists. In all his work, however, Gantt demonstrated an almost passionate concern for the worker as an individual and pleaded for a humanitarian approach. In 1908 he presented a paper to the American Society of Mechanical Engineers calling for a policy of teaching and instructing rather than of driving workers—a statement of Gantt's psychology of employee relations. In view of his untiring efforts on behalf of labor, Gantt has a place in and was responsible for part of the growth of the behavioral school.

Elton Mayo

Elton Mayo is best known as the father of the Hawthorne studies and a strong advocate of the behavioral school of thought. As we have seen, it was he, working at the Department of Industrial Research at Harvard, who led the team conducting the study at Western Electric's Hawthorne Plant to evaluate the attitudes and psychological reactions of workers in on-the-job situations. From these studies, Mayo proposed that workers constituted a culture all their own, and he developed his ideas on the sociological concepts of group endeavor. Through his work, a new dimension was added to the then existing concepts of management—that to be effective, a manager must recognize and understand the individual as a person with wants, motives, drives, and personal goals that need to be satisfied.

Today, as a result, we know among other things that worker performance is related to psychological and sociological as well as physical factors; that employees develop their own norms or output standards; that status, social satisfactions, and similar factors affect an employee's job satisfaction and output; and that informal work groups develop with their own concepts of what should be done for the company, what an employee should tell his supervisor, and what action should be taken against employees who overproduce. In other words, this school lifted the whole sociopsychological veil that had up to this time shrouded the worker and confused managers as to the best supervision.

Through Mayo's research efforts (along with those of his associate, F. J. Roethlisberger), knowledge of the behavioral school became widespread. Managers, aware of the importance of his study, gradually turned to this new trend of management thought. Today the behavioral stream is both broad and deep, fully a part of the growing field of managerial study, and rightfully commanding an important position in its totality.

Mary Parker Follett

A discussion of the behavioral stream of management thought should also include the ideas of social worker Mary Parker Follett. Virtually her entire life was given to developing a new managerial philosophy incorporating an understanding of the motivating desires of the individual and the group.

Basically, Miss Follett emphasized that a man on the job was motivated by the same forces that influence his duties and pleasures away from the job and that a manager's job was to harmonize and coordinate group efforts—not to force and drive. In her consulting work, Miss Follett recognized the need for a manager's understanding the group concept principles, which she prophesied would one day become the basis for all sound approaches to national and international order. To the behavioral school she added two new words, "togetherness" and "group thinking," which have subsequently permeated management literature.

Oliver Sheldon

Sheldon's concepts could logically place him in either the behavioral school or the process school. He established a set of management functions and principles that could place him squarely in the process school; yet his great emphasis on managerial responsibility, his view of industry not as a mass of machines but as a body of men, a complex of humanity, and his efforts to synthesize scientific management with the social ethic could also place him with the behaviorists. Though it might be debated, the weight of the behavioral school appears to be in his favor. In fact, both Sheldon and Follett predicated the subsequent emphasis on human behavior through their "men are first" concepts.

Chester I. Barnard

Chester I. Barnard's part in developing this stream of thought lay in his logical analysis of organization structure and his application of sociological concepts to management. Some scholars do not include Barnard in the behavioral school, but in a new school evolving around his social system concept. This concept is, of course, closely related to the human behavior approach and differs only in that management is looked upon as a system of cultural interrelationships. The distinction is logical, but for our purposes the overall classification of the behavioral school will suffice, including the study of management as a system of cultural interrelationships.

Chester Barnard looked upon the organization as a system of consciously coordinated activities needed by the individual to overcome his biological, physical, and social limitations. Highly sociological in his approach to management, Barnard nevertheless repeatedly emphasized the individual and his importance as the strategic factor which must be induced to cooperate.

In analyzing the qualities of forces at work in an organization, Barnard started with those of the individual, analyzed the functions of the executive, and included both in his analysis of the total organization concept. To him, an organization was a system of interactions whose continuance depended on the balance between the individual member's contributions and the satisfactions he derived. Thus, recognizing individual behavior, he saw the manager's job as one of allocating "satisfactions"—money, status, and the like—to elicit individual coordinated and prescribed behavior. By this type of analysis, Barnard brought more scholarly and scientific insight into the totality of managerial organizations than any prior individual.

As a result of the work of Mayo, Follett, Barnard, Munsterberg, and others which brought a more comprehensive insight to management, it is not unusual today to find sociologists and anthropologists employed by industry to help diagnose ills and prescribe correctives. The fields of industrial sociology and applied anthropology have emerged with particularly rewarding findings in the study of such processes and subcultures as labor-management relations, union organizations, and collective bargaining.

Contemporary Contributors

To this ever-growing behavioral school we might well add such contemporary writers as Simon, Argyris, Selekman, and Leavitt. Theirs has been the job of further rounding out various facets of this important school of thought, and their works have been of no small significance along this line. Important as they are, however, their contributions are too contemporary to have earned a precise place in a historically developed perspective. The dust, so to speak, has not settled enough yet to see their positions clearly. Thus, while we should recognize their efforts, it is still too early to classify, evaluate, and rank their several contributions. This task will devolve to subsequent students of management thought who will be able, with their vision cleared by time, to place each work in its proper perspective.

MANAGEMENT PROCESS SCHOOL

The management process school builds a theory of management around the process involved in managing, the establishment of a conceptual framework for it, and the identification of the principles underlying it.

Management is viewed as a universal and practically identical process regardless of its sphere of operation: governmental, industrial, or institutional. Because management is viewed as a process, this school approaches the analysis of the process by analyzing the manager's functions of planning, organizing, staffing, directing, and controlling. Inasmuch as these functions deal with the individuals involved, the school is somewhat eclectic in that pertinent aspects of the social sciences are recognized. Up to this point, however, they have not been actively incorporated in the process school theory.

Henri Fayol

Without doubt, Henri Fayol fathered this stream of managerial thought. His original and perceptive listing of the functions of management still reads like a current managerial treatise, and his classical analysis of managerial functions has stood the test of time. In fact, his orderly analysis of management from the board of directors down was only discovered in the United States during the 1950s.

According to Fayol, the study, analysis, and teaching of management should all be approached from its functions, which he defined as (1) forecasting and planning, (2) organizing, (3) commanding, (4) controlling, and (5) coordinating. Stressing that these functions applied to *all* managerial undertakings, Fayol foresaw the simplicity of managerial study and analysis when only this one rather than many administrative sciences would be studied.

Of these five functions, Fayol thought that planning was the most important and the most difficult. Poor planning, he reasoned, would lead to subsequent hesitations, false steps, untimely action, general weakness, and possible demise. Viewing organization as a problem involving both material and human resources, Fayol confined his discussion to the human aspects, thus marking him with a behavioral approach. To him, commanding and coordinating were necessary to initiate and effectively operate a system of work, with control as the system of checks.

Though the originator of the process school of thought, Fayol was not enthusiastically accepted or understood during his time. His concepts were ahead of his time by over thirty years. Why, we might ask, would one whose managerial philosophy was so sound be virtually ignored both in his native France and in the United States? Several factors may account for this.

A famous French engineer, Charles de la Poix de Fréminville, was so electrified by Taylor and his work that after meeting him in 1912, he propagandized for Taylor's scientific management throughout France. So effective was Fréminville that he almost singlehandedly started a scientific management movement there. In addition to this groundwork, the French were amazed at the speed and efficiency with which the United States troops in 1917 built docks, debarkation camps, railroads, and the like, needed for World War I. With Fréminville's prior teaching, the French had a word for this extraordinary feat—*Taylorism*—and by order of the French minister of war, Georges Clemenceau, all plants under his control were to study and install Taylor's methods.

In the United States high labor costs focused managerial attention upon efficient production, and Taylor's scientific management offered a ready answer. Efficiency, labor savings, and lowered costs were the vanguards. Under Taylor's system results were immediate and measurable. Not so with Fayol's concepts; his were more long-run, nebulous, and incapable of measurement. Given these choices, the average business man chose Fred Taylor.

James D. Mooney

In 1926 James D. Mooney conceived of the idea that the principles of organization employed by all great managers were the same and proceeded to prove it. His writings lent emphasis and stature to the process stream of management thought. What he came up with was a concept of organization based on scalar processes, functional definitions of jobs, and fundamental coordination. Making no mention of the human element, his was a tight engineering approach to the manager's job of getting work done through others. Today many regard his as the most complete description of classical organization analysis to be found.

QUANTITATIVE SCHOOL

The rise in importance of the quantitative school of thought since World War II has been so great that it deserves to be treated in detail as a separate chapter. However, for the sake of completeness in recognizing the existing schools, it is mentioned here as one of the strongest recent developments in the continuum of management thought.

SUMMARY

In this chapter we have attempted to classify various writers in the field of management by the type of school they represent. Obviously, our classification is perforce arbitrary, since few writers express all facets of one school to the exclusion of the others. Many of the early proponents' writings place them in two or more schools. In some instances a writer might just as surely be classified as a behaviorist as a member of the process school. Nevertheless, we have identified the various schools of management thought by essential concepts and leading contributors.

An exception has been made of the quantitative school because of its relative newness. In view of its collective and eclectic nature, the management science school might logically encompass virtually all management scholars. The next chapter is devoted to this school of thought.

11

THE QUANTITATIVE SCHOOL

The use of mixed teams of scientists from several disciplines is probably the most obvious characteristic of the quantitative school of management thought. Variously labeled operations research, operational research, and management science, this school consists of bringing the knowledge of various disciplines to bear on the study and effective solution of a problem.

It may bring together, for example, a mathematician, a physical scientist, an economist, an engineer, and a statistician to study a problem in, say, inventory management. By thus studying this problem from an operations research, or management science, point of view, the resulting solution should be much better than could be achieved otherwise. It is, therefore, a scientific method utilizing all pertinent scientific tools for providing a quantitative basis for managerial decisions. It grew out of the recognition by leading managers that closely integrated research teams were needed to fathom the diverse ramifications of various alternative paths of action.

Simply stated, the approach to solving problems using management science consists of:

1. Formulating the problem. This refers to both the consumer's (decision-maker's) problem and the researcher's problem.
2. Constructing a mathematical model to represent the system under study. This model expresses the effectiveness of the system as a function of a set of variables at least one of which is subject to control. Variables of either type

may be subject to random fluctuations, and one or more may be under control of a competitor or other "enemy."

3. Deriving a solution from the model. This involves finding the values of the "control variables" that maximize the system's effectiveness.

4 Testing the model and the solution derived from it. This involves evaluating the variables, checking the model's predictions against reality, and comparing actual and forecasted results.

5. Establishing controls over the solution. This involves developing tools for determining when significant changes occur in the variables and functions on which the solution depends, and determining how to modify the solution in light of such changes.

6. Putting the solution to work. Implementation.[1]

The construction of the mathematical model referred to above expresses the effectiveness of the system under study as a function of a set of variables at least one of which is subject to control. The general form of the operations research model is

$$E = f(x_i, y_j)$$

where E represents the effectiveness of the system (profit, cost, and the like), x_i the variables of the system that are subject to control, and y_j those variables that are not subject to control.

DEVELOPMENT OF QUANTITATIVE SCHOOL

Scientists and engineers have been involved with military activities for at least as long as recorded history. One of the best known individual instances in ancient history occurred in 212 B.C. when the city of Syracuse employed Archimedes (who was then seventy-five years old!) to devise means of breaking the naval siege of the city then under attack by the Romans.[2] It was out of this involvement by scientists in the quantitative aspects of decision making in war games that operations research, or management science, arose in the twentieth century. Many incidents, of course, contributed to its development before this time.

In the late 1880s pioneers in management consulting and industrial engineering were proving the value of scientific techniques in the fields of production planning—techniques that operations research was to refine and

[1]Russell L. Ackoff, "The Development of Operations Research as a Science," *Operations Research*, June 1956, pp. 265-66.

[2]Will Durant, *The Story of Civilization* (New York: Simon and Schuster, Inc., 1939), II, 632.

extend. Frederick W. Taylor, as we know, campaigned for the application of scientific analysis to methods of production.

Taylor's work had importance in ways directly germane to operations research. His contributions, great as they were intrinsically, were even more valuable in revealing the merit of creating elements of organization whose obect was not the *performance* of operations, but their analysis. It is difficult to overemphasize the importance of this first basic step: the formation of organizations for research on operations. The criterion for evaluating Taylor's work should not be the perfection that he seemed to claim, but only the degree to which his work led to *better decisions* than those that were possible, and in most cases, necessary before. The margin of superiority for Taylor's techniques in time study, wage incentives, and metal cutting, in these terms of relative goodness, was very great indeed.

Another point of resemblance between Taylor's work and operations research as we know it today was the mixed or multidiscipline teams which are vital to effective operations research. Taylor appeared to pioneer in this approach with at least twelve colleagues in his metalworking studies and had this to say about three of them:

> Mr. White [Maunsel White] is undoubtedly a much more accom-plished metallurgist than any of the rest of us; Mr. Gantt [H. L. Gantt] is a better all around manager, and the writer of this paper has perhaps the faculty of holding on tighter with his teeth than any of the others. . . . Mr. Barth [Carl G. Barth], who is a very much better mathematician than any of the rest of us, has devoted a large part of his time . . . to carrying on the mathematical work.[3]

Inasmuch as operations research also includes the development of mathematical models, we could say that the slide rule developed by Carl Barth appears to be a mathematical model, representative of the operations it portrays.

In 1917 A. K. Erlang, a Danish mathematician working for the telephone company, grappled with various technical problems, the first of which was to measure stray currents in the manholes of the streets of Copenhagen. He aided the engineers of the company in solving problems of a physical and mathematical nature in a Socratic manner. Instead of giving a direct solution of the problem posed, he preferred to enter into a somewhat lengthy discussion elucidating the subject from every conceivable point of view, thus aiding the inquirer to solve the problem independently. Erlang's ideas and work in telephony anticipated by almost half a century the modern concepts of waiting-line theory.[4]

[3]Frederick W. Taylor, "On the Art of Cutting Metals," *Transactions American Society of Mechanical Engineers,* XXVIII, 35, 1906.

[4]See E. Brockmeyer, H. L. Halztrom, and A. Jensen, *The Life and Works of A. K. Erlang* (Copenhagen: Copenhagen Telephone Company, 1948).

In the area of inventory control, the well-known economic lot size models have a long genealogy. Though it has been reported that G. D. Babcock developed a model stated in the form of a cubic equation, his technique was never published.[5] The first published economic lot size model for a simplified system is generally attributed to Ford W. Harris, who described his model in 1915.[6] Other early contributors to the development of inventory control models include H. S. Owen,[7] Benjamin Cooper,[8] R. H. Wilson, and W. A. Mueller.[9] Mathematical techniques of inventory control are, therefore, among the oldest of the new tools in the operations research kit.

As we have seen, the work of Taylor has also been followed by a number of other impressive aids to managerial decision making, such as the development of accounting techniques, Gantt charts, Gilbreth's micromotion studies, aptitude tests, and in a somewhat more qualitative sense by Mayo's dramatic Hawthorne experiments.

From a military standpoint, the germination of operations research occurred on both sides of the Atlantic during World War I. In England between 1914 and 1915, F. W. Lanchester attempted to treat military operations quantitatively. He obtained expressions relating to the outcome of a battle to both the relative numerical strength of the combatants and their relative firepower. Just as Newton's equation can be said to describe certain fundamental relationships between force and mass and motion, the "Lanchester equations" can be said to describe certain fundamental relationships of warfare.

During the period when Lanchester was pioneering military operations research in Great Britain, Thomas A. Edison was studying in America the process (rather than the instrumentalities) of antisubmarine warfare. He initiated the compilation of statistics to be used in analyzing maneuvers whereby surface ships could evade and destroy submarines. He devised a war game to be used for simulating problems of naval maneuver. He analyzed the merits of "zigzagging" as a submarine countermeasure for merchant ships.[10]

It must be noted, however, that the work of Lanchester and Edison did not have any noticeable impact on military operations in World War I; we must look to the period of World War II for the beginnings of effective military operations research.

[5]See F. E. Raymond, *Quantity and Economy in Manufacturing* (New York: McGraw-Hill Book Company, 1931), p. 124.

[6]*Ibid.,* p. 121.

[7]H. S. Owen, "How to Maintain Proper Inventory Control," *Industrial Management,* LXIX, 83-85, Feb. 1925.

[8]Benjamin Cooper, "How to Determine Economical Manufacturing Quantities," *Industrial Management,* LXXII, 228-33, Oct. 1926.

[9]R. H. Wilson and W. A. Mueller, "A New Method of Stock Control," *Harvard Business Review,* V, 197-205, Jan. 1927.

[10]W. F. Whitmore, "Edison and Operations Research," *Journal of the Operations Research Society of America,* February 1953, pp. 83-85.

Probability and Inference

The utilization of statistical inference and probability theory was further enhanced by the work of H. F. Dodge and H. G. Romig, co-workers with Shewhart at Bell Telephone Laboratories. They developed the technique of sampling inspection in connection with quality control, and they published statistical sampling tables which, although slowly accepted at first, are now widely used.

T. C. Fry, another Bell Telephone engineer, made additional significant contributions toward the statistical foundations of queuing theory. A series of lectures presented by Fry in 1928 concerning the engineering applications of probability theory became the basis for his important book on the subject.[11]

Our list would be incomplete without mentioning the work of Sir Ronald Fisher dealing with various modern statistical methods including chi-square tests, Bayesian statistics, sampling theory, and the design of experiments. During the mid-twenties, Fisher's work had little direct effect on management thought, but it is the basis for most of the applied statistical theory in use today.

In connection with investment decision analysis, the "Capital Goods Model" of Eugen von Bohm-Bawerk appeared in 1890.[12] Application of Bawerk's theory was made by Harold Hotelling in 1925.[13] Another early model widely applied in this area is the breakeven chart developed by Walter Rautenstrauch in the 1930s.

WORLD WAR II APPLICATIONS

Inasmuch as Britain was at war two years before the United States, it was almost inevitable that the first effective military operations research occurred there. In 1939, according to one historian, "there was a nucleus of a British operational research organization already in existence,"[14] and their contributions were quickly followed and augmented in various important ways: in improving the early-warning radar system, in antiaircraft gunnery, in antisub-

---

[11]See T. C. Fry, *Probability and Its Engineering Uses* (New York: D. Van Nostrand Co., Inc., 1928).

[12]Eugen von Bohm-Bawerk, *Capital and Interest* (London: Macmillan & Co. Ltd., 1890).

[13]Harold Hotelling, "A General Mathematical Theory of Depreciation," *Journal of the American Statistical Association,* December 1925, p. 340.

[14]Florence N. Trefethen, "A History of Operations Research," *Operations Research for Management,* ed. Joseph F. McCloskey and Florence N. Trefethen (Baltimore: The Johns Hopkins Press, 1954), I, 3-35.

marine warfare, in civilian defense, in the determination of convoy size, and in the conduct of bombing raids upon Germany.[15]

One of the most publicized of Britain's operations research groups was that under the direction of Professor P. M. S. Blackett of the University of Manchester, a Fellow of the Royal Society, Nobel laureate, and former naval officer. "Blackett's circus," as the group was called, included ". . . three physiologists, two mathematical physicists, one astrophysicist, one Army officer, one surveyor, one general physicist, and two mathematicians."[16] The value of the mixed-team approach was effectively demonstrated over and over again by this group.

Two Americans who were instrumental in the development of operations research in the United States during this time were Dr. James B. Conant, then chairman of the National Defense Research Committee, and Dr. Vannevar Bush, chairman of the Committee on New Weapons and Equipment, Joint Chiefs of Staff. These gentlemen had observed such groups in England in 1940 and in 1942 respectively.[17]

In October 1942, at the request of General Spaatz, commanding general of the Eighth Air Force, stationed in England, General Arnold (then Chief of Staff) sent a letter to all commanding generals of air force commands, recommending that they include in their staffs "operations analysis groups."[18] The first such operations team was assigned to the Eighth Bomber Command, also stationed in England. Almost simultaneously, the U.S. Navy formed operations research teams in Naval Ordinance and the Tenth Fleet. Naval mining and antisubmarine warfare were the main problems attacked by the groups.

POSTWAR USES

Operations research activity was considered to be so valuable by American military leaders that such functions were not discontinued at the end of the war. The army continued its operations research functions through the agency of the Operations Research Office (now known as the Research Analysis Corporation) in Chevy Chase, Maryland, with Dr. Ellis A. Johnson as director.

The navy established the Operations Evaluation Group under the direction of Professor Morse at M.I.T. The air force continued to employ operations analysis groups as a part of the various commands under its Operations Analysis Division. Additionally, the air force established Project RAND, administered by the Rand Corporation, for long-range studies of aerial warfare. Above the three

[15]*Ibid.*, pp. 5-10.
[16]*Ibid.*, p. 6.
[17]*Ibid.*, p. 12.
[18]*Ibid.*, p. 13.

service branches in the Department of Defense, the Weapons Systems Evaluations Group (now known as the Institute for Defense Analysis) was established
in 1948 and receives reports from ORO, OEG, OAD, and RAND. In addition,
several smaller groups of analysts work within the military service framework.[19]

Because of the rapid growth and spread of operations research activities in
military applications, many people have gained the impression that it is a type of
analysis applicable only to military problems. This is, of course, incorrect but
has been fostered by security regulations preventing the disclosure of the
effectiveness of the activities.

BUSINESS APPLICATIONS

At the close of the war, the industrial climate on both sides of the Atlantic
was ripe for the introduction of operations research into business planning. As
some of the formerly "top secret" indications of its value were released, its
possible applications to the business world became more apparent. Industry
needed to revamp its production and organization to service peacetime needs
quickly. In the United States the question of competition was paramount. In
Great Britain, a critical economic situation demanded drastic increase in
efficiency in production and in the development of new markets.

Industrial operations research in Great Britain and in the United States
developed along different lines. In Britain the nationalization of a few industries
provided a fertile field for experimentation with operations research techniques
in industries as a whole. Today, operations research groups exist in Great Britain
for the iron and steel industry, for coal, road and rail transport, textiles,
agriculture, brickmaking, shoes, and the like, with most but not all of them
under civil service sponsorship.[20]

In the United States the application of operations research techniques to
business operations was somewhat slower because many executives, already
accustomed to management consulting and industrial engineering, believed that
operations research was merely a new application of an old technique. Some
executives then (and frequently now) simply did not understand how to use
operations research techniques in their companies. Heightened competition
tended to slow down the state of the art because companies had no desire to aid
competitors by releasing the results of studies undertaken. Operations research
groups in the United States have worked upon problems in hospitals, department
stores, supermarkets, railroads, newspapers, toll bridges, electric utilities, and

[19]James C. Mouzon, "Military Operations Research," *Record of the 1957-1958
Operations Research Seminar* (The University of Michigan, 1958), pp. 189-213.

[20]Ellis A. Johnson, *The Application of Operations Research to Industry* (Chevy
Chase: The Johns Hopkins University Press, 1953), p. 48.

petroleum refining, to mention a few. Results have varied from notable to nothing, but there is a growing and impressive record of accomplishment.[21]

It is not unlikely that many of the objectives of operations research in industry had already been pursued by persons called management consultants, specialists in quality control, time and motion experts, marketing analysts, design engineers, and industrial engineers. However, the intensity and purpose of the new approach have provided broader, more precise, and always quantitative studies of industrial problems, often closer to the objectives of the *entire operation*. The executive, therefore, can more and more base his decisions on quantitative analyses having as their primary interests the objectives of the entire organization.

Recognizing the rise in quantitative analysis for managerial decision making, the Massachusetts Institute of Technology established the first course in nonmilitary applications of operations research in 1948.[22] Closely correlated with this has been the rapid growth in the number of publications on the subject.

Professor Blackett's is probably the earliest name associated with the literature, with his two papers, "Scientists at the Operational Level" (1941) and "A Note on Certain Aspects of the Methodology of Operational Research" (1943), leading the way.

ASSOCIATIONS

Another indication of the interest in operations research has been the formation in the early 1950s of two active socieites, The Operations Research Society of America, founded in 1952 (with its journal, *Operations Research*), and The Institute of Management Science, founded in 1953 (with its journal, *Management Science*). In England similar interest has been evinced by the formation in 1948 of the Operational Research Club (now known as the Operational Research Society of the United Kingdom), and the issuance in 1950 of the first periodical in the field, the *Operational Research Quarterly*.

In 1957 the First International Conference on Operations Research was held at Oxford, England, sponsored by The Operational Research Society of the United Kingdom jointly with The Operations Research Society of America and The Institute of Management Science. Delegates representing twenty-one nations reported comprehensive activity in seven countries and modest development in eleven. The Second International Conference, organized by the newly formed International Federation of Operational Research Societies, was held at the University of Aix-Marseille in Aix-en-Provence, France, in September 1960,

[21]*Ibid.*, pp. 47-48.
[22]*Ibid.*, p. 47.

hosted by the Société Française de Recherche Operationelle, and attended by 350 delegates from twenty-two countries.[23]

The growth and interest in the quantitative school is surely indicative of its widespread acceptance.

QUANTITATIVE TECHNIQUES

The number of techniques that have evolved with the quantitative school is growing rapidly and it would be impossible to include all of them. Though the table below is by no means complete, it will serve to indicate the tool, some of the people who made important contributions to its development and application, and the managerial area in which application has been made.

SUMMARY OF QUANTITATIVE TECHNIQUES

Technique	Contributors	Area of Application
Decision theory (including organization theory, learning theory, cybernetics, and suboptimization)	R. M. Thrall W. Edwards C. I. Barnard C. Hitch K. J. Arrow C. W. Churchman H. A. Simon N. Wiener	*Determination of objectives of firm, assessment of group conflicts and interactions, job performance estimates, organization analysis.*
Experimental design	R. A. Risher W. G. Cochran G. M. Cox M. G. Kendall	*The application of experimental design techniques is basic to the construction of any predictive model.*
Game theory	J. von Neumann O. Morgenstern M. Shubik	*Timing and pricing in a competitive market, military strategy.*
Information theory	C. Shannon S. Goldman W. Weaver	*Data-processing systems design, organization analysis, advertising effectiveness in market research.*
Inventory control	F. W. Harris T. W. Whitin J. F. Magee K. J. Arrow T. Harris J. Marschak	*Economic lot size and inventory control.*

---

[23]See *Proceedings of the Second International Conference on Operational Research* (New York: John Wiley & Sons, Inc., 1961).

Technique	Conbributors	Area of Application
Linear programming	L. V. Kantorovich T. C. Koopmans W. Leontieff G. B. Dantzig R. Dorfman P. A. Samuelson	*Assignment of equipment and personnel, scheduling, input-output analysis, transportation routing, product mix, allocation processes.*
Probability theory	R. A. Fisher T. C. Fry W. Feller H. Cramer	*Probability theory enters almost all areas of application.*
Queuing theory	A. K. Erlang L. C. Edie P. M. Morse M. G. Kendall	*Inventory control, traffic control, telephone trunking systems, scheduling of patients at clinics, radio communications, etc.*
Replacement theory	G. Terborgh J. Dean	*Replacement of equipment through failure and deterioration.*
Sampling theory	W. E. Deming H. F. Dodge H. G. Romig	*Quality control, simplified accounting and auditing, consumer surveys and product preferences in marketing research.*
Simulation theory (including Monte Carlo methods)	C. J. Thomas W. L. Deemer R. E. Zimmerman N. H. Jennings	*System reliability evaluation, profit planning, logistic-system studies, inventory control, and manpower requirements.*
Statistical decision theory	A. Wald E. C. Molina O. L. Davies W. A. Shewhart R. Schlaifer	*Estimation of model parameters in probabilistic models.*
Symbolic logic	G. Boole A. N. Whitehead B. Russell P. F. Strawson W. E. Cushen	*Circuit design, legal inference, e.g., checking contract consistencies.*

Of course, the techniques listed are not mutually exclusive nor are they all of equal importance; but they do serve to show the kinds of tools found in the quantitative school of management thought. Inasmuch as uncertainty and its measurement is a central problem facing management, it is not surprising that probability theory finds a use in nearly every quantitative study that is at all realistic. It is the branch of mathematics most useful in operations research.

The school has progressed from a war baby stage to rapid maturity, with its national and international societies and publications, its acceptance in learned circles and university curricula, and its adoption by business and government alike. It has provided the academician the opportunity to contribute something to the solution of real problems and has simultaneously pointed out to the populace the resources that lie behind the walls of the ivory tower.

The management science school of thought is now well entrenched, and its followers are firmly convinced that any phase of managerial organizing, decision making, or planning can be expressed in quantitative terms for a more exacting analysis. As mentioned in the preceding chapter, it is so eclectic in nature that virtually every contributor may be included in this school which offers almost unlimited promise in the development of the science of management.

12

A GENERAL THEORY OF MANAGEMENT

As we have seen thus far, people have performed managerial activities throughout history—as farmers, as army commanders, as school principals, as officeholders, as service station owners, as corporation presidents.

Various schools of management thought have emerged over the past seventy-five years. One early school, the *scientific management* approach, was sparked by Frederick W. Taylor. His introduction of scientific analysis of work methods was clearly revolutionary, and while Taylor did not emphasize the human element in his approach to management, he did not completely overlook it. The human element and the effects of social interaction are accorded the primary role in the *behavioral* school, which developed somewhat later.

In the *process* school we found that the emphasis was on the functions the manager performed, and from this approach a new theory of management evolved. Finally, and most recently, the emphasis has been on the quantification of managerial decisions, and around this new emphasis has emerged the *quantitative* school.

MASLOW AND MANAGEMENT THEORY

To a degree we can see that these developing approaches to management followed Maslow's hierarchy of needs.

Our first scientific theories centered around physiological "survival," assurance of the on-going of the concern, followed logically by elaborations dealing with physical and psychological safety and security. These theories were in turn followed by "social" theories dealing with human interaction. Perhaps, today, we are in the final stage of our search for a generally accepted theory embodying self-esteem and self-realization—a professional concept. To realize this final stage, what we may need is not another theory of management, but rather a concept that will serve to unify the generally accepted values of the previously recognized theories.

Evolving an all-encompassing and eclectic theory of management that will be general enough to apply to every managerial situation is the purpose of this chapter.

MANAGEMENT AND MANAGERS

Taylor spoke of management as knowing exactly what you want men to do, and then seeing that they do it the best and cheapest way. This definition, you will note, contains three essential elements: a goal, or an objective; a means by which that goal, or objective, can be attained; and the utilization of human effort. Today we typically add a fourth element by saying that managers are involved in the process of setting goals, or objectives, and achieving them by employing men and material resources in a compatible environment. Every activity involving human effort possesses to some degree these four facets: (1) a goal, (2) the means by which the goal can be attained, (3) the use of human effort, and (4) the creation of an environment that will induce men to participate. The emphasis that each of these facets receives, however, varies widely in complexity, depending on the managerial task.

A manager in a simple situation, for example, may be little more than a receiver, storer, translator, and communicator of information pertinent to the effective performance of the undertaking. Receiving-storing-translating, nevertheless, effects the desired end and, as such, causes the communicator to be known as a manager. In this sense, a sailor directing the boom operator in the unloading activities of a ship's hold may be thought of as a manager. His activities involve a goal, the means by which it can be attained, the use of human effort, and the creation of an environment in which the other participants will work. If he directed that the boom be overloaded, for example, he might be creating an environment that was not safe, thus causing the other sailors to refuse to participate.

Many managerial undertakings, on the other hand, are rather complex and require more than mere communication; a basic knowledge and understanding of perhaps the technical aspects of an operation may be needed, and the act of managing may also involve a more complex decision-making process than the sailor's observations and communications. This more complex type of management is the one normally ascribed to individuals such as a captain of a ship, a governor of a state, or a president of a large company.

Through the years, writers have attempted to explain what these managers do—what their job is. Taylor and his followers, of course, couched the manager's job in shop terms. Fayol explained it as a complex of administrative functions. Other writers have seen the manager simply as one who manipulates others to achieve ends—the human relations expert.

Managers as we know them today, however, cannot be classified as scientific managers or behavioral managers or quantitative managers. They are not, for example, practicing management solely on the foundations established by F. W. Taylor and his followers—though their practice may well include some of Taylor's ideas. Nor are they following solely in the footsteps of behaviorists such as Munsterberg and Roethlisberger—though surely the man and the various human wants of individuals are recognized.

Nor can we classify the contemporary manager as belonging exclusively to the quantitative school regardless of his dependence on or use of numerical calculations. Numbers cannot manage. They can only be manipulated to show certain relationships which may cause the manager to ponder, to consider, or to make a certain decision.

Finally, a manager cannot be classified solely as to the function or process he employs. Though he may perform certain functions in attempting to create an environment conducive to achieving a given objective using other individuals, today's manager is more than a functionalist. To deny this would be like classifying a symphony conductor simply as a bandleader—with none of the symphonic overtones of interpretation, dynamics, tonal qualities, and the like. Thus, the more deeply we probe the more certain we become that though they may well describe one facet of it, none of the schools of managerial thought completely describe today's manager or contemporary management. They can be compared to the blind men who went to "see" the elephant—each one describing with precision and accuracy the part that he "saw" with his hands, yet none of the men grasping a complete picture of the entire beast. This may well be where we are today in the managerial area.

Management as we know it today has moved a great distance along the continuum of development from management as it existed in 1850. The manager of that period had little concern for managerial philosophy or human relations. It is probable, therefore, that the classical, or scientific, school, for example, fairly accurately described the manager of that day, who was more technically than behaviorally oriented. He was concerned with the things of management rather than the concepts of management. He was a doer in contrast to being a thinker. But this would be an incomplete description of today's manager. Neither the quantitative nor the behavioral schools would by themselves accurately describe the modern manager. As we study this it becomes apparent that because of the complex nature of modern management, no single school of management thought appears adequate for its description or analysis. We find ourselves, instead, with many different schools or theories describing with precision some aspect of the whole—but no theory depicting the totality.

Our job, therefore, is simply to evolve a general theory that will incorporate the appropriate aspects of past theories and disciplines.

A GENERAL THEORY OF MANAGEMENT

Management, we have said, is the process of setting and achieving objectives by influencing human behavior within a suitable environment. *Managers,* on the other hand, create the environment that is conducive to the performance of acts by other individuals—acts that will accomplish the firm's objective, commonly called the firm's goal, as well as achieve one or more objectives of the participating individuals. *Determining the collective objectives of an undertaking and generating an environment for their achievement,* therefore, *is the total function of a manager.* Let us examine the environmental aspect first.

The work environment that managers are concerned with involves two parts. One, obviously, is the *physical* part and includes all the physical aspects of which it is composed: light, heat, noise, ventilation; the tools and materials that employees work with; the sequence of work performance. Everything that affects the physical environment is part of it, and these are the things that managers must utilize in the correct ratio to create a physical environment in which employees will work contentedly and productively. In generating this physical environment, today's manager borrows heavily from the classical, or scientific management, school with its emphasis on the physical aspect. In addition to heat, light, and so forth, other less obvious items such as queuing theory, probabilities, economic lot size, and work sampling contribute to the development of the physical environment through their impact on production methods, materials, schedules, and the like. The effective manager, of course, borrows these techniques from the newer quantitative, or management science, school.

The second part of the environment that managers are concerned with is *conceptual* in nature. It is the mental facet of the environment which affects an employee's attitude toward his work and his work place. This conceptual, or mental, environment that managers generate is aimed at creating a positive attitude or frame of mind for each worker which will have a salutary effect on the employee's willingness to participate in the endeavor. It aims at creating a frame of mind that will enable each worker to understand why it is to his advantage to expend his efforts to achieve the firm's objective, it being "to his advantage" only when it enables him directly or indirectly to reach his personal goal or goals.

Imperfections in this mental environment may be apparent, for example, when an employee seeks employment elsewhere or does not contribute wholeheartedly to accomplishing his task. An effective mental environment, on the other hand, makes the employee understand why he should participate in the work, why the firm needs him, and how his personal goals can be achieved through this cooperative endeavor.

A manager's prime task, therefore, is the creation of a healthy *physical* and *mental* work climate which will induce others to willingly contribute their efforts to achieve the objectives of the undertaking. Without this proper *physical-conceptual* environment, or work climate, the participant's efforts may be ineffective or even lacking.

These two facets of the environment, of course, cannot and do not exist independently. Each affects the other. A "perfect" physical environment is not perfect to an employee who perceives it to be otherwise, and this imperfection will affect his mental attitude. We may have a temperature reading, for example, that the physical scientists tell us is perfect, but if an employee *thinks* it is too hot, it *is too hot* for him to work effectively—if at all. In this case, the mental affects the physical. The reverse may also be true. In a situation where music, for example, is played over a public-address system, it may have a tranquilizing effect on an employee's work tension. Here the physical affects the mental. The announcement of prizes and awards over this same public-address system within the plant might well please the employee and cause a positive frame of mind. On the other hand, reprimands announced over the same system would have a very negative effect. Thus, the subject matter as well as how it is communicated is part of this physical-conceptual environment.

A wise manager, of course, recognizes the effect that the physical has on the mental, and vice versa. He understands psychology and human behavior well enough to know what should be communicated over public channels and what should be communicated in private. In creating the proper work environment, today's manager, therefore, borrows heavily from the physical scientists, the behaviorists, the physicists, and the psychologists because he has learned from them the critical role that their disciplines assume in creating the precisely correct atmosphere in which effective work will be accomplished.

In his involvement with all of these—in his effort to generate an environment conducive to achieving the firm's objective—the effective manager, we have said, borrows heavily from various disciplines and employs selected and appropriate parts from the classical, behavioral, and quantitative schools. In doing this he is completely enmeshed and involved in a totality of mental and physical activity which can perhaps best be described by using the functional approach first set forth by Henri Fayol.

Functional Aspects of Management

In managing any endeavor, every manager undertakes several recognizable functions. He must, for example, determine the undertaking's objective, as well as decide what needs to be done, how it should be accomplished, and when it needs implementing. Determining these facts involves a conceptual look at needed future action—be it tomorrow or next year. It involves looking ahead, conceptualizing about the future, and making plans today that will affect the future. Fayol called this aspect of managing *planning*.

Planning, of course, is not a separate recognizable act. It is a mixed part of every managerial act or function. A manager, for example, does not give a directive (or order) based solely on impulse or reflex. Instead, even a casual communication about needed action may well involve some planning *along with* the communication act itself—it may even develop into planning about the future of the employee based upon his reaction to and reception of the manager's communiqué. Every managerial act, mental or physical, is inexorably intertwined with planning. It is as much a part of every managerial act as breathing is to the living human.

We may, of course, conceptually separate planning for the purpose of theoretical discussion and analysis, but in practice neither is it a distinct entity nor is it capable of being separated. The planning function is mixed with other managerial functions and like ink once mixed with water cannot be set apart. It is spread throughout and is part of the whole of managing. For the purpose of analysis, however, let us mentally separate the managerial planning function and see how it is involved in managing.

Planning, as a conceptually separate managerial function, consists of looking ahead, "imagineering," conceptualizing, anticipating probable future events and the actions needed to cope with them. It may be nothing more than a simple plan for employee vacations next year in relation to the probable vacation schedule of other plants in the community, or it may involve a plan of action to stay competitive and minimize the impact of a possible business recession eighteen months hence. Whatever the area of consideration, managers in the performance of the planning function systematically analyze the problem in light of probable future events and make decisions regarding the action they will take if certain events come about in the future. Planning in this sense, therefore, is a rational, economic, and systematic way of making decisions today that will affect the future.

A second managerial function is that of *organizing*. Like planning, organizing can be separated only in a conceptual sense because it, too, is intertwined with planning and other managerial functions. It is part of this *mixed* and *inseparable* whole which we call managing. If we were to regard this as conceptually separable, however, we might say that when managers attempt to create an acceptable physical and mental environment, they must bring some degree of order to the chaos that happenstance effects. This ordering process, involving planning, goes by several names, the most common being that of organizing. In communicating, in directing, in fixing limits, and so on, a manager is involved with the organizing as well as the planning processes. Thoughts, for example, must be organized to some degree before they are communicated;

directing and establishing relationships or hierarchies demand system and organization; and physical environment conducive to participation shows order or organization. Thus, a manager in generating the right environment for participation is a constant organizer. Organization is involved in his every communication; organization is part of his every plan; and organization is a vital part of any attempt on his part to check or control activities.

Over and above planning and organizing, another apparent managerial function involves making objectives known to the participants. This managerial activity is frequently referred to as *directing*. Like planning and organizing, this function does not stand alone but is intermixed with others. Every student of management knows that in one way or another the individuals involved in an organizational endeavor must be told what is expected of them. These communications may involve, for example, what their specific daily tasks are, or they may involve a delineation of firm and personal goals. They may take the form of writing, nodding the head, gesturing, frowning, or simply talking. Whatever their form, their purpose is to let the participant know the action needed on his part to achieve some goal. Directing is not, however, simply or solely directing. It is, instead, a *planned* and *organized* communication to create an environment conducive to participative action, and this communication which directs is also inexorably intertwined with the planning and organizing functions previously mentioned. Unplanned, disorganized directives would be meaningless. Every directive to be understood, therefore, must possess some degree of organization, and organization in and of itself implies a plan. Thus, the managerial functions include directing which, like the others, is not a separate entity but is intermixed with planning and organizing.

The best laid plans of mice and men sometimes go astray. This seems to be particularly true in managerial endeavors involving multiple individuals. The probabilities and possibilities for incorrect or inappropriate action seem to increase geometrically with an arithmetic increase in personnel. As a result, any person directing an overall undertaking must check on the actions of the participants as well as the results that they have achieved. If either the actions or the results do not comply with preconceived or planned achievements, then planned and needed action must be communicated to the participants for them either to correct what they have done or to take remedial action during subsequent events. Frequently referred to as the *control* function, this action is likewise involved with the planning, organizing, and directing activities previously discussed and cannot stand alone without involving these three. This is readily apparent when we consider the following.

Controlling is forcing events to conform to preconceived plans. Planning, therefore, is an integral part of control. A manager controls, of course, through the actions of his employees. When preconceived objectives or plans are not achieved, a manager must communicate to his employees the action he wants them to take to remedy the situation. When a manager undertakes this action he is *directing,* and as we have seen, *directing* cannot be undertaken without involving the *planning* and the *organizing* functions. Therefore, like planning organizing, and directing, the *control* function cannot stand alone but is inseparably intertwined with these three. None of these functions can be performed independently. A plan is an *organized* course of action. To be a plan, it must be known and communicated. Employees must be told what the plan is and what they are to do. This communication, of course, is the function we call *directing,* which, we have just shown, involves *planning* and *organizing.*

The Managerial Composite

The managing process, therefore, is not a series of separate functions (planning, organizing, directing, and controlling) that can be performed independently. Instead, management is a *composite* process made up of these individual components. No one of these functions, we have said, can be performed without involving the others, but by utilizing all four as a composite process, the manager carries out his duty of generating a physical and conceptual environment conducive to the coordinated participation of team members or participants.

Every manager, of course, does not employ the same time mixture of these functions. A low-level manager such as a first-line supervisor may employ a mixture of, say, 10 per cent planning, 10 percent organizing, 50 per cent directing, and 30 per cent controlling; while a top-level manager such as a corporate president may have as his proportions 40 per cent planning, 35 per cent organizing, 20 per cent directing, and 5 per cent controlling. Thus, while the elements of the mass are constant regardless of the level on which managing is practiced, the *proportions* of the elements vary for *every* managerial job and may even vary over time for the same job. Because of this, the study of management and managers is frequently confusing to students. Management cannot be viewed simply as a given or fixed entity, an inert compound. Rather, it is a highly reactive compound that is not found twice in identical proportions.

Management in this new perspective consists of accomplishing objectives with the use of other participants by developing a physical and conceptual environment that will elicit their participation. In building this environment, managers perform an eclectic and unified process involving planning, organizing, and directing all intertwined with each other and with control. The effective performance of this managerial process in part or in whole is often dependent upon all of man's collective knowledge.

It may call upon technical knowledge for background information on which to make decisions; it may call upon quantitative theory to aid in placing parts in proper perspective for analysis and decision; it may rely on the physical sciences to aid in the development and maintenance of an acceptable physical climate; and it may rely completely on the behavioral sciences (sociology, psychology, anthropology, economics, and the like) to point the proper approach for the creation of the appropriate conceptual and emotional environment—*all of these* intended to induce coordinated associative action by participants for the effective achievement of individual as well as corporate objectives.

A manager, therefore, is not a specialist in the usual sense of the word. Instead, he is a composite specialist—one who sees and comprehends the totality of associative situations.

Completely educating such an individual would be a tremendous, almost impossible task. A lifetime of study would be insufficient. Yet we must manage, and we must also be productive even though we lack managers with this extensive knowledge. We find ourselves, therefore, having to compromise between the ultimate in education and the requirements of reality. We pay for it, of course, by relatively ineffective management which results in the inefficient utilization of resources, relative underproduction, high rates of futility and frustration, and out-of-line prices.

This is not a condemnation of the *system*. Rather, it is a recognition of a man's inability to be a perfect manager. Recognizing this, we have arrived at a satisficing position in our approach to managing—a position where we understand personal inadequacies, but where at the same time we recognize the need for managerial action that cannot wait for perfection.

Managerial Acts

A manager, using his acquired knowledge of science, human behavior, and the like, undertakes to build an environment conducive to achieving recognized and desired goals. In the process of building this environment he performs two and only two types of acts. Like the environment he builds, the acts are either *physical* or *conceptual*.

In the physical realm, a manager's acts are readily recognized. Basically, they take the form of some means of communication to other individuals: gesturing, talking, demonstrating, and the like. Managers do not *as managers* act as participants or workers in an endeavor. Instead, theirs is the task of creating an environment in which others will participate. Their one physical act in this area is communicating. They may communicate about what has to be done, the pay that will be earned, future plans, and so on. In all these communications the manager is attempting to create the appropriate environment for participation on the part of employees.

In the conceptual realm, a manager's acts are not so readily recognizable. We cannot, for example, see a manager think, evaluate, or make a decision. We can, however, observe his communications, which indicate the presence of this conceptual activity. Like the wind, we can see the effects but not the force. This conceptual aspect of a manager's job also borrows heavily from the acquired knowledge of the physical and behavioral sciences.

Some people reason that the conceptual aspect of a manager's job may be instinctive rather than reasoned. A moment's thought tells us that this cannot be true. Even though a manager cannot tell the exact process he uses in making a decision, it is a product of his knowledge and past experience. Decisions are not formed out of nothing but out of theory and reflect a manager's total mental capacity. He may not, of course, obviously or consciously enumerate every aspect of a problem and evaluate alternatives. Nevertheless, this is done in whole or in part as a reflective process of experience previously stored in his mind. Though the mind in such an instance may well be like the iceberg with 90 per cent of its capacity not apparent, it is, nevertheless, available and on call to aid the manager as a reflective storage vault for his concepts, facts, and impressions—making them available to him in his decision-making process. This decision-making process includes all mental activity. Every mental act, every concept, every thought derives from a decision—a rejection of one part and the selection of another. Managers, therefore, are basically involved with making decisions, a mental activity, and communicating to employees, a physical activity, in order to develop a climate conducive to participative action.

A MANAGEMENT MODEL

Some of us seem to think best, or understand best, when concepts are expressed quantitatively or in model form. The idea is that one model is worth a thousand words. If this be the case, we might wish to express what has been said thus far about management in some concise formula or model. One approach to building such a model could be as follows.

If we agree that managing consists of physical and conceptual acts which effect or yield physical and conceptual environments, and if we further agree that these acts and these environments are collectively a function of group (corporate) and individual objectives, *then,* we can express managing as

$$Mg = [(Ac + Ap) \longrightarrow (Ec + Ep)] f (Oi, Og)$$

where
Ac = conceptual acts
Ap = physical acts
Ec = conceptual environment
Ep = physical environment
Oi = individual objectives
Og = group (corporate) objectives
W = a weight (proportion) of P (planning), O (organizing), D (directing), and C (controlling)

Inasmuch as the physical and conceptual acts $(Ac + Ap)$ of managing (Mg) may be expressed as a compound of P, O, D, and C with varying proportions whose total is unity, *then*

$$(Ac + Ap) = W_1 P + W_2 O + W_3 D + W_4 C$$

where

$$\sum_{i=1}^{4} \qquad W_i = 1 \qquad \text{and} \qquad W_i > 0$$

Therefore

$$Mg = [(W_1 P + W_2 O + W_3 D + W_4 C) \longrightarrow (Ec + Ep)] \ f \ (Oi, \ Og)$$

We know that despite well-set goals and effective managerial actions, neither the firm's nor the individual's goals are fully realized in most instances. They are, instead, partially realized. What, we might ask, happens to our model under these conditions?

It may well be that a firm's goal is 90 per cent achieved while the individual's goals are 20 per cent realized. Under these conditions employee resistance may well result. This resistance, in turn, would cause a change in managerial actions to effect a greater achievement of individual goals.

However, if the firm's goal is only 10 per cent realized and the employees' goals are 90 per cent achieved, then some change will be made by the manager in his actions to effect a greater than 10 per cent achievement of the firm's goal.

A good manager or an effective manager, therefore, is one who promotes high achievement in a firm's as well as in an individual's goals.

Given the above, managerial achievement (MgA) may be expressed as the percentage (p) that the firm's and the employee's goals are realized. *Thus*

$$MgA = p(Oi + Og)$$

Likewise, if we recognize that managerial acts (Amg) are a function of a percentage of $Oi + Og$, then

$$Amg = f(pOi + pOg)$$

If Og is known, Oi is a function of it. *Thus*

$$Oi = f \, Og \qquad\qquad \text{and} \qquad\qquad Og = f \, Oi$$

Now, therefore, recognizing that managerial acts are functions of goals and the effectiveness of these acts is in proportion to goal achievement; then, the percentage of achievement changes a manager's conceptual and physical acts which yield the conceptual and physical environment $[(Ac + Ap) \rightarrow (Ec + Ep)]$ which is a function of the goals.

This can be expressed as a *schematic model* as follows:

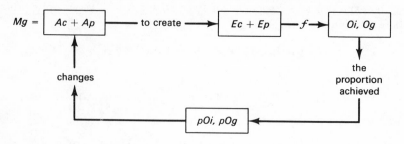

SUMMARY

The job of a manager is to create an environment conducive to the performance of acts by other individuals in order to accomplish personal as well as corporate goals. In building this environment, the manager must first recognize what he is trying to accomplish (the goals involved) so that he can generate an environment in which individuals will contribute their efforts. This environment has a physical and a conceptual aspect, and its effective development depends on contributions from various schools or streams of management thought as well as from the physical and behavior sciences.

In developing this environment managers perform a composite managerial function consisting of planning, organizing, directing, and controlling activities— all of which are interwoven into the whole cloth of management. Finally, we indicated that the acts of managers, like the environment that they build, are both physical and conceptual.

None of this is intended conceptually to place the contemporary manager on any new plane. It is not intended in any manner to minimize the contributions of the various schools of management thought or individual contributors of managerial concepts. It in no way attempts to alter the basic theory or practice of management. It is, rather, an attempt to conceptualize and explain in general terms the manager's job and how he performs it.

That concept, it is hoped, will serve to link the various schools or streams of management thought together into an understandable and meaningful whole.

13

HISTORY AND CONTEMPORARY MANAGEMENT

Management, we have said, is the determiner of our economic progress, the employer of our educated, the amasser of our resources, the strength of our national defense, and the molder of our society. It is the core of all our public as well as personal activities. And it is all these things because man has found no substitute for it in the effective achievement of his goals.

Management thought as we know it today is in some respects a twentieth-century concept. It has attained its position, however, through the efforts of a host of men working in its behalf over the centuries. It stands tall because it stands on the shoulders of past theoreticians and scholars—a meaningful product of history. By seizing an example from the past, we may solve a current problem or avoid a future catastrophe. In addition to this aid, management history provides us with a clear window for an objective evaluation; it points out the developing complexities of concepts we normally take for granted; it helps to guide us in our decision making; and in doing all these things, it may well serve to kindle in us a spark of original thought by which we can make the way clearer for those who follow.

As a result of these and other changes in management's outlook, today's business leaders bear little resemblance to the table-pounding, cigar-chewing leaders of the turn of the century.

The image of the typical manager in 1900 was fairly clear. He was the master of his fate and he ran a taut ship. Orders were to be followed, not questioned, and orders came only from the boss.

Labor was generally a plentiful commodity and treated as such. Little thought was given to improving the worker's lot in life, to say nothing of his immediate working environment. Instead, management viewed labor as a factor of production from which to extract maximum productivity with little or no regard for the whole man.

It was in this atmosphere that scientific management was born and it was in this environment that it was nurtured by its followers.

The impact of this new form of management on the practices of managers was slow to be seen. In some instances, the concepts led practice by twenty or more years; in other cases, the delay was considerably less. But the important point is that it did have an impact—one that could be seen and evaluated. To illustrate this impact, let us look at a few examples of some of the developing changes in managerial practices which evolved as a direct and obvious outgrowth of the spread of the new science of management.

PERSONNEL-HUMAN RELATIONS

About four or five years after Frederick W. Taylor published his principles of management calling for the scientific selection and placement of workers, personnel departments (or employment departments as they were generally called then) began to appear with the outward charge of careful selection and placement of workers. Having an "employment department" was a status symbol of the time, and even companies that were too small to afford one nevertheless had an employment manager.

As one would expect, these early departments or managers did little other than help make transfers between departments and help start recreational activities and other diversions at lunch periods; in general, they did what they thought best to achieve good relations between management and workers.

But with the spread of the new concepts about employee relations, these early departments began to perform duties that management recognized as of general importance. The Depression of the thirties, however, served momentarily to stop their progress. As cost reductions became necessary, these early personnel departments came in for their share of cuts. Although the departments were not dispensed with entirely, they did undergo drastic changes—probably with cause. Often ill-conceived and poorly organized, these personnel departments often lacked any depth in concepts or practices concerning employee hiring and training.

In addition to their economic troubles, management in the mid-thirties began to come under somewhat severe attack as the cause of all the country's economic ills. Business itself was held responsible by many for the economic breakdown in our system. Communications between labor and management was nonexistent or poor.

Looking for a solution to this dilemma, management listened to the preachments of leaders such as Sheldon, Follett, and Mayo. Perhaps they did have an obligation to labor and society that had long been ignored. Grabbing at straws, they started trying the human relations approach. In fact, any gimmick that worked would have been acceptable. But what started out as a gimmick turned out to be profound.

The managerial philosophers were right! Human relations became firmly established as a developing philosophy of management. And as it became better understood and appreciated, the effects on the general health of industry were salutary, causing even more interest and study. University curricula began to reflect this new human relations philosophy in courses. Industry, however, found that human relations could not be required in one area and not applied in another. To be effective it had to permeate the entire organization, particularly the foremanship levels.

The training and education of foremen at one time was not considered as even the most remote of managerial obligations. The personnel-human relations philosophy developing in the twenties and thirties, however, soon brought management to the realization of its total obligation. The incorporation of training programs for foremen followed the concepts of the new managerial approach with some success. It was the pressure for output and good supervision during the early forties, however, that hurried the pace of supervisory training. Programs of Training Within Industry, Job Relations Training, Job Instruction Training, and Job Methods Training sprang up at virtually every war production plant.

The experience with the incorporation of a real concern for employees has proved to be all that its early proponents said it would. Firmly entrenched in industry today, no manager would consider a system of supervision not incorporating the ideals and concepts of sound human relations.

NEW MANAGERIAL APPROACHES

Not only changes in personnel practices but changes, too, in managerial practices followed the concepts of scientific management. In the early thirties two new approaches to managerial organization and practice, called bottom-up management and multiple management, were introduced. Actually, the basis for each was the broadened concept of delegation and centralization. The specific practices, while interesting, are not the item of importance here. Rather, it is the indication of an overall trend that is of importance, with its shifting away from an authoritative form of management to one incorporating the individual.

EFFICIENCY

Just as scientific management affected personnel and managerial practices, it also has a real impact on the efficiency of persons and factories in the twenties and in the thirties.

With its scorn of waste and inefficiency, scientific management brought an awareness of these to management, which never before had been aware of them or had expressed much concern over them. Fanned by the experience of managerial applications, the interest in management efficiency and conservation caused a large portion of the First National Management Congress held in Chicago in March 1930 to be devoted to the discussion and analysis of these factors. As the Depression wore on, the interest in efficiency heightened, with its successes serving to underscore the validity of the claims of scientific management.

Cost minimization was a common and proud boast. It was not unusual for companies to report "sales down—profits up." J. C. Penney, for example, in 1931 reported gross sales off 9.5 per cent with profits up 23 per cent. Once tried and found good, managers on every hand turned to the practices of scientific management for waste reduction and conservation—both in labor and in materials. This preachment of the new management caught hold in the thirties and was largely the causal factor for our phenomenal productive output during the war years. The flame of scientifically eliminating waste has burned brightly ever since.

EMPLOYEE WELFARE

Following the publications of the managerial scholars urging management's awakening to its multiple responsibilities and obligations, many leading managers became aware of the plight of their employees. For the first time they began to feel and understand their needs and turned to hiring physicians and nurses to look after their employees' health problems. They added cafeterias, installed recreational facilities, and generally improved working conditions by better lighting, better ventilation, and cleaner surroundings. All of this, of course, did not occur at a signal. Instead, it took place gradually during a decade or more prior to World War II.

Concern for employees off the job was also manifest. Their home life, standard of living, leisure, and acceptable level of income came in for discussion.

In 1930 Henry Ford echoed the thesis of Sheldon, Gantt, and others when he said that the abolition of poverty was the only worthwhile end for business.

This was truly a milestone in the expression by business leaders of a philosophy set forth twenty years earlier, a clear indication of management's impact on the total thinking of business leaders.

Along with this came the newer ideas of job security—a guaranteed annual wage. Why, such leaders as W. M. Leiserson were asking in 1931, should labor be paid by the hour or piece when management's pay did not fluctuate with the weather, or seasons, or output, or profit, or introduction of labor-saving equipment? A few companies between 1930 and 1950 sought to introduce a policy of guaranteed wages, recognizing a moral obligation to their employees as well as to the community for economic well-being. But it took virtually three decades before the Ford Motor Company established the first plan that would offer a guaranteed annual wage, as much of an innovation as Ford's five-dollars-per-day wage.

WAGES

Wages, too, were prominent in the news. Prior to Taylor's time, management had regarded long hours and low wages as a prime principle for low production costs. Following Taylor's pronouncements of high wages and low labor costs, management by the late twenties began to question their long-held but erroneous principle. In the decade or two following this questioning, their principle was virtually reversed: the way to high production and low unit cost was through short hours and high wages.

This reversal, however, did not happen because of a spiritual awakening on management's part. On the contrary, it happened because managers found that Frederick W. Taylor was right. They began to see that high pay among other things affected a man's outside environment as well as his mental attitude toward his work. And, in addition, they saw that the composite of internal and external environmental influences coupled with the worker's psychological outlook had a direct and pronounced effect on the quantity and quality of his work.

Here again is another example of the philosophy of management reversing by degrees a long-held policy.

DECISION MAKING

The managerial decision-making process likewise has undergone changes through time. Apparently, in the early days, managers made decisions based to a large degree on hunch, intuition, and guess. F. W. Taylor recognized this and preached the word of scientific analysis instead of rule of thumb. Gradually through the years managers have turned to the scientific rather than the intuitive approach to problem solving, as did Taylor. And once they recognized the value of the scientific approach to making decisions, managers have continued to develop their skills in the use of scientific rather than haphazard decision-making models.

The development of the computer, of course, has done much to change management's approach to decision making, inasmuch as it has made it possible for a manager to have vast quantities of information about both internal and external operations of the firm at his call. He is, as a result, learning to scientifically synthesize, interrelate, and use knowledge from diverse sources in the form of quantitative models. Many of the models now used by management grew out of the quantitative approaches and activities described in Chapter 11. Linear and nonlinear programming are examples of those used today, as are integer programming, dynamic programming, transportation models, waiting-line models, critical-path models; and thus the list goes on.

To the student of management history the importance of the use of models and other quantitative techniques is the recognition of the impact that these new approaches have had on the management process. Here again we see a further refinement in management, particularly in that aspect dealing with decision making, which has resulted from a gradual application of quantitative techniques and theories evolved since Taylor first insisted on science instead of rule of thumb.

SOCIAL RESPONSIBILITY

For years the managerial philosophers had called management's attention to its total responsibility. The indication of a moral oughtness was there, they stressed. As stewards for stockholders, managers had a prime responsibility to the employees, the customers, and the community—along with their well-recognized responsibility to the owners. By and large, these early pronouncements apparently fell on deaf ears. By the mid-thirties, however, heartening signs began to appear. In 1937, for example, Raymond Moley declared that while management remained legally and ethically a primary agent of the investor, its secondary responsibility to the public and labor had become relatively greater.[1] Four years later Roger D. Lapham asserted that in the narrow sense of the past, management had been considered solely responsible to its ownership—its stockholders—but there was a growing conviction that in the broader sense management's duty to its customers, to the public, and to its employees came first![2]

[1]Raymond Moley, "Industrial Leadership, 1937 Model," *Vital Speeches of the Day*, *III*, January 1, 1937, p. 186.

[2]"The Trading Post," *Business Week*, May 24, 1941, p. 67.

By 1951 this view was well established, and Frank Abrams writing in the *Harvard Business Review* for May of that year enunciated the new philosophy when he indicated that the job of management was to conduct the affairs of the enterprise in such a way as to maintain an equitable balance among the claims of the variously interested groups.

In the mid-sixties and early seventies we have again recognized changes in philosophy that reflect management's gradual assumption of its moral and social obligation of good corporate citizenship. We see it, for example, in management's assuming its social responsibility by cooperating with the federal government in withholding goods from countries if those goods would jeopardize our national security; in maintaining prices at a level consistent with a healthy economy, not raising them to a point considered critically inflationary; in training the unemployed; in cleaning up city ghettos; and in recognizing and acting upon pollution problems. More examples could be cited, but the point of the broadened view taken by management of its total responsibility has been made. It took almost half a century for the change to come about, but the managerial philosophers won again.

THE CONTEMPORARY MANAGER

Today's manager recognizes his multiple obligations because of his peculiar place of stewardship over vast resources. The employees' and the community's well-being takes equal or greater precedence over owners and customers in many matters. Managers today must exercise all the wisdom of Solomon in allocating scarce resources with relative equality among the many demands on industry.

This, then, is today's manager—a product of the prime concepts proposed by the early managerial philosophers. Borrowing from all schools of managerial thought, today's manager is eclectic in his practice. We might call his new brand of management a somewhat scientifically humanized approach—one incorporating all the findings of the sociologists and the psychologists, yet still managing to be quantitatively oriented with a goodly portion of scientific methodology. Imbued with the idea of research, today's manager is open minded in virtually all spheres, standing ready to promote change if his "science" shows it to be more effective.

Along this line, there is arising today a discrete, learnable, and organized body of management thought which is evident in the existence and growth of a body of literature. Research, both pure and applied, is taking place in the area of management with applications in virtually every field of man's endeavor. And further evidence of this body of thought is afforded through the growth in professional meetings where management thought is discussed, analyzed, enlarged upon, and explained in the hope of furthering the growing profession. The concepts of management have shifted today from the level of gang bosses to the systems concept because growing complexities in our society have moved management from a relatively simple task to that of evolving information systems, and of organizing these systems into patterns of management.

Today's managers, however, with all their eclecticism and comprehension do not really understand their developing profession. It is still too nebulous. Nor do they understand some of their motives, some of their actions, their relative position in society, or their future position. In fact it is doubtful at this time that any one individual has all the answers. Nor has management thought, with its evolution and forward development, provided all the answers. But this we do know: Good theory will provide good practice, and it is this developing area of management theory and history to which we must turn for guidance and partial answers to our current questions.

Today's manager, therefore, must become a student of history and a managerial theorist who deals in environmental generalities in contrast to the owner-manager who had to deal in specifics and odd facts about particular cases. Only when today's manager keeps theory and practice in proper perspective, therefore, can he manage the ever-developing, complex information-systems type of business conglomerations. And the keeping of this proper perspective, we know, can be achieved not by viewing each situation *de novo*, but by viewing it diagnostically in light of already developed and tried theory. Managerial history, therefore, puts present-day managers on the shoulders of past learning, making it unnecessary for every manager to find his way anew from the labyrinth of managerial theory.

The history of management thought, then, finds its value in placing current problems in proper perspective and in providing advanced points of departure for managerial decision making.

SELECTED BIBLIOGRAPHY
OF MANAGEMENT LITERATURE

500-002 B.C.

Ramaswamy, T. N., *Essentials of Indian Statecraft.* London: Asia Publishing House, 1962.

Roman Farm Management, The Treatises of Cato and Varro, trans. by a Virginia farmer. New York: The Macmillan Company, 1913.

Shamasastry, R., trans., *Kautilya's Arthasastra.* Mysore: Sri Raghuveer Printing Press, 1956.

Xenophon, *Memorabilia and Oeconomicus,* trans. E. C. Marchant, Loeb Classical Library edition. Cambridge: Harvard University Press, n.d. Also published London: William Heinemann, Ltd., 1923,.

800-900 A.D.

Hammon, Robert, *The Philosophy of Alfarabi.* New York: The Hobson Book Press, 1947.

1000-1100

Bagley, F. R. C., trans., *Ghazali's Book of Counsel for Kings (Nasihat al-Muluk).* London: Oxford University Press. 1964.

1300-1350

Whitting, C. E. J., *Al Fakhri.* London: Luzac & Co., Ltd., 1947.

1400-1550

Machiavelli, Niccolo, *The Prince.* New York: Modern Library, Inc., 1940.
More, Sir Thomas, *Utopia,* ed. Edward Surtz, New Haven, Conn.: Yale University Press, 1964.
Pacioli, L., *Summa de arithmetica, geometria, proportioni, et proportionalia,* trans. R. G. Brown and K. S. Johnston in *Paciolo on Accounting.* New York: McGraw-Hill Book Company, 1963. Original published in Venice in 1494.

1675-1775

Savary, Jacques, *Le Parfait Negociant.* Paris: J. Guignard Fils, 1675.
——, *Universal Dictionary of Trade and Commerce,* with improvements by Malachy Postlethwayt. Paris: J. Guignard, 1755.
Steuart, Sir James, *An Inquiry into the Principles of Political Economy.* London: A. Millar & T. Cadell, 1767.
Turgot, Anne Robert, *Reflections on the Formation and the Distribution of Riches.* New York: The Macmillan Company, 1922. Original published in 1770.

1800-1850

Babbage, Charles, *On the Economy of Machinery and Manufactures.* London: Charles Knight, 1832.
Clausewitz, Karl von, *Principles of War.* Harrisburg: Military Service Publishing Company, 1832.
——, *On War.* New York: Barnes & Noble, Inc., n.d.
Dupin, Charles, *Discours sur le sort des ouvriers.* Paris: Bachelier, Libraire, 1831.
Mill, James, *Elements of Political Economy* (3rd ed.). London: Baldwin, Cradock, and Joy, 1826.
Newman, Samuel P., *Elements of Political Economy.* Andover: Gould and Newman, 1835.
Owen, Robert, *A New View of Society.* New York: E. Bliss & E. White, 1825.
Ricardo, David, *The Principles of Political Economy and Taxation.* New York: E. P. Dutton & Co., Inc., 1960. Original published in 1817.
Say, Jean Baptiste, *Catechism of Political Economy,* trans. John Richter. Philadelphia: M. Carey & Son, 1817.
Smith, Frederic, *Workshop Management: A Manual for Masters and Men* (3rd ed.). London: Wyman and Son, 1832.
Ure, Andrew, *The Philosophy of Manufactures.* London: Charles Knight, 1835.
Wilkinson, Sir Gardner, *Manners and Customs of Ancient Egyptains* (2nd ed.). London: John Murray (Publishers) Ltd., 1842.

1851-1875

Babbage, Charles, *Passages from the Life of a Philosopher.* London: Longmans Green & Co. Ltd., 1864.

Bishop, J. Leander, *A History of American Manufactures,* 2 vols. Philadelphia: E. Young and Company, 1861.

Bowen, Francis, *American Political Economy.* New York: Charles Scribner's Sons, 1870.

Denslow, van Buren, *Principles of the Economic Philosophy of Society, Government, and Industry,* London: Cassell & Co. Ltd., 1868.

Freedley, Edwin T., *A Practical Treatise on Business.* Philadelphia: J. B. Lippincott Co., 1854.

Owen, Robert, *The Life of Robert Owen,* 2 vols. London: Effingham & Wilson, 1857-8.

1876-1900

American Economic Association, *The Adjustment of Wages to Efficiency.* New York: The Macmillan Company, 1896.

Bohm-Bawerk, Eugen von, *Capital and Interest.* London: Macmillan & Co. Ltd., 1890.

Bowker, R. R., *Economics for the People.* New York: Harper & Bros., 1886.

Cooke-Taylor, R. W., *Introduction to a History of the Factory System.* London: Richard Bentley and Sons, 1886.

Dodge, Theodore A., *Great Captains.* Boston: Houghton Mifflin Company, 1892.

Durfee, W. F., "The History and Modern Development of the Art of Interchangeable Construction in Mechanism," *Journal of the Franklin Institute,* CXXXVII, No. 2.

Emerson, Harrington, *Efficiency as a Basis for Operation and Wages.* New York: The Engineering Magazine Co., 1900.

Erman, Adolf, *Life in Ancient Eygpt,* trans. Helen M. Tirard. London: Macmillan & Co. Ltd., 1894.

Gilman, Nicholas Paine, *Profit Sharing between Employer and Employee, A Study in the Evolution of the Wage System.* New York: Houghton Mifflin Company, 1889.

Ireland, G. H., *The Prevention and Causes of Diseases in Mills and Factories.* Washington, D.C.: American Public Health Association, 1886.

———, *The Preventable Causes of Disease, Injury and Death in American Manufactories and Workshops.* Concord, N.H.: Republican Press Association, 1886.

Jevons, W. S., *Theory of Political Economy.* London: Macmillan & Co. Ltd., 1888.

Laughlin, J. Lawrence, *The Elements of Political Economy.* New York: American Book Company, 1896.

Laveleye, Emile de, *The Elements of Political Economy,* trans. Alfred W. Pollard. New York: G. P. Putnam's Sons, 1884.

Marshall, Alfred, *Elements of Economics of Industry.* London: Macmillan & Co. Ltd., 1892.

Metcalfe, Henry, *The Cost of Manufactures and the Administration of Workshops Public and Private.* New York: John Wiley & Sons, Inc., 1885.

Watson, Rev. J. S., *Xenophon's Minor Works.* London: G. Bell & Sons, Ltd., 1898.

———, and Henry Dale, trans., *Xenophon's Cyropaedia and the Hellenics.* London: G. Bell & Sons, Ltd., 1898.

Wright, Carroll D., *Report on the Factory System of the United States.* Washington, D.C.: Government Printing Office, 1884.

1901-1905

Chapman, Sydney J., *The Lancaster Cotton Industry.* Manchester: University Press, 1904.

Cunningham, William, *The Growth of English Industry and Commerce in Modern Times.* London: Cambridge University Press, 1903.

Factory Sanitation and Labor Protection, U.S. Bureau of Labor, Bulletin No. 44. Washington, D.C., 1903.

Harper, Robert F., *The Code of Hammurabi, King of Babylon.* Chicago: University of Chicago Press, 1904.

Taylor, Frederick W., *Shop Management.* New York: Harper & Bros., 1903.

———, and S. E. Thompson, *Concrete, Plain and Reinforced.* New York: John Wiley & Sons, Inc., 1905.

Unwin, George, *Industrial Organization in the 16th and 17th Centuries.* Oxford: At the Clarendon Press, 1903.

Woods, C. E., *Organizing a Factory.* New York: The System Company, 1905.

1906-1910

Breasted, James H., *Ancient Records of Egypt.* Chicago: University of Chicago Press, 1906.

Buying: Purchasing for Factory, Store, and Office, Purchase Correspondence, Files and Systems. Chicago: A. W. Shaw Co., 1908.

Carpenter, Charles U., *Profit Making in Shop and Factory.* New York: The Engineering Magazine Co., 1908.

Diemer, Hugo, *Factory Organization and Administration.* New York: McGraw-Hill Book Company, 1910.

Galloway, Lee, *Organization and Management.* New York: McGraw-Hill Book Company, 1910.

Gantt, Henry Laurence, *Work, Wages and Profits.* New York: The Engineering Magazine Co., 1910.

Gilbreth, Frank B., *Bricklaying System.* New York: The Myron C. Clark Publishing Co., 1909.

——, *Concrete System.* New York: The Engineering New Publishing Co., 1908.

Tolman, William H., *Social Engineering.* New York: McGraw-Hill Book Company, 1909.

1911-1915

Blackford, K. M. H., and Arthur Newcomb, *The Job, The Man, The Boss.* New York: Doubleday & Company, Inc., 1915.

Brandeis, Louis D., *Business—A Profession.* Boston: Small, Maynard and Co., 1914.

——, *Scientific Management and Railroads.* New York: The Engineering Magazine Co., 1911.

Brisco, Norris A., *Economics of Efficiency.* New York: The Macmillan Company, 1914.

Business and the Public Welfare. New York: The Academy of Political Science, 1912.

Church, Alexander Hamilton, *The Science and Practice of Management.* New York: The Engineering Magazine Co., 1914.

Clark, J. B., *Social Justice without Socialism.* Boston: Houghton Mifflin Company, 1914.

Clewell, C. E., *Factory Lighting.* New York: McGraw-Hill Book Company, 1913.

Cooke, Morris L., "Spirit and Social Significance of Scientific Management," *Journal of Political Economy,* June 1913, p. 481.

Diemer, Hugo, *Factory Organization and Administration.* New York: McGraw-Hill Book Company., 1914.

Dodge, J. A., "A History of the Introduction of a System of Shop Management," in *Scientific Management,* C. Bertrand Thompson. Cambridge: Harvard University Press, 1914.

Drury, Horace B., *Scientific Management: A History and Criticism.* New York: Columbia University Press, 1915.

Duncan, John C., *The Principles of Industrial Management.* New York: D. Appleton and Company, 1911.

Emerson, Harrington, *Efficiency as a Basis for Operation and Wages.* New York: The Engineering Magazine Co., 1911.

——, *The Twelve Principles of Efficiency.* New York: The Engineering Magazine Co., 1913.

Ennis, W. D., *Works Management.* New York: McGraw-Hill Book Company, 1911.

Gilbreth, Frank B., *Motion Study.* New York: D. Van Nostrand Co., Inc., 1911.

——, *Primer of Scientific Management.* New York: D. Van Nostrand Co., Inc., 1912.

Gilbreth, L. M., *The Psychology of Management.* New York: Sturgis and Walton Co., 1914.

Godwin, E. B., *Developing Executive Ability.* New York: The Ronald Press Company, 1915.

———, *The Executive and His Control of Man.* New York: The Macmillan Company, 1915.

Going, C. B., *Principles of Industrial Engineering.* New York: McGraw-Hill Book Company, 1911.

Goldmark, Josephine, *Fatigue and Efficiency.* New York: Russell Sage Foundation, 1912.

Hartness, J., *The Human Factor in Works Management.* New York: McGraw-Hill Book Company, 1912.

Hoxie, R. F., *Scientific Management and Labor.* New York: D. Appleton and Company, 1915.

Huan-Chang, Chen, *The Economic Principles of Confucius and His School.* New York: Columbia University Press, 1911.

Jones, Edward D., *Industrial Leadership and Executive Ability.* New York: The Engineering Magazine Co., 1913.

———, *Industrial Leadership and Executive Ability: Its Models in War, Statecraft and Science.* New York: The Engineering Magazine Co., 1914.

Kendall, H. P., "Unsystematized, Systematized, and Scientific Management," in *Scientific Management,* C. Bertrand Thompson. Cambridge: Harvard University Press, 1914.

Kimball, D. S., *Principles of Industrial Organization.* New York: McGraw-Hill Book Company, 1913.

Law, Narendra Nath, *Studies in Ancient Hindu Polity.* London: Longmans, Green and Company, 1914.

Munsterberg, Hugo, *Psychology and Industrial Efficiency.* Boston: Houghton Mifflin Company, 1913.

Scientific Management, Addresses and discussions of the conference on scientific management held October 12-14, 1911. Hanover, N.H.: Amos Tuck School of Administration and Finance, Dartmouth College.

Scott, Walter Dill, *Increasing Human Efficiency in Business.* New York: The Macmillan Company, 1913.

Taylor, Frederick W., *The Principles of Scientific Management.* New York: Harper & Bros., 1911.

———, and S. E. Thompson, *Concrete Costs.* New York: John Wiley & Sons, Inc., 1912.

Technology and Industrial Efficiency, Section C, Proceedings of the Congress of Technology. New York: McGraw-Hill Book Company, 1911.

Thompson, C. Bertrand, *Scientific Management.* London: Oxford University Press, 1914.

Van Deventer, J. H., *Handbook of Machine Shop Management.* New York: McGraw-Hill Book Company, 1915.

1916-1920

Barrett, H. J., *Modern Methods in the Office.* New York: Harper & Bros., 1918.

Berriman, A. E., *et al.*, *Industrial Administration.* London: Longmans, Green & Co. Ltd., 1920.

Bloomfield, Daniel, *Selected Articles on Modern Industrial Movements.* New York: H. W. Wilson Co., 1919.

Bloomfield, Meyer, *Labor and Compensation.* New York: Industrial Extension Institute, Inc., 1917.

——, *Management and Men.* New York: The Century Company, 1919.

Cannons, H. G. T., *Bibliography of Industrial Efficiency and Factory Management.* London: Routledge & Kegan Paul Ltd., 1920.

Case, W. L., *The Factory Buildings.* New York: Industrial Extension Institute, Inc., 1919.

Chaney, L. W., and H. S. Hanna, *Accidents and Accident Prevention in Machine Building.* Washington, D.C.: Government Printing Office, 1917.

Church, Alexander Hamilton, *The Proper Distribution of Expense Burden.* New York: The Engineering Magazine Co., 1916.

——, *The Science and Practice of Management.* New York: The Engineering Magazine Co., 1916.

Clark, Victor, *History of Manufactures in the United States, 1607-1860.* New York: McGraw-Hill Book Company, 1916.

Clewell, C. E., *Handbook of Machine Shop Electricity.* New York: McGraw-Hill Book Company, 1916.

Cole, G. D. H., *The Payment of Wages.* London: George Allen and Unwin Ltd., 1918.

Denning, A. Du Pré, *Scientific Factory Management.* London: Nisbet & Co., 1919.

Dicksee, L. R., *Business Organization.* London: Longmans, Green & Co. Ltd., 1919.

Diemer, Hugo, *Industrial Organization and Management.* Chicago: LaSalle Extension University, 1919.

Emerson, Harrington, *Efficiency as a Basis for Operation and Wages.* New York: The Engineering Magazine Co., 1919.

Fayol, Henri, *Administration industrielle et générale.* Paris: Dunod, 1925. First English trans. 1929; 2nd trans. by Constance Storrs, London: Sir Isaac Pitman & Sons Ltd., 1949.

Fish, E. H., *How to Manage Men.* New York: The Engineering Magazine Co., 1920.

Galloway, L., *Office Management.* New York: The Ronald Press Company, 1919.

Gantt, Henry L., *Industrial Leadership.* New Haven, Conn.: Yale University Press, 1916.

——, *Organizing for Work.* New York: Harcourt, Brace and Howe, 1919.

Gerstenberg, C. W., *Principles of Business.* Englewood Cliffs, N.J.: Prentice-Hall, Inc., 1918.

Gilbreth, Frank B., *Fatigue Study.* New York: Sturgis & Walton Company, 1916.

Gilbreth, Frank B., and Lillian M. Gilbreth, *Applied Motion Study*. New York: Sturgis & Walton Company, 1917.

——, *Fatigue Study* (2nd ed.). New York: The Macmillan Company, 1919.

Gowin, E. B., *The Selection and Training of the Business Executive*. New York: The Macmillan Company, 1918.

Hammond, J. L., and Barbara Hammond, *The Town Laborer, 1760-1832*. London: Longmans, Green & Co. Ltd., 1917.

Herford, R. O., H. T. Hildage, and H. G. Jenkins, *Outlines of Industrial Administration*. London: Sir Isaac Pitman & Sons Ltd., 1920.

Hollingworth, H. L., and A. T. Poffenberger, *Applied Psychology*. New York: D. Appleton and Company., 1918.

Industrial Efficiency and Fatigue in British Munition Factories. Washington, D.C.: Government Printing Office, 1917.

Industrial Health and Efficiency, Ministry of Munitions. Washington, D.C.: Government Printing Office, 1919.

Jones, E. D., *The Administration of Industrial Enterprises*. New York: Longmans, Green & Co. Ltd., 1916.

Kimball, Dexter S., *Plant Management*. New York: Alexander Hamilton Institute, 1918.

Knoeppel, C. E., *Installing Efficiency Methods*. New York: The Engineering Magazine Co., 1919.

Lawson, F. M., *Industrial Control*. London: Sir Isaac Pitman & Sons Ltd., 1920.

Leffingwell, W. H., *Making the Office Pay*. Chicago: A. W. Shaw Co., 1919.

——, *Scientific Office Management*. Chicago: A. W. Shaw Co.

MacDonald, D. J., *Executive Training for Foremen*. New York: The Ronald Press Company, 1920.

Merrick, D. V., *Time Study as a Basis for Rate Setting*. New York: The Engineering Magazine Co., 1920.

Muscio, B., *Lectures on Industrial Administration*. London: Sir Isaac Pitman & Sons Ltd., 1920.

Parkhurst, F. A., *Applied Methods of Scientific Management*. New York: John Wiley & Sons, Inc., 1917.

Parsons, C. S., *Office Organization and Management*. Chicago: LaSalle Extension University, 1918.

Ripley, C. M., *Life in a Large Manufacturing Plant*. Schenectady: General Electric Co., 1919.

Scientific Business Management, Ministry of Reconstruction, Great Britain, 1919.

Shepard, George H., *The Application of Efficiency Principles*. New York: The Engineering Magazine Co., 1917.

Sparling, S. E., *Introduction to Business Organization*. New York: The Macmillan Company, 1919.

Szepesi, E., *Modern Methods in Textile Mills*. New York: Westinghouse Lamp Co., 1917.

Tead, Ordway, *Instincts in Industry*. Boston: Houghton Mifflin Company, 1918.

The Human Factor in Industrial Preparedness. Chicago: Western Efficiency Society, 1917.

The Practical Application of the Principles of Industrial Engineering. Chicago: Society of Industrial Engineers, 1920.

Thompson, C. B., *How to Find Factory Costs*. Chicago: A. W. Shaw, 1916.

———, *The Theory and Practice of Scientific Management*. Boston: Houghton Mifflin Company, 1917.

Wace, W. L., *The Factory Buildings*. New York: Industrial Extension Institute, 1919.

Webb, Sidney, *The Works Manager Today*. London: Longmans, Green & Co. Ltd., 1917.

Williams, Whiting, *What's on the Worker's Mind*. New York: Charles Scribner's Sons, 1920.

1921-1925

Alford, L. P., *Management's Handbook*. New York: The Ronald Press Company, 1923.

Allen, C. R., *The Foreman and His Job*. Philadelphia: J. B. Lippincott Co., 1922.

Ashley, Sir William, *The Economic Organization of England*. London: Longmans, Green & Co. Ltd., 1922.

Basset, W. R., *The Organization of Modern Business*. New York: Dodd, Mead & Co., 1921.

———, and J. Heywood, *Production Engineering and Cost Keeping for Machine Shops*. New York: McGraw-Hill Book Company, 1922.

Bloomfield, Daniel, *The Modern Executive*. New York: H. W. Wilson Co., 1924.

Bowden, Witt, *Industrial Society in England towards the End of the 18th Century*. New York: The Macmillan Company, 1925.

Budge, E. A. Wallis, *Babylonian Life and History* (2nd ed.). London: Religious Tract Society, 1924.

Cartmell, M., *Stores and Materials Control*. New York: The Ronald Press Company, 1922.

Church, Alexander H., *The Making of an Executive*. New York: D. Appleton and Company, 1923.

Clark, Wallace, *The Gantt Chart*. New York: The Ronald Press Company, 1922.

Cooke-Taylor, R. W., *Introduction to a History of the Factory System*. London: Longmans, Green & Co. Ltd., 1924.

Copley, Frank B., *Frederick W. Taylor: Father of Scientific Management*, Vols. I and II. New York: Harper & Bros., 1923.

Crowther, Samuel, *John H. Patterson: Pioneer in Industrial Welfare.* Garden City: Doubleday Page, 1923.

Drever, J., *The Psychology of Industry.* London: Methuen & Co. Ltd., 1921.

Dutton, H. P., *Business Organization and Management.* Chicago: A. W. Shaw Co., 1925.

———, *Factory Management.* New York: The Macmillan Company, 1924.

Edie, L. D., *Practical Psychology for Business Executives.* New York: H. W. Wilson Co., 1922.

Farnham, D. T., *America vs. Europe in Industry.* New York: The Ronald Press Company, 1921.

Fayol, Henri, *L'Incapacité administrative de l'état—les postes et télégraphes.* Paris: Dunod, 1925. (Originally published in *Revue Politique et Parlementaire,* March 1921).

Fleming, A. P. M., and H. J. Brocklehurst, *An Introduction to the Principles of Industrial Administration.* London: Sir Isaac Pitman & Sons Ltd., 1922.

Florence, P. S., *Economics of Fatigue and Unrest and the Efficiency of Labour in English and American Industry.* New York: Henry Holt and Co., 1924.

Fordham, T. B., and E. H. Tingley, *Organization and Budgetary Control in Manufacturing.* New York: The Ronald Press Company, 1924.

Gardiner, G. L., *Management in the Factory.* New York: McGraw-Hill Book Company, 1925.

Gerstenberg, C. W., and W. S. Johnson, *Business Organization.* New York: Alexander Hamilton Institute, 1921.

Gilbreth, Frank B., and Lillian M. Gilbreth, "Scientific Management in Other Countries than the United States," *Taylor Society Bulletin,* June 1924, p. 132.

———, "The Achievements of Motion Psychology," *Taylor Society Bulletin,* December 1924, p. 322.

Gilbreth, Lillian Moller, *The Quest of the One Best Way.* Chicago: Society of Industrial Engineers, 1924.

Grimshaw, R., *The Modern Foreman.* New York: Biddle Business Publications, Inc., 1921.

———, *Why Manufacturers Lose Money.* New York: D. Van Nostrand Co., Inc., 1922.

Hazard, Blanche, *The Organization of the Boot and Shoe Industry in Massachusetts before 1875.* Cambridge: Harvard University Press, 1921.

Hiscox, W. J., *Factory Administration in Practice.* London: Sir Isaac Pitman & Sons Ltd., 1921.

Hotelling, Harold, "A General Mathematical Theory of Depreciation," *Journal of the American Statistical Association,* December 1925, p. 340.

Hunt, Edward E., *Scientific Management Since Taylor.* New York: McGraw-Hill Book Company, 1924.

Kendall, H. P., "A Decade's Development in Management," *Taylor Society Bulletin,* April 1924, p. 55.

Knoeppel, C. E., *Organization and Administration.* New York: Industrial Extension Institute, 1921.

Lansburgh, R. H., *Industrial Management.* New York: John Wiley & Sons, Inc., 1923.

Lee, John, *Industrial Organization, Development and Prospects.* London: Sir Isaac Pitman & Sons Ltd., 1923.

——, *Management. A Study of Industrial Organization.* London: Sir Isaac Pitman & Sons Ltd., 1921.

Lichtner, W. O., *Planned Control in Manufacturing.* New York: The Ronald Press Company, 1924.

——, *Time Study and Job Analysis as Applied to Standardization of Methods and Operations.* New York: The Ronald Press Company, 1921.

Lord, John, *Capital and Steam Power.* London: P. S. King & Son, Ltd., 1923.

Marshall, L. C., *Business Administration.* Chicago: University of Chicago Press, 1921.

McKinsey, J. W., *Business Administration.* Cincinnati: South-Western Publishing Co., 1924.

Metcalf, H. C., and L. Urwick, *Dynamic Administration. The Collected Papers of Mary Parker Follett.* New York: Harper & Bros., 1924.

Munsterberg, Margaret, *Hugo Munsterberg, His Life and Work.* New York: D. Appleton and Company, 1922.

Myers, C. S., *Mind and Work.* New York: G. P. Putnam's Sons, 1921.

On the Extent and Effects of Variety in Repetitive Work, Industrial Fatigue Research Board. London: H. M. Stationery Office, 1924.

Owen, H. S., "How to Maintain Proper Inventory Control," *Industrial Management,* LXIX, 83.

Parsons, F. W., *American Business Methods for Increasing Production and Reducing Costs in Factory, Store and Office.* New York: G. P. Putnam's Sons, 1921.

Person, Harlow S., "On the Contribution of Scientific Management to Industrial Problems," *Taylor Society Bulletin,* June 1923, p. 116.

Porosky, M., *Practical Factory Administration.* New York: McGraw-Hill Book Company, 1923.

Power, E. E., *Medieval People.* Garden City: Doubleday Anchor Books, 1924.

Radford, G. S., *The Control of Quality in Manufacturing.* New York: The Ronald Press Company, 1922.

Robinson, Webster, *Fundamentals of Business Organization.* New York: McGraw-Hill Book Company, 1925.

Rose, H. W., *Primitive Culture in Greece.* London: Methuen & Co. Ltd., 1925.

Rowntree, B. S., *The Human Factor in Business.* London: Longmans, Green & Co. Ltd., 1921.

Schnell, E. H., *The Technique of Executive Control.* New York: McGraw-Hill Book Company, 1924.

Sheldon, Oliver, "The Art of Management," *Taylor Society Bulletin,* December 1923, p. 209.

——, *The Philosophy of Management.* London: Sir Isaac Pitman & Sons Ltd., 1923.

——, "Taylor the Creative Leader," *Taylor Society Bulletin,* February 1924, p. 5.

Timbie, W. H., *Industrial Electricity: Direct Current Machines.* New York: John Wiley & Sons, Inc., 1924.

Time and Motion Study, Industrial Fatigue Research Board. London: H. M. Stationery Office, 1921.

Towne, Henry R., "The Evolution of Industrial Management," *Factory and Industrial Management,* April 1921, p. 231.

Unwin, George, *Samuel Oldknow and the Arkwrights.* Manchester: The University Press, 1924.

Veblen, Thorstein, *The Engineers and the Price System.* New York: B. W. Huebsch, Inc., 1921.

Vernon, H. M., *Industrial Fatigue and Efficiency.* New York: E. P. Dutton & Co., Inc., 1921.

Ware, Norman J., *The Industrial Worker, 1840-1860.* Boston: Houghton Mifflin Company, 1924.

Waste in Industry, Federated American Engineering Societies. New York: McGraw-Hill Book Company, 1921.

Weaver, A., *Office Organization and Practice.* Boston: Ginn and Company, 1923.

Wera, E., *Human Engineering.* New York: D. Appleton and Company, 1921.

1926-1930

Alford, L. P., *Laws of Management Applied to Manufacturing.* New York: The Ronald Press Company, 1928.

——, *Henry Laurence Gantt, Leader in Industry.* New York: Harper & Bros., 1934.

Anderson, A. C., *Industrial Engineering and Factory Management.* New York: The Ronald Press Company, 1928.

Atkins, P. M., *Factory Management.* Englewood Cliffs, N.J.: Prentice-Hall, Inc., 1926.

Austin, B., and W. F. Floyd, *The Secret of High Wages.* New York: Dodd, Mead & Co., 1926.

Bangs, J. R., and C. F. Hart, *Factory Management.* New York: Alexander Hamilton Institute, 1930.

Bowers, E. L., *Is It Safe to Work?* Boston: Houghton Mifflin Company, 1930.

Business Management as a Profession, ed. Henry C. Metcalf. Chicago: A. W. Shaw Co., 1927.

Calhoun, George M., *The Ancient Greeks and the Evolution of Standards in Business.* Boston: Houghton Mifflin Company, 1926.

Chi-Chao, Liang, *History of Chinese Political Thought.* New York: Harcourt, Brace & Co., 1930.

Cooper, Benjamin, "How to Determine Economical Manufacturing Quantities," *Industrial Management,* LXXII (1926) 228.

Cornell, William B., *Organization and Management in Industry and Business.* New York: The Ronald Press Company, 1928.

Davis, Ralph C., *The Principles of Factory Organization and Management.* New York: Harper & Bros., 1928.

Devinat, P. E., *Scientific Management in Europe.* Geneva: International Labor Office, 1927.

Erman, Adolf, *The Literature of the Ancient Egyptians.* New York: E. P. Dutton & Co., Inc., 1927.

Fry, T. C., *Probability and Its Engineering Uses.* New York: D. Van Nostrand Co., Inc., 1928.

Glotz, Gustave, *Ancient Greece at Work.* New York: Alfred A. Knopf, Inc., 1926.

Hamilton, Henry, *The English Brass and Copper Industries to 1800.* London: Longmans, Green & Co. Ltd., 1926.

Keir, Robert Malcolm, *Manufacturing.* New York: The Ronald Press Company, 1928.

Kendall, H. P., "Development of the Art and Science and Philosophy of Management Since Taylor," *Coal Age,* March 1930, p. 163.

Lewis, W., "Fifty Years of Scientific Management," *Manufacturing Industries,* April 1928, p. 249.

Metcalf, Henry C., *Scientific Foundations of Business Administration.* Baltimore: The Williams & Wilkins Co., 1926.

Mill, John Stuart, *Principles of Political Economy,* ed. Sir W. J. Ashley. London: Longmans, Green & Co. Ltd., 1926.

Person, H. S., ed., *Scientific Management in American Industry.* New York: Harper & Bros., 1929.

Recent Economic Changes in the United States, Vols. I and II. New York: McGraw-Hill Book Company, 1929.

Roe, Joseph W., *English and American Tool Builders.* New York: McGraw-Hill Book Company, 1926.

Roll, Erich, *An Early Experiment in Industrial Organization.* London: Longmans, Green & Co. Ltd., 1930.

Saunders, Alta G., ed., *The Literature of Business* (3rd ed.). New York: Harper & Bros., 1928.

Schell, E. H., and H. H. Thurlby, *Problems in Industrial Management.* Chicago: A. W. Shaw Co., 1927.

Schwenning, G. T., ed., *Management Problems.* Chapel Hill: The University of North Carolina Press, 1930.

Toutain, Jules, *The Economic Life of the Ancient World.* New York: Alfred A. Knopf, Inc., 1930.

Usher, Abbott P., *A History of Mechanical Inventions.* New York: McGraw-Hill Book Company, 1929.

Wu, Kuo-Cheng, *Ancient Chinese Political Theories.* Shanghai: The Commercial Press, Ltd., 1928.

1931-1935

Alford, Leon P., *Henry Laurence Gantt, Leader in Industry.* New York: Harper & Bros., 1934.

Balderston, C. C., V. S. Karabasz, and R. P. Brecht, *Management of an Enterprise.* Englewood Cliffs, N.J.: Prentice-Hall, Inc., 1935.

Barnes, Ralph M., *Industrial Engineering and Management, Problems and Policies.* New York: McGraw-Hill Book Company, 1931.

Benge, E. J., *Cutting Clerical Costs.* New York: McGraw-Hill Book Company, 1931.

Burn, D. L., "The Genesis of American Engineering Competition," *Economic History,* Vol. II, January 1931.

Dennison, H. S., *Organization Engineering.* New York: McGraw-Hill Book Company, 1931.

Dutton, H. P., *Principles of Organization as Applied to Business.* New York: McGraw-Hill Book Company, 1931.

Gaillard, J., *Industrial Standardization.* New York: H. W. Wilson Co., 1934.

Gras, N. S. B., "The Rise of Big Business," *Journal of Economic and Business History,* Vol. IV., (1932), p. 381.

Lane, Frederic C., *Venetian Ships and Shipbuilders of the Renaissance.* Baltimore: The Johns Hopkins Press, 1934.

Mayo, George Elton, *The Human Problems of an Industrial Civilization.* Boston: Division of Research, Harvard Business School, 1933.

Mooney, J.D., and A. C. Reiley, *Onward Industry!* New York: Harper & Bros., 1931.

Raymond, F. E., *Quantity and Economy in Manufacturing.* New York: McGraw-Hill Book Company, 1931.

Shlakman, Vera, *Economic History of a Factory Town.* Northhampton, Mass.: Smith College Studies in History, 1934.

Tead, Ordway, *The Art of Leadership.* New York: McGraw-Hill Book Company, 1935.

——, *Creative Management.* New York: Association Press, 1935.

Viteles, Morris S., *Industrial Psychology.* New York: W. W. Norton & Company, Inc., 1932.

Ware, Caroline F., *The Early New England Cotton Manufacturer.* Boston: Houghton Mifflin Company, 1931.

Westbrook, F. A., *Industrial Management in This Machine Age.* New York: Thomas Y. Crowell Company, 1932.

1936-1940

Alford, L. P., *Principles of Industrial Management for Engineers.* New York: The Ronald Press Company, 1940.

Anderson, E. H., *The Process of Internal Organization.* Chapel Hill: The University of North Carolina Press, 1937.

——, and G. T. Schwenning, *The Science of Production Organization.* New York: John Wiley & Sons, Inc., 1938.

Baldwin, Summerfield, *Business in the Middle Ages.* New York: Henry Holt and Co., 1937.

Barnard, Chester I., *The Functions of the Executive.* Cambridge: Harvard University Press, 1938.

——, *The Nature of Leadership.* Cambridge: Harvard University Press, 1940.

Barnes, H. E., *An Economic History of the Western World.* New York: Harcourt, Brace & Co., 1937.

Durant, Will, *The Story of Civilization,* Vol. II, *The Life of Greece.* New York: Simon and Schuster, Inc., 1939.

Gillespie, James J., *The Principles of Rational Industrial Management.* London: Sir Isaac Pitman and Sons Ltd., 1938.

Gilson, Mary B., *What's Past Is Prologue: Reflections on My Industrial Experience.* New York: Harper & Bros., 1940.

Gulick, L., and L. Urwick, eds., *Papers on the Science of Administration.* New York: Institute of Public Administration, Columbia University, 1937.

Lipson, Ephraim, *An Introduction to Economic History of England.* London: A. & C. Black, Limited, 1937.

McCormick, Charles P., *Multiple Management.* New York: Harper & Bros., 1938.

Mitchell, W. N., *Organization and Management of Production.* New York: McGraw-Hill Book Company, 1939.

Mooney, J. D., and A. C. Reiley, *The Principles of Organization.* New York: Harper & Bros., 1939.

Phillips, T., *Roots of Strategy.* Harrisburg: Military Service Publishing Co., 1940.

Roethlisberger, F. J., and W. J. Dickson, *Management and the Worker.* Cambridge: Harvard University Press, 1939.

Smith, Adam, *An Inquiry into the Nature and Causes of the Wealth of Nations.* New York: Modern Library, Inc., 1937.

Spaulding, O., *Pen and Sword in Greece and Rome.* Princeton, N. J.: Princeton University Press, 1937.

1941-1945

Benge, E. J., *Job Evaluation and Merit Rating.* New York: National Foreman's Institute, 1941.

Benson, B. E., *Music and Sound Systems in Industry*. New York: McGraw-Hill Book Company, 1945.

Bienstock, G., *et al., Management in Russian Industry and Agriculture*. London: Oxford University Press, 1944.

Burnham, James, *Managerial Revolution*. New York: The John Day Company, Inc., 1941.

Cochran, Thomas C., and William Miller, *The Age of Enterprise*. New York: The Macmillan Company, 1944.

Dietz, Frederick C., *An Economic History of England*. New York: Henry Holt and Co., 1942.

Gardner, B. B., *Human Relations in Industry*. Homewood, Ill.: Richard D. Irwin, Inc., 1945.

Holden, P. E., L. S. Fish, and H. L. Smith, *Top Management Organization and Control*. Stanford, Calif.: Stanford University Press, 1941.

Lane, Frederic C., *Andrea Barbarigo: Merchant of Venice (1418-1449)*. Baltimore: Johns Hopkins Press, 1944.

Mayo, George Elton, *The Social Problems of an Industrial Civilization*. Boston: Division of Research, Harvard Business School, 1945.

Metcalf, Henry C., and Lyndall Urwick, *Dynamic Administration—The Collected Papers of Mary Follett*. New York: Harper & Bros., 1942.

Roethlisberger, F. J., *Management and Morale*. Cambridge: Harvard University Press, 1941.

Sloan, Alfred P., Jr., *Adventures of a White Collar Man*. New York: Doubleday & Co., Inc., 1941.

Urwick, L., *The Elements of Administration*. New York: Harper & Bros., 1944.

Wright, C. W., *Economic History of the United States*. New York: McGraw-Hill Book Company, 1941.

1946-1950

Arakelian, A., *Industrial Management in U.S.S.R.* Washington, D.C.: Public Affairs Press, 1950.

Bakke, E. Wight, *Bonds of Organization*. New York: Harper & Bros., 1950.

Barnard, Chester I., *Organization and Management*. Cambridge: Harvard University Press, 1948.

Beishline, John R., *Military Management for National Defense*. Englewood Cliffs, N. J.: Prentice-Hall, Inc., 1950.

Bower, M., *The Development of Executive Leadership*. Cambridge: Harvard University Press, 1949.

Brech, E. F. L., *Management: Its Nature and Significance*. London: Sir Isaac Pitman & Sons, 1946.

Brockmeyer, E., H. L. Halztrom, and A. Jensen, *The Life and Works of A. K. Erlang*. Copenhagen: Copenhagen Telephone Co., 1948.

Brown, Alvin, *Organization of Industry*. Englewood Cliffs, N.J.: Prentice-Hall, Inc., 1947.

Burlingame, Roger, *Backgrounds of Power.* New York: Charles Scribner's Sons, 1949.

Chase, S., S. H. Ruttenberg, E. G. Nourse, and William Given, Jr., *The Social Responsibility of Management.* New York: New York University, School of Commerce, Accounts and Finance, 1950.

Chevalier, J., and Louis Pehuet, *L'Organisation du travail en France depuis cent ans.* Paris: Comité National de l'Organisation Française, 1949.

Cleeton, G. U., and C. W. Mason, *Executive Ability.* Yellow Springs, Ohio: The Antioch Press Publishers, 1947.

Dalla Valle, J. M., *The Industrial Environment and Its Control.* New York: Pitman Publishing Corp., 1948.

Drucker, Peter, *Concept of the Corporation.* New York: The John Day Company, Inc., 1946.

Filipetti, George, *Industrial Management in Transition.* Homewood, Ill.: Richard D. Irwin, Inc., 1946.

Follett, Mary Parker, *Freedom and Coordination.* London: Management Publications Trust, 1949.

Gilbreth, L. M., and A. R. Cook, *The Foremen in Manpower Management.* New York: McGraw-Hill Book Company, 1947.

Hammond, Robert, *The Philosophy of Alfarabi.* New York: The Hobson Book Press, 1947.

Hittle, J. D., *The Military Staff: Its History and Development.* Harrisburg: Military Service Publishing Co., 1949.

Hopf, Harry A., *Historical Perspective in Management.* New York: Hinkhouse, Inc., 1947.

Johnson, Gerald W., *Liberal's Progress.* New York: Coward-McCann, Inc., 1948.

Larson, Henrietta, *Guide to Business History.* Cambridge: Harvard University Press, 1950.

LePawsky, A., *Administration, The Art and Science of Organization and Management.* New York: Alfred A. Knopf, Inc., 1949.

Machiavelli, Niccolo, *The Prince and the Discourses.* New York: Random House, Inc., 1950.

Martindell, Jackson, *The Scientific Appraisal of Management.* New York: Harper & Bros., 1950.

McCormick, Charles P., *The Power of People, Multiple Management Up to Date.* New York: Harper & Bros., 1949.

McDonald, John E., *Strategy in Poker, Business and War.* New York: W. W. Norton & Company, Inc., 1950.

Mooney, James D., *Principles of Organization* (rev. ed.). New York: Harper & Bros., 1947.

Navin, Thomas R., *The Whitin Machine Works Since 1831.* Cambridge: Harvard University Press, 1950.

Nehru, Jawaharlal, *The Discovery of India.* London: The Signet Press, 1946.

Piggot, Stuart, *Prehistoric India.* Middlesex: The Penguin Books, Ltd., 1950.

Simon, Herbert A., *Administrative Behavior. A Study of Decision-Making Processes in Administrative Organization.* New York: The Macmillan Company, 1947.

Swann, Nancy Lee, *Food and Money in Ancient China.* Princeton, N.J.: Princeton University Press, 1950.

Urwick, Lyndall, and E. F. L. Brech, *The Making of Scientific Management,* Vol. III. London: Management Publications Trust, 1948.

Watts, Thomas, *An Essay on the Proper Method for Forming the Man of Business 1716.* Boston: The Kress Library of Business and Economics, 1946.

Whitting, C. E. J., *Al Fakhri.* London: Luzac & Co., Ltd., 1947.

Yutang, Lin, *The Gay Genius.* New York: The John Day Company, Inc., 1947.

1951-1955

Allen, Frederick L., *The Big Change.* New York: Harper & Bros., 1952.

Argyris, Chris, *Executive Leadership.* New York: Harper & Bros., 1953.

Berle, Adolf, Jr., *The 20th Century Capitalist Revolution.* New York: Harcourt Brace Jovanovich, Inc., 1954.

Bowen, H. B., *Social Responsibilities of the Businessman.* New York: Harper & Bros., 1953.

Bright, James R., *Automation and Management.* Boston: Division of Research, Graduate School of Business Administration, Harvard University, 1954.

Caldwell, W., and W. McDermott, *Readings in the History of the Ancient World.* New York: Holt, Rinehart, 1951.

Childe, V. G., *Man Makes Himself.* New York: The New American Library, 1951.

Clough, Shepard B., *The Rise and Fall of Civilization: An Inquiry into the Relationship between Economic Development and Civilization.* New York: McGraw-Hill Book Company, 1951.

Cole, Margaret, *Robert Owen of New Lanark.* London: Batchworth Press, 1953.

Contenau, Georges, *Everyday Life in Babylon and Assyria.* London: Edward Arnold (Publishers) Ltd., 1954.

Dale, Ernest, *Planning and Developing the Company Organization Structure.* New York: American Management Association, 1952.

Davis, Ralph C., *Industrial Organization and Management.* New York: Harper & Bros., 1951.

——, *The Fundamentals of Top Management.* New York: Harper & Bros., 1951.

Diebold, John, and George Terborgh, *Automation—the Advent of the Automatic Factory.* New York: D. Van Nostrand Co., Inc., 1952.

Drucker, Peter F., *The Practice of Management.* New York: Harper & Bros., 1954.

Friedman, Georges, *Industrial Society.* Glencoe, Ill.: The Free Press, 1955.

Given, William B., Jr., *Reaching Out in Management.* New York: Harper & Bros., 1953.

Glover, J. G., *Fundamentals of Professional Management.* New York: Republic Book Company, 1954.

Growth of the American Economy (2nd ed.), ed. Harold Williamson. Englewood Cliffs, N.J.: Prentice-Hall, Inc., 1951.

Hodnett, Edward, *The Art of Problem Solving.* New York: Harper & Bros., 1955.

Jacques, Elliott, *The Changing Culture of a Factory.* London: Tavistock Publications, Ltd., 1951.

Johnson, Ellis A., *The Application of Operations Research to Industry.* Chevy Chase: Operations Research Office, 1955.

Koontz, H., and C. O'Donnell, *Principles of Management.* New York: McGraw-Hill Book Company, 1955.

Lane, F. C., and J. Riemersma, *Enterprise and Secular Change.* Homewood, Ill.: Richard D. Irwin, Inc., 1953.

Learned, E. P., D. N. Ulrich, and D. R. Booz, *Executive Action.* Boston: Graduate School of Business Administration, Harvard University, 1951.

Lincoln, James F., *Incentive Management.* Cleveland: The Lincoln Electric Co., 1951.

McCloskey, Joseph F., and Florence N. Trefethen, eds., *Operations Research for Management.* Baltimore: The Johns Hopkins Press, 1954.

Mirsky, J., and Allan Nevins, *The World of Eli Whitney.* New York: The Macmillan Company, 1952.

Nadworny, Milton J., *Scientific Management and the Unions, 1900-1932.* Cambridge: Harvard University Press, 1955.

Newcomer, Mabel, *The Big Business Executive.* New York: Columbia University Press, 1955.

Newman, William H., *Administrative Action. The Techniques of Organization and Management.* Englewood Cliffs, N.J.: Prentice-Hall, Inc., 1951.

Osborn, Alexander F., *Applied Imagination, Principles and Procedures of Creative Thinking.* New York: Charles Scribner's Sons, 1953.

Rose, T. C., *A History of the Institute of Industrial Administration.* London: Sir Isaac Pitman & Sons Ltd., 1954.

Ross, J. B., and M. M. McLaughlin, *The Portable Medieval Reader.* New York: The Viking Press, Inc., 1953.

Sampson, Robert C., *The Staff Role in Management.* New York: Harper & Bros., 1955.

Smiddy, Harold F., and Lionel Meum. "Evolution of a Science of Managing in America," *Management Science,* Vol. I, October 1954.

Stevens Institute of Technology, *Classified Guide to the Taylor Collection.* New York: American Society of Mechanical Engineers, 1951.

Tead, Ordway, *The Art of Administration*. New York: McGraw-Hill Book Company, 1951.

Terry, George R., *Principles of Management*. Homewood, Ill.: Richard D. Irwin, Inc., 1953.

The Development of Executive Talent, ed. J. Dooher. New York: American Management Association, 1952.

The Writings of the Gilbreths, ed. William R. Spriegel and Clark E. Myers. Homewood, Ill.: Richard D. Irwin, Inc., 1953.

Wilson, John A., *The Culture of Ancient Egypt*. Chicago: University of Chicago Press, 1951.

1956-1960

Ackoff, Russell L., "The Development of Operations Research as a Science," *Operations Research*, IV, June 1956, 265.

Aitken, Hugh G. J., *Taylorism at Watertown Arsenal*. Cambridge: Harvard University Press, 1960.

Allen, Louis A., *Management and Organization*. New York: McGraw-Hill Book Company, 1958.

Argyris, Chris, *Personality and Organization*. New York: Harper & Bros., 1957.

Barnett, Homer G., *Anthropology in Administration*. Evanston, Ill.: Row, Peterson & Company, 1956.

Beer, Stafford, *Cybernetics and Management*. New York: John Wiley & Sons, Inc., 1959.

Bendix, Reinhard, *Work and Authority in Industry*. New York: John Wiley & Sons, Inc., 1956.

Berliner, Joseph S., *Factory and Manager in the U.S.S.R.* Cambridge: Harvard University Press, 1957.

Bowman, E. H., and R. B. Fetter, *Analysis for Production Management*. Homewood, Ill.: Richard D. Irwin, Inc., 1957.

Brech, E. F. L., *Organization: The Framework of Management*. London: Longmans, Green & Co. Ltd., 1957.

Bright, James R., *Automation and Management*. Cambridge: Harvard University Press, 1958.

Business and Religion: A New Depth Dimension in Management, ed. Edward C. Bursk, New York: Harper & Bros., 1959.

Butterfield, H., *The Statecraft of Machiavelli*. London: G. Bell & Sons, Ltd., 1960.

Chandler, Alfred D., "Beginnings of Big Business," *Business History Review*, XXXIII, No. 1.

Churchman, C. West, Russell L. Ackoff, and E. Leonard Arnoff, *Introduction to Operations Research*. New York: John Wiley & Sons, Inc., 1957.

Cochran, Thomas C., *The American Business System: An Historical Perspective, 1900-1955*. Cambridge: Harvard University Press, 1957.

Cordiner, Ralph J., *New Frontiers for Professional Managers.* New York: McGraw-Hill Book Company, 1956.

Cornford, Francis, *The Republic of Plato.* New York: Oxford University Press, Inc., 1959.

Dale, Ernest, "DuPont: Pioneer in Systematic Management," *Administrative Science Quarterly,* Vol. II, June 1957.

——, *The Great Organizers.* New York: McGraw-Hill Book Company, 1960.

Dalton, Melville, *Men Who Manage.* New York: John Wiley & Sons, Inc., 1959.

Dimock, Marshall E., *A Philosophy of Administration toward Creative Growth.* New York: Harper & Bros., 1958.

"Early Phases of the Management Movement," *Administrative Science Quarterly,* Vol. V.

Elliott, Osborn, *Men at the Top: A New Look at American Enterprise and the Men Who Run It.* New York: Harper & Bros., 1959.

Fifty Years of Progress in Management, ed. O. Sizelove and M. Anderson. New York: American Society of Mechanical Engineers, 1960.

Gager, Curtis H., "Management throughout History," in *Top Management Handbook,* H. B. Maynard, ed. New York: McGraw-Hill Book Company, 1960.

Ginzberg, Eli, and Dwing W. Reilley, *Effecting Change in Large Organizations.* New York: Columbia University Press, 1957.

Goodman, L. Landon, *Man and Automation.* London: Pelican Books, 1957.

Granick, David, *The Red Executive.* Garden City, N. Y.: Doubleday & Company, Inc., 1960.

Green, Constance, *Eli Whitney and the Birth of American Technology.* Boston: Little, Brown and Company, 1956.

Greenwalt, C. H., *The Uncommon Man.* New York: McGraw-Hill Book Company, 1959.

Haire, Manson, *Modern Organization Theory.* New York: John Wiley & Sons, Inc., 1959.

Harbison, Frederick H., and Charles A. Myers, *Management in the Industrial World: An International Analysis.* New York: McGraw-Hill Book Company, 1959.

Hartman, Heinz, *Authority and Organization in German Management.* Princeton, N.J.: Princeton University Press, 1959.

Hays, Samuel P., *The Response to Industrialiam, 1885-1914.* Chicago: University of Chicago Press, 1957.

Hesiodus, *Works and Days,* trans. Richmond A. Lattimore. Ann Arbor: The University of Michigan Press, 1959.

Houser, Theodore V., *Big Business and Human Value.* New York: McGraw-Hill Book Company, 1957.

Jaffee, William J., *L. P. Alford and the Evolution of Modern Industrial Management.* New York: New York University Press, 1957.

Jones, Manley H., *Executive Decision Making.* Homewood, Ill.: Richard D. Irwin, Inc., 1957.

Jucius, Michael J., and William E. Schlender, *Elements of Managerial Action.* Homewood, Ill.: Richard D. Irwin, Inc., 1960.

Kirkland, Edward C., *Dream and Thought in the Business Community, 1860-1900.* Ithaca: Cornell University Press, 1956.

Kosambi, D. D., *Indian History.* Bombay: Popular Book Depot, 1956.

Latil, Pierre de, *Thinking by Machine.* Boston: Houghton Mifflin Company, 1957.

Leavitt, Harold J., *Managerial Psychology.* Chicago: University of Chicago Press, 1958.

Littleton, A. C., and B. S. Yamey, *Studies in the History of Accounting* Homewood, Ill.: Richard D. Irwin, Inc., 1956.

Long Range Planning for Management, ed. David W. Ewing. New York: Harper and Bros., 1958.

Management's Mission in a New Society, ed. Dan H. Fenn, Jr. New York: McGraw-Hill Book Company, 1959.

March, J. G., and H. A. Simon, *Organization.* New York: John Wiley & Sons, Inc., 1958.

McFarland, Dalton E., *Management Principles and Practices.* New York: The Macmillan Company, 1958.

McGregor, Douglas, *The Human Side of Enterprise.* New York: McGraw-Hill Book Company, 1960.

Merrihue, Willard V., *Managing by Communication.* New York: McGraw-Hill Book Company, 1960.

Merrill, Harwood F., ed., *Classics in Management.* New York: American Management Association, 1960.

Mills, Charles Wright, *The Power Elite.* New York, Oxford University Press, Inc., 1956.

Morley, Felix, *Essays on Individuality.* Philadelphia: University of Pennsylvania Press, 1958.

Neuschel, Richard F., *Management by System.* New York: McGraw-Hill Book Company, 1960.

Niles, Mary C., *The Essence of Management.* New York: Harper & Bros., 1958.

Oliver, John W., *History of American Technology.* New York: The Ronald Press Company, 1956.

Pigors, Paul, and Charles A. Myers, *Personnel Administration.* New York: McGraw-Hill Book Company, 1956.

Richards, M. D., and W. A. Nielander, *Readings in Management.* Cincinnati: South-Western Publishing Co., 1958.

Roethlisberger, F. J., and W. Dickson, *Management and the Worker.* Cambridge: Harvard University Press, 1956.

Rowland, Virgil K., *Improving Managerial Performance.* New York: Harper & Bros., 1958.

Roy, Robert H., *The Administrative Process.* Baltimore: The Johns Hopkins Press, 1958.

Sasieni, M., A. Yaspan, and L. Friedman, *Operations Research.* New York: John Wiley & Sons, Inc., 1959.

Selekman, Benjamin M., *A Moral Philosophy for Management.* New York: McGraw-Hill Book Company, 1959.

Selekman, Sylvia K., and Benjamin M. Selekman, *Power and Morality in a Business Society.* New York: McGraw-Hill Book Company, 1956.

Selznick, Philip, *Leadership in Administration.* Evanston, Ill.: Row, Peterson & Company, 1957.

Shartle, Carroll, *Executive Performance and Leadership.* Englewood Cliffs, N. J.: Prentice-Hall, Inc., 1956.

Shull, Fremont A., Jr., *Selected Readings in Management.* Homewood, Ill.: Richard D. Irwin, Inc., 1958.

Simon, Herbert A., *Administrative Behavior: A Study of Decision-Making Processes in Administrative Organization* (2nd ed.). New York: The Macmillan Company, 1957.

——, *Models of Man.* New York: John Wiley & Sons, Inc., 1957.

——, *The New Science of Management Decision.* New York: Harper & Row, 1960.

Strauss, Leo, *Thoughts on Machiavelli.* Glencoe, Ill.: The Free Press, 1958.

Summer, Charles E., Jr., *Factors in Effective Administration.* New York: Graduate School of Business, Columbia University, 1956.

Sutton, Francis X., *et al., The American Business Creed.* Cambridge: Harvard University Press, 1956.

Tarn, W. W., *Alexander the Great.* Boston: Beacon Press, 1957.

Thompson, Stewart, *Management Creeds and Philosophies.* New York: American Management Association, 1958.

Toynbee, Arnold, *The Industrial Revolution.* Boston: Beacon Press, 1956.

Urwick, L., *The Golden Book of Management.* London: Newman Neame, Ltd., 1956.

——, *The Pattern of Management.* Minneapolis: University of Minnesota Press, 1956.

Von Frange, Eugene K., *Professional Creativity.* Englewood Cliffs, N.J.: Prentice-Hall, Inc., 1959.

Weber, Clarence A., and J. W. Karnes, *Industrial Leadership.* Philadelphia: Chilton Book Division, 1959.

1961-1965

Ackoff, Russell L., and Patrick Rivett, *A Manager's Guide to Operations Research.* New York: John Wiley & Sons, Inc., 1963.

Albers, Henry H., *Principles of Organization and Management* (2nd ed.). New York: John Wiley & Sons, Inc., 1965.

Argyris, Chris, *Integrating the Individual and the Organization.* New York: John Wiley & Sons, Inc., 1964.

Bagley, F. R. C., trans., *Ghazali's Book of Counsel for Kings.* London: Oxford University Press, 1964.

Bartels, Robert, *The Development of Marketing Thought.* Homewood, Ill.: Richard D. Irwin, Inc., 1962.

Beard, Miriam, *A History of Business,* Vols. I and II. Ann Arbor: The University of Michigan Press, 1962 and 1963.

Bittel, Lester R., *Management by Exception.* New York: McGraw-Hill Book Company, 1964.

Blake, Robert R., Herbert A. Shepard, and Jane S. Moulton, *Managing Intergroup Conflict in Industry.* Houston, Texas: Gulf Publishing Co., 1964.

Blau, Peter M., and W. Richard Scott, *Formal Organizations.* San Francisco: Chandler Publishing Co., 1962.

Borow, Henry, ed., *Man in a World at Work.* Boston: Houghton Mifflin Company, 1964.

Boulding, Kenneth E., Carl H. Voss, and Walter A. Kaufmann, *Ethics and Business.* University Park: College of Business Administration, Pennsylvania State University, 1962.

Brown, R. G., and K. S. Johnston, *Paciolo on Accounting.* New York: McGraw-Hill Book Company, 1963.

Chandler, Alfred D., Jr., *The Railroads—The Nation's First Big Business.* New York: Harcourt, Brace & World, Inc., 1965.

Clough, Donald J., *Concepts in Management Science.* Englewood Cliffs, N.J.: Prentice-Hall, Inc., 1963.

Daiute, Robert James, *Scientific Management and Human Relations.* New York: Holt, Rinehart & Winston, Inc., 1964.

Dale, Ernest, *Readings in Management: Landmarks and New Frontiers.* New York: McGraw-Hill Book Company, 1965.

Dauten, Paul M., Jr., ed., *Current Issues and Emerging Concepts in Management.* New York: Houghton Mifflin Company, 1962.

Drucker, Peter, *Managing for Results: Economic Tasks and Risk-Taking Decisions.* New York: Harper & Row, Publishers, 1964.

Ewing, John S., and Frank Meissner, *International Business Management.* Belmont, Calif.: Wadsworth Publishing Co., 1964.

Garret, T. M., *Ethics in Business.* New York: Sheed & Ward, 1963.

George, Claude S., *Management in Industry* (2nd ed.). Englewood Cliffs, N.J.: Prentice-Hall, Inc., 1964.

Golembiewski, Robert T., *Men, Management and Morality.* New York: McGraw-Hill Book Company, 1965.

Granick, David, *The European Executive.* Garden City, N.Y.: Doubleday & Company, Inc., 1962.

Haber, Samuel, *Efficiency and Uplift: Scientific Management in the Progressive Era, 1890-1930.* Chicago: University of Chicago Press, 1964.

Haimann, Theo., *Professional Management—Theory and Practice.* Boston: Houghton Mifflin Company, 1962.

Haire, Mason, *Organization Theory in Industrial Practice*. New York: John Wiley & Sons, Inc., 1962.

Haynes, W. Warren, and Joseph L. Massie, *Management Analysis, Concepts and Cases*. Englewood Cliffs, N.J.: Prentice-Hall, Inc., 1961.

Houn, Franklin W., *Chinese Political Traditions*. Washington, D.C.: Public Affairs Press, 1965.

Juran, J. M., *Managerial Breakthrough*. New York: McGraw-Hill Book Company, 1964.

Koontz, H., ed., *Toward a Unified Theory of Management*. New York: McGraw-Hill Book Company, 1964.

Kosiol, Erich, *Organization der Unternehmung*. Wiesbaden: Betriebswirtschaftlicher Verlag Dr. Th. Gabler GmbH., 1962.

Lemke, B. C., and James D. Edwards, *Administrative Control and Executive Action*. Columbus, Ohio: Charles E. Merrill Books, Inc., 1961.

Likert, Rensis, *New Patterns of Management*. New York: McGraw-Hill Book Company, 1961.

Litterer, Joseph A., *Organizations: Structure and Behavior*. New York: John Wiley & Sons, Inc., 1963.

——, *The Analysis of Organizations*. New York: John Wiley & Sons, Inc., 1965.

Littleton, A. C., *Essays on Accountancy*. Urbana: University of Illinois Press, 1961.

Machiavelli: The Chief Works and Others, trans. Allan Gilbert. Durham, N.C.: Duke University Press, 1965.

Madeheim, Huxley, Edward M. Mazze, and Charles S. Stein, eds., *Readings in Organization and Management*. New York: Holt, Rinehart & Winston, Inc., 1963.

Maier, Norman, and John J. Hayes, *Creative Management*. New York: John Wiley & Sons, Inc., 1962.

Mantoux, Paul, *The Industrial Revolution in the Eighteenth Century*. London: Jonathan Cape Limited, 1961.

Maslow, A., *Motivation and Personality*. New York: Harper & Row, Publishers, 1964.

Massie, Joseph L., *Essentials of Management*. Englewood Cliffs, N.J.: Prentice-Hall, Inc., 1964.

Mee, J. F., *Management Thought in a Dynamic Society*. New York: New York University Press, 1963.

Mellaart, James, *Earliest Civilizations of the Near East*. London: Thames and Hudson, 1965.

Newman, William H., and Charles E. Summer, Jr., *The Process of Management: Concepts, Behavior and Practice*. Englewood Cliffs, N.J.: Prentice-Hall, Inc., 1961.

Odiorne, George S., *Management by Objectives*. New York: Pitman Publishing Corp., 1965.

Randall, Clarence B., *The Folklore of Management*. Boston: Little, Brown and Company, 1961.

Schleh, Edward C., *Management by Results.* New York: McGraw-Hill Book Company, 1961.

Schuchman, Abe, *Scientific Decision Making in Business.* New York: Holt, Rinehart & Winston, Inc., 1963.

Simon, Herbert, *The Shape of Automation for Men and Management.* New York: Harper & Row, Publishers, 1965.

Srivastava, A. L., *History of India: 1000-1707.* Jaipur: Shiva Lal Agarwala & Co., 1964.

Towle, Joseph W., *et al., Ethics and Standards in American Business.* Boston: Houghton Mifflin Company, 1964.

Uris, Auren, *The Management Makers.* New York: The Macmillan Company, 1962.

Woodward, Joan, *Industrial Organization.* London: Tavistock Publications, 1961.

1966-1971

Azreal, Jerry R., *Managerial Power and Soviet Politics.* Cambridge: Harvard University Press, 1966.

Beer, Stafford, *Cybernetics and Management.* London: English University Press, Ltd., 1968.

Bell, Gerald D., *Organizational Flexibility.* Chicago: Rand McNally & Co., 1968.

Brech, E. F. L., *Organisation: The Framework of Management* (2nd ed.). London: Longmans, Green & Co., Ltd., 1966.

Chamberlain, Neil W., *Enterprise and Environment.* New York: McGraw-Hill Book Company, 1968.

Dale, Ernest, *Organization.* New York: American Management Association, 1967.

——, and L. C. Michelson, *Modern Management Methods.* New York: World Publishing Co., 1966.

Flippo, Edwin B., *Management: A Behavioral Approach.* Boston: Allyn & Bacon, Inc., 1966.

Gellerman, Saul W., *Management by Motivation.* New York: American Management Association, 1968.

——, *The Management of Human Relations.* New York: Holt, Rinehart & Winston, Inc., 1966.

George, Claude S., Jr., *Management for Business and Industry.* Englewood Cliffs, N.J.: Prentice-Hall, Inc., 1970.

Glotz, Gustave, *Ancient Greece at Work.* New York: Barnes & Noble, Inc., 1967.

Grosset, Serge, *Management: American and European Styles.* Belmont, Calif.: Wadsworth Publishing Co., 1970.

Hare, Van Court, Jr., *Systems Analysis: A Diagnostic Approach.* New York: Harcourt, Brace & World, Inc., 1967.

Heald, Morrell, *The Social Responsibilities of Business.* Cleveland: Press of Case Western Reseserve University, 1970.

Jay, Antony, *Management and Machiavelli.* New York: Holt, Rinehart & Winston, Inc., 1967.

Kakar, Sudhir, *Frederick Taylor: A Study in Personality and Innovation.* Cambridge, Mass.: MIT Press, 1970.

Keay, Fred, *The Numerate Manager.* London: Allen & Unwin, Ltd., 1969.

Killian, Ray A., *Managing by Design.* New York: American Management Association, 1968.

Lay, Bierne, *Someone Has to Make It Happen.* Englewood Cliffs, N.J.: Prentice-Hall, Inc., 1969.

Likert, Rensis, *The Human Organization: Its Management and Values.* New York: McGraw-Hill Book Company, 1967.

Marrow, Alfred J., David G. Bowers, and Stanley E. Seashore, *Management by Participation.* New York: Harper & Row, Publishers, 1967.

McFarland, Dalton E., ed., *Current Issues and Emerging Concepts in Management.* Boston: Houghton Mifflin Company, 1966.

McGregor, Douglas, *The Professional Manager.* New York: McGraw-Hill Book Company, 1967.

Mosson, T. M., ed., *Teaching the Process of Management.* London: George G. Harrap & Co. Ltd., 1967.

Odiorne, George ´S., *Management Decision by Objectives.* Englewood Cliffs, N.J.: Prentice-Hall, Inc., 1969.

Peters, Lynn H., *Management and Society.* Belmont, Calif.: Dickinson Publishing Co., 1968.

Petit, Thomas A., *The Moral Crisis in Management.* New York: McGraw-Hill Book Company, 1967.

Richards, Max D., and Paul S. Greenlaw, *Management Decision Making.* Homewood, Ill.: Richard D. Irwin, Inc., 1966.

Roethlisberger, F. J., *Man-in-Organization.* Cambridge: Harvard University Press, 1968.

Schafer, Edward H., *Ancient China.* New York: Time-Life Books, 1967.

Sheldon, Oliver, *The Philosophy of Management.* New York: Pitman Publishing Corp., 1966.

Strauss, George, and Leonard R. Sayles, *Personnel: The Problems of Management.* Englewood Cliffs, N. J.: Prentice-Hall, Inc., 1967.

Suojanen, Wains W., *The Dynamics of Management.* New York: Holt, Rinehart & Winston, Inc., 1966.

Terborgh, George, *Business Investment Management.* Washington, D.C.: Machinery and Allied Products Institute and Council for Technological Advancement, 1967.

Toutain, Jules, *The Economic Life of the Ancient World.* New York: Barnes & Noble, Inc., 1969.

Voich, Dan, Jr., Daniel A. Wren, and Robert L. Froemke, *Principles of Management . . . Resources and Systems.* New York: The Ronald Press Company, 1968.

Wadia, Maneck S., ed., *The Nature and Scope of Management.* Chicago: Scott, Foresman & Company, 1966.

Walton, Clarence C., *Business and Social Progress.* New York: Frederick A. Praeger, Inc., 1970.

——, *Corporate Social Responsibilities.* Belmont, Calif.: Wadsworth Publishing Co., 1967.

Weissman, Jacob, *The Social Responsibilities of Corporate Management.* Hempstead, N.Y.: Hofstra University, 1966.

Yoshino, M. M., *Japan's Managerial System.* Cambridge, Mass.: MIT Press, 1969.

Young, Stanley, and Charles E. Summer, *Management: A Systems Analysis.* Glenview, Ill.: Scott, Foresman & Company, 1966.

INDEX

A

Abrams, Frank, xiii, 187
Accounting control, ix, 39-40
Ackoff, Russell L., 158
Akkadian Code, 9
Alexander the Great, viii, 22
Alfarabi, viii, 31
Alford, L. P., 10
American system of scientific manage-
    ment, 64-5
    Eli Whitney, 64-5
Ancient civilizations, 3-27
    Babylonia, 9-10
    China, viii, 11-14
    Egypt, vii, 4-9
    Greece, viii, 14-18
    Hebrews, vii, 11
    India, 18-20
    Military contributions, 20-23
    Rome, 23-26
    Sumer, vii, 3-4
Argyris, Chris, xiii, 154
Arsenal of Venice, ix, 35-41
    assembly line, 37-8

Arsenal of Venice (cont.)
    control, 39-40
    cost control, 41
    inventory, 40
    inventory control, 40-41
    personnel, 38-39
    standardization, 39
    warehousing, 36-7
Arkwright, Richard, 57-8
Ashley, Sir William, 54
Authority, 55
    acceptance theory, 45
Automation, 55, 73

B

Babbage, Charles, X, 75-77, 149
    motion study, 76
    proposals, 77
    scientific investigation, 76
    time study, 76-7
Babylonia, 9-10
    Hammurabi, vii, 9-10
    Nebuchadnezzar, vii, 10

Bagley, F. R. C., 32
Barbarigo, ix
Behavioral school, 150-154
Barnard, Chester I., xii, 153-4
   (*see also* Behavioral school)
   executive functions, 140
   Barnard, Chester I., 153-4
   Follett, Mary Parker, xii, 152-3
   Gantt, Henry L., 151-2
   Mayo, Elton, xii, 152
   Munsterberg, Hugo, 151
   Sheldon, Oliver, xii, 153
Blackett, P. M. S., xii, 162
Bloomfield, Meyer, xii, 122-3
Bohm-Bawerk, Eugen von, 161
Bookkeeping, viii, 34
Boulton, Matthew, ix, 59-62
Boulton, Watt, and Sons, ix, 59-62
   (*see also* Soho Foundry)
Bowen, Frances, 71
Bowker, R. R., 68
Brandeis, Louis D., 120-21
Breasted, J. H., 7
Brockmeyer, E., 159
Brown, R. E., 32
Budge, E. A. Wallis, 10
Burnham, James, 141-2

C

Cato, viii, 24
   on planning, 25
Caveat emptor, 53
Child labor, 62
Childe, V. G., 3
China, viii, 11-14
   Chow, 11-12
   Mencius, viii, 13
   Sun Tzu, viii, 14
Christ, viii
Church, Alexander H., xi, 117-19
   functional approach, 118
   laws of effort, 118
Chow, 11-12
Classical economists, 67-70
Clausewitz, Carl von, 74
Code of Hammurabi, 9
Cohesiveness, 45
Conceptual acts, 177
Conceptual environment, 172
Constitution of Chow, 11-12

Contemporary manager, 187-8
Contenau, Georges, 9
Contemporary management, 181-8
Continuum of management (table),
   vii-xiii
Controlling, vii, 175-6 (*see also*
   Managerial functions)
Coordination, types of, 139
Cooke, Morris L., xii, 125-26, 150
Cooke-Taylor, R. W., 58
Cooper, Benjamin, 160
Cornford, Francis, 16
Cost control, 41
Cunningham, William, 54
Cyclegraph, 100
Cyrus, viii, 20-21

D

Dale, Ernest, 82
Dale, Henry, 20
Decision making, 185-6
Decision theory, 165
de Laveleye, Emile, 70-72
Denslow, van Buren, 71
Diemer, Hugo, xi, 119
Dietz, Frederick C., 52
Di Marco, F., viii
Diocletian, viii
Directing, 13, 175
Direction as a managerial function, 54
Division of labor, 15, 56-7, 72
Dodge, H. F., xii, 161
Domestic system, 50-51
Drucker, Peter, 150
Drury, Horace B., xi, 86, 124-5
Duncan, John C., xi, 119-20
Dupin, Charles, 75
Durant, Will, 158

E

Early writings, 31-33
Edison, Thomas A., xi, 160
Education for management, xi, 87,
   111-14
   Fayol, Henri, 111-14
   Wharton School, 87
Efficiency, 184

Egypt, vii, 4-9
  Ptah-hotep, 6
  Pharoah, 8
  structures, 4-5
  writings, 5-7
Emerson, Harrington, xi, 107-9, 150
  principles of efficiency, 108
  contributions, 109
Employee selection, 26
Employee welfare, 184-5
Environment, 172-3
  conceptual, 172
  physical, 172
Erlang, A. K., xi, 159
Erman, Adolf, 5-6
Estate management, 23
  incentives, 23
  organization, 23
Experimental design, 165

F

Factory system, 52
Fayol, Henri
  career, 110-11
  contributions, xi, 111-14
  and management process school, 154-5
  managerial concepts, 111-14
  managerial functions, 112
  principles of management, 113
  teaching management, 112
Feudal organization, 29-31
Financial control, 53
Fisher, Sir Ronald, xii, 161
Follett, Mary Parker, 138-9, 152-3 (*see also* Behavioral school)
  types of coordination, 139
Formula for management, 178-9
Fry, T. C., xii, 161
Functional aspects of management, 173-6
Functions of the executive, 140
Functions of management, 112
Functions of manager, 172

G

Gager, Curtis H., 15
Game theory, 165
Gantt chart, 104

Gantt, Henry L., 103-105, 151-2 (*see also* Behavioral school)
  contributions, 104-5
  training employees, 105
General theory of management, 169-80
Ghazali, viii, 32
Gilbreths, Frank B. and Lillian M., xi, 99-101
  bricklaying, 99
  contributions, 101
  cyclegraph, 100
  microhronometer, 100
  motion pictures, 100
  motion study, 100
  "one best way," 100
  and scientific management, 149
  therbligs, xi, 100
Glotz, Gustave, 15
Greece, viii, 14-18
  art of management, 18
  principles of management, 15-18
Greene, Constance McL., 64
Group endeavors, 136

H

Halsey, Frederick, x, 86-7
  premium incentive plan, 86-7
Halztrom, H. L. 159
Hammond, Robert, 31
Hammurabi, vii, 9-10
Harper, Robert F., 9
Harris, F. W., xi
Hartness, James, 121-2
Hawthorne study, 136-137
Hebrews, xviii, 11
Heilbroner, Robert L., 63
Herford, R. O., 127-8
Hildage, H. T., 127-8
History and management, 181-8
Hittle, J. D., 22
Hotelling, Harold, 161
Hoxie, Robert F., xi, 123-4
Huan-Chang, Chen, 13
Human relations, 20, 182-3

I

Incentives, 23
Incentive wages, 10

India, viii, 18-20
Industrial psychology, 105-6
Information theory, 165
Interchangeable parts, 63-4
Inventory control, 40, 165

J

Jay, Anthony, 45
Jefferson, Thomas, ix, 63
Jenkins, H. G., 127-8
Jensen, A., 159
Jevons, W. S., xviii, 77-79, 149
    motion study, 78
Job specification, xviiiv, 19, 25
Johnson, Ellis A., 163
Johnston, K. S., 32

K

Kautilya, viii, 18-20

L

Lane, Frederic C., 32, 33, 35
Laughlin, J. Lawrence, xxv, 68, 70
Leadership, xiv, 45-6
Leffingwell, William H., xii, 127
Leggee, James, 12
Leavitt, Harold J., xiii, 154
Likert, Rensis, xiii
Linear programming, 166
Littleton, A. C., 35
Lynch, Edmund C., 123

M

Machiavelli, Niccolo, ix, 43-7
Management
    beginning of, 1-27
    decision making, 185-6
    early writers, 67-79
        Babbage, Charles, x, 75-7
        classical economists, 67-73
        Clausewitz, Carl von, 74
        Dupin, Charles, 75
        Jevons, W. S., x, 77-9
        early writings, 31-33

Management (cont.)
    efficiency, 184
    a formula (model) of, 178-9
    and social responsibility, 186-7
    theory, 169-80
Management process school, 154-6
    Fayol, Henri, 154-5
    Mooney, James D., 155-6
Manager, traits of, viii, 31-3
Managerial acts, 177-8
    conceptual, 177-8
    physical, 177
Managerial composite, 176-7
Managerial functions, 68-72
    controlling, ix, 175-6
    direction, 54
    organizing, 71, 174
    planning, xiii, 70, 174
    staffing, 70
    systems approach, 72
Managerial philosophers, 131-43
    Barnard, Chester I., xii, 140-41
    Burnham, James, 141-2
    Follett, Mary Parker, xii, 138-9
    Mayo, Elton, xvii, 136-7
    Mooney, James D., xii, 138
    Sheldon, Oliver, xii, 132-6
    Urwick, Lyndall, xii, 142-3
Managers and management, 170-72
Mantoux, Paul, 58
Manufacture de Versailles, 62
Marshall, Alfred, xv, 71
Maslow and management theory,
    169-70
Materials handling, 21
Mayo, Elton, xii, 136-7, 152 (*see also*
    Behavioral school)
    Hawthorne study, 136-7
McCallum, Daniel C., x, 82-3
    control, 83
    delegation, 83
Medieval period, 29-47
    early writings, 31-33
        Alfarabi, viii, 31
        Ghazali, xviiix, 32
    Feudal organization, 29-31
    Venetian arsenal, ix, 35-41
    Venetian merchants, 33-5
Mellaart, James, 2
Mencius, viii, 13
    need for system, 13
Merrill, Harwood F., 63

Metcalfe, Henry C., x, 85
Microchronometer, 100
Military contributions, 20-23
　Cyrus, xiv, 20-21
　staff principle, xviiiv, 22-3
　uniform methods, xviiiv, 21-2
Mill, James, ix, 69-70, 149
　motion and time study, 69-70
Mill, John Stuart, 70, 71, 73
Minor writers, 117-29
　Bloomfield, Meyer, 122-23
　Brandeis, Louis D., 120-21
　Church, Alexander H., xi, 117-19
　Cooke, Morris L., xii, 125-26
　Diemer, Hugo, 119
　Drury, Horace B., xi, 124-5
　Duncan, John C., xi, 119-20
　Hartness, James, 121-22
　Herford, Hildage, and Jenkins, 127-8
　Hoxie, Robert F., xi, 123-4
　Leffingwell, William H., 127
　Parsons, Carl C., xii, 126
　Tead, Ordway, xii, 125
Model of management, 178-80
Moley, Raymond, 186
Mooney, James D., xii, 30-138 (see also Process school)
More, Sir Thomas, ix, 41-3
Motion and time study, 69-70
Motion pictures, 100
Motion study, x, xi, 21, 76, 77-79
　shoveling, 77
　therbligs, 100
Mouzon, James C., 163
Mueller, W. A., 160
Munsterberg, Hugo, xi, 105-6, 151 (see also Behavioral school)
Music and work, 15
Myers, Charles A., 6

N

Nebuchadnezzar, viii, 10
New Lanark, ix, 62-3
　child labor, 62
　homes, 62
　personnel management, 63
New managerial approaches, 183
Newman, Samuel P., 67, 68, 73

O

"One best way," 100
Operations research, 157-67 (see Quantitative school)
Organization, vii, 14
Organizing, 71, 174 (see also Managerial functions)
Overtime, 61
Owen, H. S., 160
Owen, Robert, ix, 149

P

Paccioli, L., viii, 32
Parsons, Carl C., xii, 126
Payback, 54
Person, Harlow S., xi, 98, 109, 150
Personnel, 38-9
Personnel-human relations, 182-3
Personnel management, ix, 62-3
Personnel selection, 26
Phillips. Thomas P., 14
Philosophers, managerial; 131-43 (see also Managerial philosophers)
Physical acts, 177
Physical environment, 172
Pigors, Paul, 6
Planning, xviii, 14, 20, 54, 70, 174 (see also Managerial functions)
　and uncertainty, 74
Plato, viii, 15
Poor, Henry, x, 82
Prehistoric era, 2-3
Principles of management, x, 93, 113
Probability theory, 166
Process school, 154-6
　Fayol, Henri, xi, 154-5
　Mooney, James., 155
Production control, vii, 10, 53
Psychology in management, 105-6, 125
Putting-out system, 51-2

Q

Quantitative school, 157-67
　associations, 164-5
　business applications, 163-4
　development of, 158-60

Quantitative school (cont.)
  postwar uses, 162-3
  probability and inference, 161
  techniques, 165-6
  World War II applications, 161-2
Queuing theory, 166

R

Raymond, F. E., 160
Reiley, Alan C., 30, 138
Reliance on mass consent, 45
Replacement theory, 166
Ricardo, David, 70
Roll, Erick, 59
Rome, 23-26
  empire organization, 23-24
  farm management, 24-26
Romig, H. G., xii, 161

S

Sampling theory, 166
Say, Jean Baptiste, 68
Scheaifer, Robert, xiii
Schools   of   management   thought,
  145-67
  background, 146-7
  behavioral school (see Behavioral
    school)
  management process school (see
    Management process school)
  quantitative school (see Quanti-
    tative school)
  scientific management school (see
    Scientific management school)
  traditional school (see Scientific
    management school)
Scientific investigation, 76
Scientific management
  aims, 97-98
  beginnings of, 81-88
  early forms, 59-65
    American system, 64-5
    interchangeable parts, 63-4
    New Lanark, 62-3
    Soho Foundry, 59-62
  early managerial practices, 53-55
    caveat emptor, 53

Scientific Management (cont.)
  early managerial practices (cont.)
    direction, 54
    financial control, 53
    payback, 54
    planning, 54
    production control, 53
  in England, 127-8
  impact, 96-7
  interest in, 94-5
  mechanisms, 94
Scientific   management   movement,
  83-7
  education for, 87
  Halsey, Frederick, 86-7
  Metcalfe, Henry, 85
  Towne, Henry R., 84-5
Scientific management school, 147-50
  Babbage, Charles, 149
  Cooke, Morris L., 150
  Drucker, Peter, 150
  Emerson, Harrington, 150
  Gilbreths, the, 149
  Jevons, W. S., 149
  Metcalfe, Henry, 150
  Mill, James, 149
  Owen, Robert, 149
  Person, Harlow S., 150
  Poor, Henry, 149
  Smith, Adam, 149
  Taylor, Frederick W., 147-49
Scientific method, 15
Scott, Walter D., xi, 106-7
Seleckman, Benjamin N., xiii, 154
Shamasastry, R., 19
Shannon, Claude, xiiii
Sheldon, Oliver, xii, 132-6, 153 (see
  also Behavioral school)
  contributions, 135-6
  managerial philosophy, 133
Shewhart, W. A., xii, 161
Shish, Hu, 14
Shop management, 91
Simon, Herbert, xiii, 154
Simulation theory, 166
Smith, Adam, ix, 54, 56, 57, 68, 149
Social responsibility, 186-7
Socrates, viii, 16-18
Soho Foundry, ix, 59-62
  control, 61
  housing, 61

Soho Foundry (cont.)
  overtime, 61
  piece rates, 60
  standard data, 61
  standard time, 60
Solomon, 3
Soranzo Brothers, viii
Spaulding, O. 21
Specialization, ix, 13, 15, 72
Staff principle, viiiiv, 12, 22, 23
Staffing, 70 (*see also* Managerial functions)
Standard data, 61
Standard motions, xiv-xvi, 15
Standard time, xv, xvi, 61
Standardization, 39
Statistical decision theory, 166
Steuart, Sir James, ix, 55-6, 149
Sumer, vii, 3-4
Sun Tzu, viii, 14
Symbolic logic, 166
Synthesizing motions, xv, 69-70
System in management, 13
Systems s approach, cl 72 (*see also* Managerial functions)

T

Tarn, W. W., 22
Taylor, Frederick W., x, 76, 90-4, 147-50, 159
  concepts of management, 92-3
  papers, 91-2
  principles of management, 93
  scientific management school, 147-50
  shop system, 91
  testimony, 95-96
Teaching management, 112, 114
Tead, Ordway, xii, 125
Theory of management, 169-80
Therbligs, xi, 100
Time study, 76-7
Toutain, Jules, 15
Towne, Henry R., x, 84-5, 150
Traditional school (*see* Scientific management school)
Traits of a manager, xiv, 67-8

Trefethen, Florence N., 161
Turgot, Anne Robert Jacques, 68-70
Tzu, Sun, viii, 14

U

Uniform methods, ix, 21
Universality of management, 16
Urwick, Lyndall, xii, 110, 142-3

V

Varro, viii, 26
Venice, ix, 32-41
  arsenal, ix, 35-41
  merchants, 33-35
Villers, Raymond, 75

W

Wage payment, 72-3
Wages, 185
Watson, J. S., 18, 20
Watt, James, ix, 59
Watts, Thomas, 53
Weber, Max, xiii
Wharton, Joseph, x, 87
White, Maunsel, 159
Whitmore, W. F., 160
Whitney, Eli, 64-5
Wiener, Norbert, xiii
Wilkinson, Sir Gardner, 9
Will to survive, 46-7
Wilson, John A., 6
Wilson, R. H., 160
Work tempo, 15
Wu, Juo-Cheng, 12

X

Xenophon, viii, 16-18, 23

Y

Yao, 12